CW01612721

PHYLLIS: MEMOIRS OF A MISFIT

Cover photo by Jennifer Holly, 1996

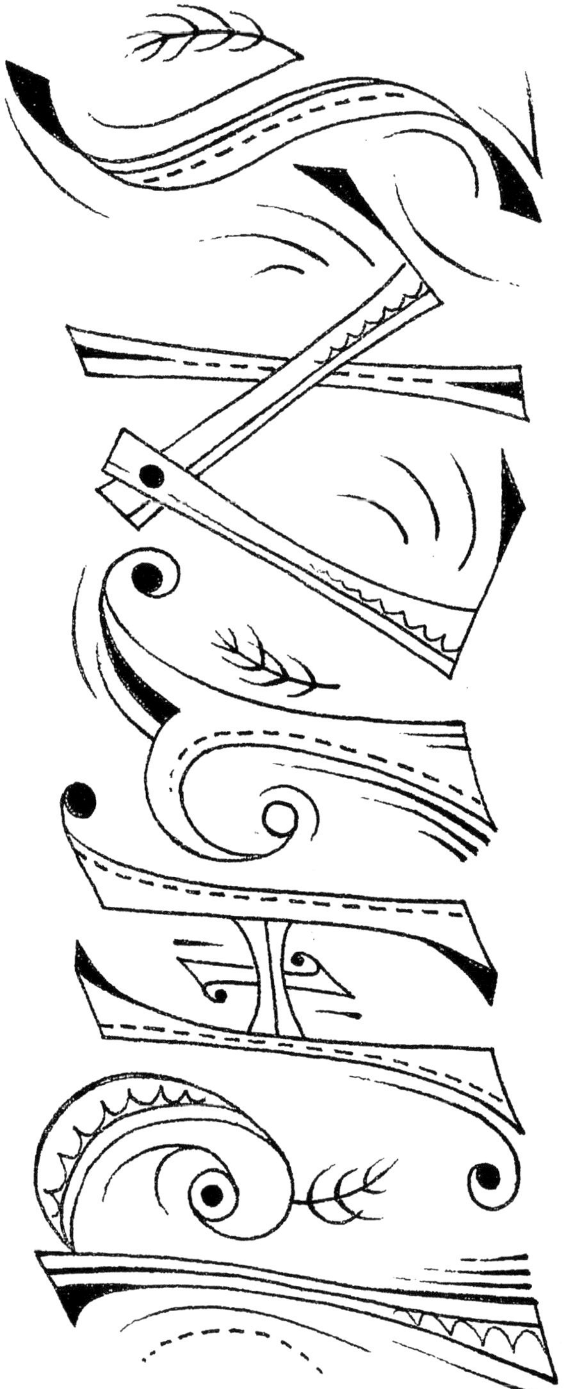

PHYLLIS

Memoirs of a Misfit

Phyllis Castle

Phyllis.

ELSP

Published in 2003 by
ELSP
1 The Shambles
Bradford on Avon
Wiltshire
BA15 1JS

All enquiries and coorrespondence
regarding this book should be directed
to its author: Phyllis Castle
26 The Ropewalk
Bradford on Avon
Wiltshire
BA15 1LQ

Design and typesetting by
Ex Libris Press

Printed in Britain by
Copytech (UK) Ltd.
Peterborough

Typeset in 10/13 Souvenir

ISBN 1 903341 84 1

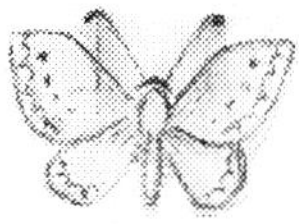

The butterfly, a common white,
(His honest idiocy of flight)
Will never now it is too late,
Master the art of flying straight,
Yet has - who knows as well as I? -
A just sense of how not to fly:
He lurches here and there by guess
And God and hope and hopelessness.
Even the aerobatic swift
Has not his flying crooked gift.

Robert Graves

CONTENTS

INTRODUCTION

Phyllis was born in Richmond, Surrey, on 13 September 1909. She was the daughter of Florence E. Castle (1867-1960), a portrait, landscape and still-life painter and an illustrator, trained at the Lambeth School of Art and in Paris. Florence exhibited at the Lambeth School of Art, the Royal Society of British Artists, the Walker Art Gallery, and the Royal Institute of Oil Painters.

Phyllis and Florence were re-united when Phyllis was four years old. They lived together on 'shoe-strings' for many years, at addresses in Kensington, Hampstead and in Oxfordshire. During her youth, Phyllis attended many different primary and secondary schools. After leaving school she became a student at the Ruskin Drawing School, followed by nearly four years at the Royal College of Art, where she gained a Principal's Prize. Phyllis had her first post as assistant art editor at the *Radio Times*, B.B.C.

In 1938 Phyllis escaped from 'work' and travelled solo, hitch-hiking round the U.S.A. Returning to England as war clouds were gathering, she applied to join the W.A.A.Fs but was unsuccessful. She joined the Land Army and served throughout World War II. Then came ten years of teaching in seventeen different schools! Phyllis has always been a voracious reader, loving words and phrases, and enjoying writing, both prose and poetry. In 1945 she had a piece published in *The Convoy File* and in 1947 two pieces in *Leaves in the Storm*.

By 1957 Phyllis was ready for a change, trained as an occupational therapist, and took up an appointment in North Cornwall, learning to drive so that she could visit home-bound patients in the rural areas. She shared a home with a friend, in Wadebridge. On retirement she developed new interests, travelling often to London which involved long journeys. She moved to a house in Frome with a large vegetable garden. It was about this time that her sight began to fail but this did not deter her from studying calligraphy and continuing her search for a personal philosophy by exploring Buddhism. Phyllis moved to Bradford-on-Avon in 1993 where she continues to write, especially poetry, and enjoys long walks. She was registered blind in 2001.

Phyllis kept her writings, some in type and later ones in long hand, and at New Year 2003 decided to self-publish her memoirs. This book is the result. It has been my pleasure and privilege to order her material and to prepare it for the publisher. She has a remarkably keen memory. The illustrations come from old photographs, many originally taken of original paintings and pastel drawings, and from Phyllis's own early line drawings of which, sadly, more could not be found.

The title reflects how Phyllis feels about herself - a Misfit. I prefer to describe her as a free spirit - something of a rebel - very conscious of failure - an outsider - BUT, resilient, resourceful and courageous throughout her long life.

Rosemary F. Carr
17 The Ropewalk
Bradford-on-Avon

May 2003

ACKNOWLEDGEMENTS

The author wishes to thank those who have given generously of their time and skills to make this book possible:-

Christine Pictor for transferring the text to computer disk,

Roger Jones for agreeing to help with the publishing,

and, especially,

Rosemary Carr who assembled the papers and illustrations with endless patience, good humour and understanding.

The extract from *The Expense of Glory*, a life of John Reith by Ian McIntyre, pub. Harper Collins 1993 on page 79 is reproduced with permission.

I

BEGINNINGS
1909-1939

Florence Castle – self-portrait; oil on canvas, exhibited at the Royal Academy Summer Exhibition, 1904

1

Not a bad start really

A divided home - a damaged child. Common knowledge. I must have known - read of it many times, but I hadn't taken it in. That is, till the day I entered the crowded staffroom of a large girls' boarding school bitterly complaining about what a nuisance so-and-so was. It was the end of term with folders of foolscap sheets piled up on cupboards. From the other side of the room, her form mistress called across, 'Two reports; two envelopes; two addresses!' And suddenly I saw it all, not only for the particular girl and most of the other excitable nuisances and bold bad characters that upset and enlivened (school) life, but with a shock of recognition, for myself also - and me too.

Looking back, useful consciousness seems to have arisen when I was four. It was also the time of a sudden radical change in circumstances. Up till this time I'd been fostered. It seemed I didn't much care for the first home. I screamed so hard I ruptured myself and was hastily handed back at the end of the week. The second encounter was different. It was love at first sight for us both. How to describe this all-encompassing warmth and affection that is everywhere and always ... how lucky I was. Or to look at it another way - how well I had chosen, for hardly dry from the womb had I not made myself unmistakably clear?

What would I have been like, I wonder, without those first few years in a normal, stable, loving two-parent family? Yet on being suddenly plucked away into a totally different world, this time the transition was seamless. Not a murmur.

We were always moving. Life was now lived in a succession of rooms - one large, or two could be called a flat. To begin with we seemed to be camping out in an open area without walls or ceiling, called by my new aunty her studio. It was a far cry from the neat bedroom in the little house where I woke to walls of pink roses in baskets and bluebirds flying. But wherever we were the performance was always the same. There'd be a period of false peace, followed by a blinding row with the landlady. I would dash for cover, fingers in ears, wishing myself dead. But I soon learned that these eruptions were as sure to pass as they were bound to come. She was always right. Other people's points of view were a personal affront: **crowned** with indignation she grew inches. My aunt was meant to battle, a good row set her up.

The trouble was usually over arrears in rent. We were always running out of money. Every week she wrote to my father demanding more and every week he replied enclosing the same amount. It became a comic set piece. She never gave up. He never gave in. It expect it was enough, for most of the time we lived quite merrily on our shoestring. The relationship between us developed into a conspiracy of two, in which I much appreciated the importance of my role and she obviously enjoyed having someone to confide in.

You would have thought that a portrait painter would be passionately interested in people, I dare say some are, my aunt was only passionately interested in painting. As to people, there were those who commissioned portraits and those who bowed down before her work. The rest were a waste of time.

She'd been something of a beauty in her youth, with corn-coloured hair, forget-me-not blue eyes and a noble Roman nose. She never married, you were given to understand because no suitor could be found who measured up. An impoverished Polish count came nearest, till it was discovered that he drank. He was then discarded on the grounds that this would interfere with her work. It was obvious to me from the very beginning that 'my work' was aunt's world, just as she was mine. It enveloped us both. And if at this time she was seldom painting, it was still clearly understood as the reason for living. I heard about it often enough. How she'd lived from portrait to portrait with occasional moonlight flits when in trouble with the rent. When times got really hard, she'd go for a walk in Kensington Gardens and mooch around eyeing the children out with their nurses. Public parks and gardens are notorious happy hunting grounds, but my aunty's angle was unusual. A child would be selected for its looks, while the nurse was used as a pointer to the income level. It only remained to follow them home and offer to paint a portrait on spec. As at the time she was regularly exhibiting on the line at the Royal Academy it was an attractive proposition. Then came the 'Studied in Paris gained medals there' bit and surprisingly often it was in the bag. It was from one of these commissions that she went on to paint the grand-parents, a retired colonel with splendid handlebar whiskers and his still pretty wife, two of her finest portraits.

The four-square solid oak easel invariably positioned in the middle of the studio-bed-cum-living room was our most important piece of furniture, portraits might be scarce, but one way or another it was much in use. For most of the morning it would be covered in bedclothes while the mattress was aired, sometimes the greater part of the day was spent in circumnavigation of this strange mountain. The mattress itself was a vast voluminous feather bed which she energetically smacked about and left in a rough dough-like mound. Later in the day when the bed was made it was tenderly kneaded into a trough-shaped nest. She believed strongly in nature: air, cold water, exercise and fruit and nuts. After the easel, the next most important piece of equipment was an aristocratic-looking hip bath that had seen better days. By the time I came to be acquainted with it much of the enamel had worn away and little cloth flags sprouted out of the base where a number of leaks had been plugged with bits of rag: when the bath was filled with water they waved gently to and fro like seaweed in a rock pool.

My aunt's bath was a vital daily ritual and double event. In bath 1 she went to work under the direction of an audible drill. Areas and limbs were announced and given a count. 'Arms! Right: 1 2 3 4 Left: 1 2 3 4 Chest!' And so on. Otherwise owing to absent-mindedness she was liable to lose the place and end up unevenly finished. Bath 2 was filled with cold water and she got right in. Hissing and gasping and sponging hard in all directions, she kept right on till she reaped her rich reward and stepped out 'glowing all over' Nor was this all, for in between, while baling out bath 1 and filling up bath 2, she sang in a well-rounded mezzo-soprano voice trained by an Italian master. Only a drawing-room voice he had told her to her great disappointment. To fall short of the rafters of the roof at Covent Garden was not to be a singer. My aunt was nothing if not professional in outlook.

As for me, a steady passion for the press began early. My failed to drag me on as I stooped to peel a grimy sheet of coloured pictures from the damp pavement. It was a piece of the front page of *The Rainbow*, which I forthwith demanded. Tiger Tim was my first great fictional character. Nothing else in the paper mattered. I had to have the Bruin

Boys every night till the next copy came out. Lying in bed afterwards I tirelessly wove myself into their adventures. It wasn't that I no longer delighted in my aunt's standard bedtime reading: fairy stories, *The Arabian Nights*, *A Child's Garden of Verses*, Wordsworth's *Poems for the Young*. I knew 'My Shadow' and all sixteen verses of 'Lucy Grey' by heart. But books came off the shelves over my head. They were nourishment. The immediately exciting, ongoing appeal of coloured animals on cheap paper was on my own level, - you could say, along with ginger beer and ice cream.

Wherever we were it would be near Kensington Gardens. We couldn't get outside quickly enough for me. But there was never any hope of rushing my aunt through her going-out routine: 'Pursekeyhandkerchief-andglasses,' she would murmur, posed on the step by the still open front door. There followed an interval while she checked on each of these, then the door slammed and we were off. I bowled my hoop down the Broad Walk and lost many cheap sailing boats in the Round Pond. Then after a fizzy drink in Lyons, we sat on a seat and shared Bath buns with the birds. Farther away, the swings in the recreational area were a special treat. The ropes ran up as it seemed to me into outer space; slim bars of wood came down to cage me in. Such high flying tended to induce transportation and on one occasion, as the swing was brought to rest, I assured my aunt that I would stay with her always - I'd never get married and leave her.

So. A bad beginning? The first four years!? How could that be seen as anything but good? And when you look into it, neither is there anything damaging about the blithely eccentric lifestyle that followed. We were a pair of innocents.

There is one other factor, though, possibly of more importance than I realize. This account begins with birth, - **a** - not **the** beginning. What about the previous nine months in residence? At least equally important as physical nourishment, there's bound to be ongoing communication on the finer levels of thought and feeling. I'm illegal - my mother obvious. Under the circumstances and understandably, I can't imagine there's have been much going for me at this particular period. That said, remembering l'affaire foster mothers, who knows?, I may well have been capable of throwing up an effective defence or taking reciprocal counter-measures even then.

What is certain, is that as I grew older, nothing from my background ever bothered me. Far from it. And as appreciation developed I came to see myself as a figure of romantic interest. On top of this, bastards, I read, tended to high intelligence, were often geniuses. Leonardo da Vinci...

The Colonel with handlebar whiskers. Portrait painted by Florence Castle

Portrait of Mary, wife of the Colonel. Potrait painted by Florence E. Castle

Phyllis, c. 1916

2

So what went wrong?

"I have a little shadow that goes in and out with me"
Robert Louis Stevenson

I was happy enough, for never having other children to play with I couldn't miss their company. All the same out in the park I must have studied them carefully, because there was this particular anatomical area of absorbing interest: the backs of their knees. I admired and envied all those excited, laughing children whose knees were backed by a firm bun-like pad of flesh. My own, I knew, had sad shady hollows. If I had no friends, the same could be said of my aunt, though she did occasionally visit. Once or twice a year we went to see the colonel with splendid handlebar whiskers and his wife whose portraits she had painted. While aunty took tea upstairs, I had mine downstairs with the kind housekeeper and maid. This was popular as I was allowed into the larder to choose whatever I fancied, and after tea there was always a present for me. It was usually only some small thing, but we all thoroughly enjoyed it. That is, until the awful occasion when it was announced that they'd found something special. A pretty china doll. Unfortunately I didn't care for dolls and said so. To my bewilderment all-round upset followed and I was taken home in disgrace. *'What a thing to say! - had I no idea how to behave?'*

I seemed only to care for toys connected with physical exercise. In a city flat there wasn't much scope for this. Teddy bears passed, a bear had appeal and could be put to a variety of uses quite outside the range of a sickly-looking doll. All the same there'd been one, a Japanese doll, that I'd tolerated for a time, caught by the novelty of the black shining hair and neat features; till one day, on impulse, it was suddenly thrown down and broken. By this time it was established that I didn't like dolls. Well then, what was I doing with this one?: *crash*. But as I'd seen myself do it I knew I was guilty; and for some time afterwards I would wake in the night and cry bitterly, upset by a picture of it lying there cracked cross - through no fault of its own. The only doll that lasted was stuffed stockinette, that could be tossed up and caught, bent double, sat on and rolled over. Later, when I was sent to boarding school, this tattered object went with me. But I never played with it, and there were nights when I lay in bed thinking about this, seeing it lying in the grit at the bottom of the big toy-box with all the other children's thing piled up on top of it. And again I was shaken by sobs at the unfairness of it all, for what had it ever done to me - to anyone, that it should be failed so utterly?

When the First World War was declared my aunt took a post. Aside from art and music, she had a flair for mathematics. She went into the Ministry of Pensions. I went to boarding school, to a Roman Catholic abbey where my aunt had once given private lessons in drawing to a specially talented pupil; and where I was accepted, due to considerations outlined by my aunt, at reduced fees. It was having so much room that was so marvellous. The long dormitories, spacious refectory, corridors and cloisters and seemingly endless grounds. I was always rushing about. I remember rushing out of the dormitory with a sister in pursuit, and being hauled back to pick up my cast-off combinations left stretched across the floor. I remember rushing into chapel with my head through a tear in my veil and being hastily ushered out. She arrived a lamb and turned into a young lion!, my aunt was told. I was always being found where I was not supposed to be - usually exploring the huge kitchens where I did wonderfully well with new sticky buns and apples for my bloomers pocket. Another highlight was a proper bath - it was their only complaint - presumably the duty sister was drenched. I was the youngest in the school and being small looked less than my age. There were five of us in the lowest form, including Dora. Dora was a dominant child twice my size and of a certain maturity. She was far from forward in learning, however, as from the start I wore the form badge denoting the first position. Air raids were usually at night: when the alarm sounded we gathered in the assembly hall. On these occasions if I didn't look out I got carried downstairs by a prefect and ended up imprisoned on a lap. I preferred to hare down on my own two feet, and by myself could usually obtain - illegally, of course - two lots of biscuits and cocoa.

So much for the joy. Now for the fall. I went home for the holidays with aunt still in the Ministry of Pensions. There was no keeping me in now, and in no time at all I was in possession of a garbled version of the facts of life as described by a boy from the area of a house further down the road. The meaning completely passed me by, what did not was the urgency of the telling. Here, clearly, was an important lead. Back at school, full of expectancy, I lost no time in passing the story on. The only reaction came from Dora where its effect was striking. In a matter of moments freedom was stripped from me. The threat of dreadful disgrace and instant expulsion hung over me. She had only to speak. The price of silence was revealing. I must no longer be top of the form. I complied with fearful servility. Then one Saturday morning when certain adventurous middle-school elements raided the orchard, I had to turn informer. She was obliged to push me into the arms of the sister on duty, '*She has something to tell you!*', to get this result, which she at once spread round the school. I dare say that up till then I'd enjoyed some measure of popularity. I enjoyed none thereafter.

Enthusiastically stoked up by Dora, the affair was always with us. Crushed and spiritless, mortally ashamed, my spare time was spent locked in a cubicle in the cloakroom, not on the seat, but on my knees, asking forgiveness. At other times, collared by Dora, we were shepherded into the chapel. On the stone steps in front of the altar, we prayed, not for me, but for guidance for her. Her final lead was undeniably inspired. Instead of directly informing authority, she leaked the story to the senior school and then sat back. It quickly spread, lightening the hearts and lifting the spirits of all who heard. But not the holy sisters. In due course the summons came and the last telling of my by now celebrated account was knocked out of me by the Mother Vicaress. As I stuck, so she struck. As for the substance of the story: as I understood it, it seemed that a lively approximation of parts was immediately followed by the desired result, the emergent infant on a line. At the time my informant claimed to be in possession of the parts concerned - in my mind's eye, unattached - and I was promised a demonstration. It was never forthcoming: he put it off and put it off, till in the end I was forced to conclude that he lied and had none. I would gladly have accepted expulsion. It didn't come, nor was anything said to my aunt. I went home for the weekend at half term in the usual way. All Saturday was spent plucking up courage to tell aunt - not what had happened, that would have been unthinkable - simply that I didn't want to go back to school. At last, before the cloth was removed after supper I crawled under the table, and thus protectively veiled gave out that in my considered opinion I'd been long enough at the Abbey - didn't aunty think it was time I went to another school? To my surprise it was ridiculously easy, as it turned out that every time she reached for something with me in range, I shot up an arm to ward off a blow. The glory was over. The tumble taken. The next years were shabby and depressed. First came a short spell at an Anglo-Catholic day school where the nuns were shocked to discover that I had never been Christened, and hastened to put this right. They prepared me themselves. Every morning I spent half an hour on a nun's knee. I disliked the position and the proposition made no impression.

My aunt was still in the Ministry of Pensions. She left the flat before me in the morning and returned two hours later than the end of afternoon school. I was given a key but preferred to play in the streets. The climax came when the woman in the flat below us reported seeing me out in the road hanging on the back of a horse-drawn cart. It was a favourite pastime: in fact it was the most exciting form of physical exercise to be found on the city streets of that time, made even more thoroughly dangerous by less adventurous kids on the pavement yelling at the driver to '*Whip behind gov'nor!*' The ground-floor lady recommended a small inexpensive boarding school in the suburbs, and my aunt felt she had no alternative.

The Laurels was a private establishment, half school, half home, where holiday boarding accommodation could also be provided. The motherless niece of the woman in the ground-floor flat was there at reduced fees, and it was soon arranged for me to be accepted at the same cut-rate. Aunty took me along. The principal was large and loud; she and aunt boomed at each other across the tiny visitors' room while I sat out of the way on a hair chair, feeling more and more uneasy. It was plain to me that my aunt was about to make a serious mistake: that what we had been given to understand suited the niece we had yet to meet of a woman we hardly knew, was on any score quite clearly not going to suit me. It was equally obvious that nothing of this could be got across to the trumpeters who were now sounding more than ever satisfied with each other. As I saw it, there was only one way out - through the door. Delicate-looking I might be, but I was not wanting in agility. I was off my mark in a flash, but only into the hall, stopped in my tracks by the battery of elaborate fastenings on the front door. The next I knew was a fierce grip on my coat collar as kicking and struggling I was yanked back into the visitors' room. And aunt sat and never made a move - not a word, not a look...this **couldn't** be! But it was. It was this that hurt. An acute sense of outrage lasted long enough for there to be talk of having to send me home. Night after night I cried myself to sleep. Then suddenly I adapted and settled into a numbed state of existence.

The school was run by a widow and her three unmarried daughters. Miss Charlotte taught the juniors; she was a tall, well-made, imposing woman with a high colour and resonant voice. Miss Ann had short hair and marched about with a hand stuffed in her skirt pocket. She taught the seniors, gave music lessons, and was easily the most popular. As I didn't take music I never came under her possibly leavening influence. But I enjoyed hearing her play the piano. She usually practised just after we'd gone to bed and was fond of a forceful rendering of Rachmaninov's *Prelude in C sharp Minor*. Miss Mary was matron. This one was different from the others: not modish like Miss Charlotte, not dashing like Miss Ann. She was rarely out of an overall, always busy, often untidy, and, to us - on the quiet - frequently kind. Mother cooked, dealt with parents, and ruled from behind the scenes like some terrible god. Only on more than usually shattering and historic occasions did she appear before us. Many stayed for the holidays. The majority of parents were in vaudeville and more often than not on tour. The parents of others were abroad. The motherless niece of the lady in the flat below us introduced herself. She was older than me, a pale, spiritless girl who seldom smiled.

At this school we went to church once a week. It has been chapel every day and three times on Sunday at the Abbey, but they were short hospitable sessions of thy will be done even while we fidget. The Protestant church I now found myself attending wasn't like this, and I thought the service was never going to end. At first I was one of a small group ushered out before the sermon began. As soon as I realised I had to stay I was caught in the chest by acute pain on Sunday morning. When it happened again at precisely the same time exactly a week later the game was up. Saturday darning and Sunday sermons were to me life lived at its lowest ebb.

At *The Laurels*, the worst experience that could come your way and one that few escaped if they stayed long enough, was that of having your parents publicly helped up to revile and ridicule. This usually took place after a visit or letter, one that contained some criticism or a request or demand that did not find favour with the family. Nothing was said to the proper people at the time, but at some stage afterwards the family would get together in a dangerous state of simmer, and the pressure would go up and up till the point was reached when one of them suddenly split off and burst in on us, and it all descended on some unsuspecting child. The parents or guardian would be dragged all ways in the mire as insult piled up on abuse overlaid with derision. It was a dangerous situation for us all as at any time it could spill over and spread. For the child concerned it amounted to the pillory. My first experience of one of these outpourings came during recreation. We were all busily occupied. I was on my knees working my way between the floorboards, prodding out tiny glass beads with a pin. It was amazing how many you could find. I was making a necklace for aunty, someone had given me a few big ones to put in at intervals. I was thinking how surprised and pleased she would be when Miss Ann threw open the door and stamped in. In dead silence we listened to thestream of accusations. A senior girl, sewing by a window, sat frozen leaning over her work. I quickly sensed danger. I had heard it all before. Miss Ann, catching my quailing eye, interrupted the flow to inform us that the new girl's aunt didn't come flouncing in giving herself airs and graces. I was not comforted: it was in my mind that she would be likely to display altogether more catastrophic qualifications. Miss Charlotte, at all times emphatic and eloquent, excelled herself on these occasions. Her bosom swelled and curls shook loose from her bun as she stood, vibrating with indignation, at the head of the huge school table with all of us little juniors grouped cringing round it. The beginning of morning school was her favourite time. It came, of course, as I had known that it would. And it wasn't my parents, so much as parentage that was held up in question. But even as I snivelled under cover of an exercise book, and later somehow swallowed my portion of dumplings and stew, the misery was lightened by a measure of relief. I had come through: the worst was over.

The schooling was as stodgy as the diet. English was dictation, history learned by heart. We were never praised or encouraged, only corrected. But youthful buoyancy found a way through. For drawing we made copies from a portfolio of reproductions of classical ornament, and towards the end of my stay at *The Laurels*, when I was nine, I remember gazing with admiration at my work on one of these, and as I reflected on the progress made - in this and other areas as well - I came to the conclusion that very soon there would be little that I could not do. Although when I look back it seems as if there was nothing but constraint and confinement, it can't have been entirely like that, for there was the time when a leg of my bed went through the dormitory floor, and it then came to light that I was in the habit of taking off from across the room into a splendid spread-eagled pancake, landing on to the bed. My aunt refused to pay the for the new floorboard. As she put it to me afterwards, she didn't feel that replacements to an early Victorian family house in use as an institution was her responsibility - good gracious, there were seven beds in the room concerned - it only surprised her that all the floorboards did not give. The end of *The Laurels* came when my father discovered where I was.

'Do you like it there?', he asked.

'Yes'

'Do they tell you to say that?'

To say the least, the approach was unfamiliar. As something of the implication sank in, I stood speechless, filled with ever widening rings of amazement. He pointed out to my aunt that I would have to earn my living. A good school with qualified staff was essential. At the new London secondary schools, girls could be prepared for the universities and the fees were reasonable. It was necessary, however, to pass an entrance test. He did not seem much cheered by what he learned of teaching methods at *The Laurels*.

Visits to my father were widely spaced and it was just as well. According to my aunt all men were dictators - they thought they knew - but this was nothing to the exaltation of the medical profession who held themselves up as gods - they **knew** they knew. Aunty knew they didn't know. My father, therefore, she dismissed as a little tin god laying down the law. His speeches simply rebounded. Unfortunately, it was not the same with me. It was this way from the beginning, and so it remained to the end; and I am almost as much at a loss to explain it now as I was then. I felt no animosity towards him. The trouble began when he got down to lecturing aunty, and it was certainly not what was said for I could not have understood. I was upset by what I was unable to avoid - the tone. With unfailing regularity, all too soon after I'd been dumped in the big leather armchair in the consulting room, I would start to cry. And as I grew older I could only hold this off for rather longer periods. I remember lying back in the hugely accommodating chair, desperately trying to fix my attention away on a wall of books: red book, green book, three black books, one brown book, two fat blue books, and so on. I tried calling to my aid the framed sepia print over the mantlepiece of a rough sea lashing a rocky shore. But no matter how hard I worked that tone came pounding through till it obliterated all else. It was an extraordinary experience - intense and precise - of being literally rammed in the breast-bone and relentlessly ground down. As in some terrible dream, I felt it, heard it and saw it. I was still not being spoken to, and as understanding advanced, I studiously avoided listening. When directly addressed, it didn't happen, but then nothing that mattered was said to me.

I think now that our visits to him were a mistake. Unquestionably he meant to do right, but the situation accentuated what was wrong. Not that they were seen by anyone as social events. I was subjected to a brief physical examination, and then he settled back and the trouble began. I feel sure my father, a keen psychologist (as I later discovered), was only trying to get across to my mother the sort of direction he firmly believed I should be having, and knew I wasn't. It made no impression on her, while the thrust and tenor of it came unerringly through to me. His tone clearly revealed that something was wrong. Despite my acute reaction, I didn't take this to myself, neither did I ascribe it to another: it was simply there. He knew it. Aunty disregarded it. I was unable to support it. It wasn't until much later that I came to see my father in a less than flattering light. During my schooldays he featured as someone colourful and exciting. I knew so little about him, and most of it at secondhand, that inevitably he was more legend than person. He was born in a remote village, overlooking the Atlantic, in wild craggy country where the doctor did his rounds on a horse. My father had a passion for horses, and, after horses, travel. For the best part of his life he travelled widely and rode strongly, supported by tropical medicine. He came home to settle down at forty, and was in-toed as a jockey to the end. This last I considered so dashing, I even reproduced it for a time. Till one morning, an irritable old man, surveying the world from his garden gate, suddenly shouted, *'Turn your feet out like a lady!'* I had no particular wish to be so described but the shock tactics worked.

I remember my father telling us that an Arab could be slashed in the stomach and ride forty miles to a medical post, holding his gut in one hand, reins in the other, be stitched up and straightway ride off again. They lived a hard life on a handful of dates, he said' and then suddenly, switching to the here and now, he remarked that it was possible to sustain life on garibaldi biscuits. He said this so severely I took it to mean that our sumptuous diet of eggs, cheese, peas and beans was costing him too much. Probably the biscuits were purely defensive, set up to known down what he knew only too well was about to follow, for every time his path crossed ours aunty did her best to touch him for an extra pound or two. This was on one of his exceedingly rare visits to us and I was eyeing out of the window his successor to the horse. Not luxurious, no, but chauffeur-driven nontheless. Aunty had come up behind me. *'Doubles as gardener and polishes the shoes'*, murmured my father aside, as he pocketed his wallet and stepped smartly through the door.

3

Playing the Game in the Right School and a Cottage in the Country

I came home from *The Laurels* to find we had moved again. The nearest suitable school was the *Latimer and Godolphin* in Hammersmith. My aunt went to look it over and returned full of enthusiasm. The headmistress was a fine woman of brilliant intellect and interested in art. *'I suggested that she might like to come and see my work, she would make an excellent portrait.'* But at the entrance test I dashed all our hopes by not getting one mark for arithmetic. Aunty's second journey in search of a school took her to Fulham. This headmistress, while not having quite the dazzle of the previous one - there was no mention of a portrait - was nonetheless an interesting and intelligent woman, *She was very ready to acknowledge the importance of the artist.'* It was the importance of arithmetic that was the trouble. Journey three took aunty to Putney. She returned, furious. It was plain that the interview hadn't gone according to plan. Not only was this headmistress no art-lover, she was no lady either. But for me a miracle had happened. For if art had gone overboard, so also had the entrance test for without even seeing me this headmistress was giving me a place. It was the importance of education that mattered at last, in this school, administered with humanity and insight. Almost certainly it was the first time that this combination of qualities had come my way, and as I look back it seems to me now that at this point the mist lifted and the first light appeared.

The school was an immediate success. It was that larger life again, glimpsed at the Abbey. I was all appetite and energy. The journey alone required a certain stamina. Believe it or not, we had moved yet again, and as far as I was concerned not in the right direction. The road we now lived in was a long one: I started off with a sprint down this - out of Kensington into Shepherds Bush where I caught a bus for

Hammersmith Broadway - here I changed to a tram for the main part of the journey through Fulham into Putney - I jumped off at Wandsworth High Street and rushed up West Hill. To run rather than walk came naturally to me, though at the time I was left with little choice as no-one in our household was much good at getting up in the morning. The school main building was at the top of the hill, the junior department occupied a private house further along the Upper Richmond Road. It was at the end of a long drive, past an ancient spreading mulberry tree, staple diet of countless munching silkworms in cardboard boxes and discarded tins.

I quickly found I did well where speed and agility counted. I became form vice-captain of games. I was captain for a term, but it was a relief when this came to an end - I had no idea of leadership. In the field, the only competition came from a half-French girl in a parallel form, who was even smaller than me and just as fleet. The game of games was the match between our respective forms with the two of us facing each other across the centre. I remember accompanying the games staff back to the school after the first of these matches. *'A good game'*, she remarked, and I could not have been more mystified - could she have forgotten the score already? *'But we didn't win!'*, I said. . A similar situation had occurred when we'd voted for the captains. We closed our eyes, and as the nominees were read out, raised an arm. I knew no better than to vote for myself - it seemed to me the natural thing to do. Till some Peeping Tom volunteered the information. I can still remember my amazement and see my form mistress's thoughtful face as, without a word, she directed a second voting.

Nothing in my background had prepared me for standards such as these, but assimilation was rapid, and after that there can have been no more devoted follower. To have a yardstick at all gave a wonderful feeling of support, but to me it was more than this: it was a shining code of behaviour that exalted the person - you told the truth; you owned up; you never informed; you controlled your feelings; and in competition it was the fair trial of strength that mattered more than the result. In addition, identification with my form gave an unprecedented feeling of belonging. It was like living in a glow. There were also revelations in the gym. On our first visit we were lined up for inspection. In front of me the mistress halted. *'Is this your tunic?'* It was a Central European version, cut low at the neck, laced to the waist and set on a gathered skirt. Aunty was a dab hand at running up frocks from remnants, often with knickers to match from bits left over. At least it was navy blue. On another occasion I was upside-down on the ribstalls when she lingered. *'Do you always wear plaid knickers for gym?'*, she inquired. There was no censure in the light-dropped, faintly quizzical remark, to the suspended junior yet another fascinating token of the new civilization.

At this school lessons were delightful adventures. We were encouraged to express and expand. You could draw for history and draw for geography. There was botany and gardening, and - most wonderful of all - language was made to come alive. Before long I was coping with arithmetic. By the end of the year my place in the form was second. If this headmistress had taken a chance on my ability, as surely she must have done, I like to think she might have felt some gratification as she signed my summer-term report. I had two outstanding form mistresses. The first was very young, the other a much older woman who left to become headmistress of a similar school. I don't remember anything in particular that they said or did, it was the wonderful feeling of being accepted as a person, even one that mattered. Whereas at *The Laurels* the family and children were in opposing camps, here I knew they were for me and it was like waking up in a new beneficent world. And if I revelled in it so much that at times I stood on my head, there was an intelligent and sympathetic understanding even of this. I wished with all my heart that I could stay at this school for the holidays.

All too quickly, the time came when the small group with its open range activities was at an end. We left the Junior House to join hundreds of others in the main building. We now trod the separate corridors of the specialist powers, and I found it uncomfortable at first. There could be no doubt the elderly English staff held an excellent record of sixth-form scholarships: she had scant patience with immaturity. It was no longer possible to ignore your set prep and hand in a play instead. In literature itself, the same transition had to be made. From the marvels of *Hiawatha, The Lays of Ancient Rome, The Forsaken Merman* and *A Midsummer Night's Dream*, to a trifle called *Home Thoughts from Abroad*, - as far as I could see quite the most feeble poem ever written. I joined the school library. And soon afterwards came the never-to-be-forgotten moment when I turned the last page of *Treasure Island*, the first full-length book I'd read on my own. I retired to sit on the old black trunk, shunted out of the way up a dark passage, the better to savour the sheer magnitude of the experience. I was in no two minds about this. I saw myself seated in the middle of a spacious salon under a high glass dome, with all round me, edge to edge, doors that I knew could be opened at will on to an infinity of horizons.

The revelations continued. Quite out of the blue I was struck by another, even more extraordinary, experience. I stayed for school dinner. At the end of each table a senior presided: the head of ours was a nice-looking girl with dark eyes and I fell in love. Here was another awakening. This time in a different dimension. In some mysterious way I found myself in alignment with another, someone I hardly knew in the only sense I was familiar with. The thing was so direct it didn't matter that we had no shared experiences - these were no longer the stuff of companionship, merely embellishment. There was hardly the need to say anything, though I chattered away. But most amazing of all it marked the end of isolation. My own precious me that I clung to with all my might was now in active extension, and far from its being - as you would have thought - the end of everything, here I was tingling all over with joyful delight! And now I became aware of myself from the outside. I saw her in a blaze of light - it was as if I had never really looked at anyone before, and I saw myself in the surrounding illumination almost equally transformed and made notable. It was like being on a stage that went round with you everywhere. But I was soon to find that even so exalted a state could bring in its train fatiguing complications, for the light that lit my love and me shone on other phenomena as well, some of an earthy nature. It became necessary to tidy myself up; worse, wash my neck every morning. I could laugh with the rest at her cropping plan for the area, but the point was taken. How splendid - heroic even, it all was.

At home it was different. It was about this time that I began to suffer from irrational fears. The trouble could have stemmed from a shock. I was in a tram struck by lightning and as I watched with objective interest long flames shoot up from the end of it, the woman in the seat beside me stood up and screamed, and in that instant I was filled with terror. It was unfortunate that shortly after this there was another storm, particularly violent, that continued for most of that night. It featured forked lightning with mauve and turquoise iridescence - according to aunty. I was under the bedclothes, curled up to present as small a target as I could against the possible descent of a thunderbolt. And as the fear spread to include the constellations, this posture became a regular feature. For it was strongly felt that the heavenly bodies were not secure. I had noted shooting stars; what was there to stop one shooting down on me? The sight of them coldly glittering right up there, surely only just eluding gravity, was deeply disturbing. On clear nights, if I had to go out, I was careful to concentrate on the pavement.

Noise, too, was troubling. Buffeting winds were particularly noticeable round the back of the flat where we slept, and on these occasions a bed had to be made up for me in the studio. Things that go bump in the night had always been a feature of our household. It was usually either the *Self Portrait*, a six-foot-square painting of my aunt in evening dress, draped across a Chippendale armchair, or the *Singing Girl*, a composition almost as large that took in a grand piano. Or it might be a pastel, if anything worse as they were glass-covered, and usually in heavy ornate frames. These crashed had always brought me out in a sweat, but now they had become entangles with premonitions of the end of the world. There were even intimations of other worlds. Aunty had started a weekly art class, and when this group of maiden ladies tired of fruit and flowers, I was roped in (heavily bribed) as model. The numbers ebbed and flowed, but chiefly ebbed till it was down to one. This was a woman older than my aunt, patently sincere, and gifted - who can for sure say not - in matters beyond normal comprehension. Her nights, it seemed, were peopled with spirits. Unfortunately, she chose to describe all this one Saturday afternoon as she worked. Aunty found it enjoyable, even reassuring, whereas to the already morbidly neurotic model it came as a most untimely introduction to transcendental affairs.

But while on the one hand I seemed to be the victim of a disordered imagination, on the other I appeared able - equally unconsciously - to work creatively with it. From another of my aunt's pupils, now no longer living in London, came an invitation to spend a sketching holiday on the Somerset coast. And since I couldn't be left behind I had to be included, which was hard on the pupil, a large unbending lady who didn't greatly care for the young. I didn't care for the pupil, or her newly-built house, her dog had fleas and where was the sea? I had brought my bathing costume, but every time we went down to the front it was just a wet stony waste with no water in sight. My aunt and the pupil painted and mild walks were taken; but Exmoor, the area I wished to visit, was summarily ruled out. People were always getting lost. It wasn't my holiday, I understood that, however on the last day a safe motor coach trip to Oare and the Doone Valley was allowed. I had just read the book. To this day any isolated moorland fold in low hills suggests the valley where the Doones were supposed to have had their farm. Though I'm not certain now whether this corresponds to what was seen then, or the one I saw when I read the book. Similarly, *Wuthering Heights* is called to mind by a certain pitch in the sound of the wind. It is hard to say now how much of this mixture of literature and physical geography led to the idea of living in the country. It surely contributed.

A Cottage in the Country

What a divine idea! I believe I thought it original as well. Unquestionbly it fell on fertile ground. All my resources, every reserve was pressed into service. Not only was the subject not allowed to drop, on every possible occasion it was craftily grafted into quite other conversation and discussions. After some initial astonishment, my aunt took it well. On the surface it was all good fanciful fun and we both enjoyed it, but as the weeks passed and I still held on, I had the satisfaction of seeing it fill in and become something of a project. I could see that it was beginning to take; it was as if wanting something hard enough, long enough, was working like a magnetic field to attract the desired result. The prospect was almost beyond conception. A place on its own. And as if this wasn't enough - like being on holiday all the time. Think of all the money we'd save by never needing to go away. Think of all the lovely landscapes aunty could paint - portraits were few and far between - and instead of having to buy flowers from a shop, she could pick them from the garden. It was all so simple and obvious.

In due course the right-sounding advertisement appeared, and the further particulars were equally inviting. It was a charming, three-bedroomed thatched cottage, two miles from an historic market town forty miles from London. There was a cobblestone path and honeysuckle round the door. It had just been done up: three coats of paint, and each bedroom colour-washed a different pastel shade. A sudden switch in circumstances required the owner to go abroad. The rent was less than half the amount we were paying for the London flat. After this it was in the nature of things that my aunt should go and see it. It turned out to be two cottages, with the ground floor still in a state of division. One front door opened into the living-room, the other into the sitting-room. It was therefore necessary to go out of the living-room into the elements to get to the sitting-room. Not that the inclination to enter the sitting-room was likely to arise often as it had no floor, just earth. Upstairs, one bedroom led off another and the floor boards were patched with tin. The garden was full of nettles. Finally, it was a sub-let: it belonged to the farmer up the hill. In view of all this the rent was plainly extortionate.

The next weeks were sad and subdued. So sure had I been that this was our cottage, I was quite unable to bring any other possibility into focus. Neither could I think of a way to defend a place I'd never seen. It seemed as if there was nothing I could do. But I had done all I needed to do. I had only to wait. One morning I woke up to find something special in the air again. I could detect a small shift in the climate of opinion. The reaction was setting in. Of course it was still maintained that the cottage was far from perfect, but this was not to say that it was without possibilities. The farmer up the hill had been righteously indignant at what he considered to be his tenant's double-dealing. *'All that money for two years for paint and colour-wash!'* And he had told my aunt that he would be delighted to have her as his tenant as soon as the other agreement ran out. Further, he would see what could be done about the sitting-room floor. And to help pay for this she was sure she could knock down the rent by a handy half-crown. There were other possibilities; she thought she might advertise with a view to getting a holiday sketching class going. And now it came to light that while she was in the historic market town she had called on the headmistress of the Girls' Grammar School. She had also ferreted out a thriving art club, while a quotation from Bourlet had shown that the cost of sending pictures to town for exhibition was not as excessive as she had feared.

Finally, as if to set the seal on our plans for an exciting - by now almost **beckoning** future, the large lady on the Somerset coast made a dramatic re-entry into our affairs. Her brother in New Zealand had just got married and built a house, and was now demanding the family portraits. How did my aunt feel about making copies? There were ten! In those days a hundred pounds was a tidy sum. To us it was a fortune. And so, at last, the decision was made. As aunty put it, *'If it is to be, it is to be!'*

It was to be.

It is hard to credit that I never faltered, never paused, at the prospect of moving away from that fine school where I'd so generously been given a place - literally lifted into another world - and where I was so happy. But by this time it was being taken for granted. Taken for granted also that it was bound to be even better in some pastoral vale or heathery heath.

Woodbine Cottage

4

Woodbine Cottage - Another School - a Different Game

The head removal man was appalled twice. First as he slammed shut and bolted the back of his van and was saying goodbye to my aunt. It was in his mind that we were about to part and meet again at the cottage that afternoon. It was in her mind that this was a quite unnecessarily roundabout and expensive procedure - we were accompanying the furniture. *'No, madam, that is not allowed!'* But by the time she had finished with him he was only too willing to settle for the easy way out. He slid back the bolts and made space for us to sit on my grandfather's old black trunk. The domed lid of this ancient cabin monster made a most uncomfortable seat, but neither of us minded this. I was only concerned about being seen coming out of the back with the furniture when we got there. A wholly unworthy thought, I knew, and one which would be most unlikely to occur to my aunt, or to trouble her if it did.

The removal man was even more appalled when he saw the cottage. *'I would not live in it, madam.'* He was not alone in this. The farmer's wife had felt the same. They lived at the top of the hill in a newly-built redbrick house, to us ugly and jerry-built. And we were to find that this was the pattern of change going on all round us. As the villagers moved out into council houses, so residents moved delightedly into the cottages. *The Singing Girl* just got in through the door. The full-length *Self Portrait* ended up across the rafters of an adjacent barn, as no way short of knocking down a wall could it be got inside. There was probably no more space in the cottage than in the London flat. It was the space all round that made the difference. And as for the first time I was having a bed to myself in a room of my own, there was valuable personal detachment as well. The best view was said to be from my room. It was pleasant enough, away across flat country to the soft blue outline of distant hills. What I didn't exactly relish was the much vaunted honeysuckle which was all bare

The kitchen range

peeling legs round the front door and came to a bushy head under my window. If it had any scent it was never wafted in my direction, and the flowers were followed by unsavoury-looking berries. It also provided access for wild life. Energetic and adventurous earwigs made regular unwelcome appearances in my socks, my sponge and my bed.

There was also wild life in the living room, where a small kitchen range had been built into a huge open fireplace, leaving dark impenetrable ingle-nooks. Out of these in peaceful moments would silently appear enormous, spine-chilling spiders with hairy legs and eyes that hung down on hooks. The cottage walls were so thick, deep cupboards were flushed into them and window seats cut out. Off the living-room was a scullery with an attractive checkered sink of red and blue quarry tiles and a hardwood surround. Out of the scullery, the larder was large enough to walk about in, with, across one wall, an enormous slate slab above our eye-level and stretching back beyond arm's-length. It was necessary to mount a block, kindly supplied by the nice young farmer. At a later date the far larder wall was knocked out to provide access to the earth sitting-room by that time tiled. Opposite the front door was the well. It had a ground-level lid on long iron hinges, and behind it lay a hooked pole. We had known about the well. That it was the only source of drinking water for seven cottages, we had not known. Worst of all it was necessary to pass in front of our living-room window to get to it. The cottagers were soon divided into those who always looked in and those who never did. But it was splendid sparkling water, ice-cold in the hottest weather, and if the occasional bucketful presented us with a frog or two, we were never any the worse for it. The 'hovel' was a lean-to shed with a beaten earth floor where we kept coal and wood. In a far corner was a sentry-box with a wooden seat and bucket under, with to hand another bucket filled with earth. One day that never came we were going to have an Elsan.

The cottage was called *Woodbine* after the honeysuckle. This didn't find favour with my aunt who wanted it called *The Cottage*. I couldn't think of anything dottier myself: fortunately there was one already. She then wanted *Hillside Cottage* but there was one of these too. In the end she settled for *Hillside*, in my opinion every bit as weak. To finalize the matter she put out a unique sign, impressionistically lettered on a piece of untrimmed canvas stretcher. This was altogether more than I could stand, so stealthily, by night, I took it off and slung it in a ditch.

Immediately on top of the hill was the manor house. We were on the edge of the manor spinney with its white violets and wild arum. Inside was cool and quiet and dimly lit. A shallow stream ran through it and came out to cross a narrow neck of field where it was full of watercress and enclosed a secluded grassy opening popular with rabbits: with any luck, a careful approach on a fine day revealed them enjoying the sun like people on a beach. This spinney, hardly farther away than the bottom of our garden, was regarded as being as much my domain as the farm, to which it was preferred, being both less domesticated and more private. More private, certainly, for the day came when I encountered a stranger with a gun and was ordered off. Of course I knew that the spinney was private property, but so were the fields - they all belonged to some farmer or other - this part of the estate was wild. From then on I reconnoitred with care before going in and went forward with caution thereafter. The manor was at this time the property of a well-to-do widow, a lady seldom seen, whose sole concession to the social life of the village was the traditional annual fête held in the grounds. My aunt, however, had already successfully pressed in and made a drawing of one of her boys.

My aunt liked to go to town on market day for the cheaper shopping. Although on this day there was a bus, we walked. Besides the obvious perennial consideration, it was good, healthy exercise, so either way we couldn't lose. There was nothing hidden or apart about the market-place in our little town. The wide main street islanded the town hall and beyond it spread still further to accommodate the cattle market. It was fine open planning, open also to rousing occasions of much good cheer to the young, as it was not unknown for a lively bullock to break loose and charge, bellowing down the High Street. A non-stop rattle of running commentaries arose from along by the town hall where most of the vendors had their stalls. Some of the regular traders arranged their wares on the road. The man with china seconds was one of these. Aunty bought, piece by piece, week by week, a nice, imperfect dinner service with octagonal vegetable dishes that she fancied.

The season advanced with a rush of growth, and soon it was high summer with poppies like flecks of paint in fields of hay that rippled in the wind like the sea, and the hedgebanks too, grew high and lush with waving grasses. Then just as it was at its peak, a roadman shaved it down to a mat of bare spiky stalks and I suffered an acute sense of loss. It was always the same; followed by relief and wonder as the grassy wilderness grew again and once more all was right with the world.

I was to have a bicycle. Meanwhile, I walked to school. In good weather it was possible to short-cut across country. One morning I was struck by the lustre of the field and when I stopped for a closer look found millions of daddy-long-legs daintily settled on gently waving grasses, the sheen of their wings like mother-of-pearl in the slanting sun. On another occasion I was late returning. I had to cross over a river, and by the time I reached the bridge it was dark. The river had flooded the meadows on either side, a double row of leaning willows marked its winding course and the fields were mapped by the straggling tops of hedgerows transfixed in the still water. But the marvel was myself, standing on the bridge as suspended in the universe. For as far as you could see everywhere you looked it was the same. The river and fields were filled with the whole starry sky in reproduction, as perfect as in the original. These were moments of pure reception, free from distorting fears. Only a short while before, the night sky had seemed so menacing I dared not even look up. Soon after this, I was whizzing to school on two wheels, full of thrills of a different kind.

While the Girls' Grammar School in the small market town served the local community, it was primarily a boarding school. Compared with London there was less teaching, much more physical education, with games every day, and a striking amount of prep. It was also a private school, jointly owned by the headmistress and housemistress. But the most important difference lay in the discipline. At the London school discipline had been not so much implemented as understood. At the Girls' Grammar School it was expressed in a network of rules and regulations with the headmistress seen to be in charge of the staff as well as the children. True, many of the staff were straight from college: they came to gain experience for a year or two before going on to better things. During my four years in this school there was a complete turnover - not one there when I arrived was still there when I left. To begin with I sat silently back, taking stock. I was staggered at what I saw. You could play the fool *ad lib*, to answer back was routine. Where I had come from to be rude to the staff was unthinkable, here there was open defiance, and with the headmistress behaving as she did it wasn't altogether surprising to find the qualifications of the staff to teach held in question. *'She likes to tell us about the fun she had at college - it's easier than teaching!'* She did, and when you looked at it like that, it was. Though not all the staff were like this. My first form mistress wasn't one of the inexperienced or defenceless ones, she had hard bright eyes and a whiplash tongue, and I rejoiced greatly when she left conveniently soon after my arrival.

And so I came to the conclusion that this, too, in its different way, was a wonderful school, and as soon as I had my bearings I plunged in. To the staff I was selfish, a show-off, a rebel. I was all of these. Yet it seemed to me then that my behaviour was natural enough, given such phenomenally rewarding opportunities. The more rules and regulations, the more merrily I set about kicking over the traces. As far as I was concerned, to cut down on transgression by blocking opportunity was to stimulate ingenuity and daring. I possessed abundant energy and a lively, growing appetite for recognition and applause. I became the form fool. *'Ay, now am I in Arden; the more fool I'* (we were doing *As you Like It.*) The idea was to have as much fun as possible while doing as little work as possible, and as far as this aim was concerned I was extraordinarily successful over a surprisingly long period.

At the Grammar School we had weekly class marks, grading the whole school, read out every Monday morning at assembly. In this scheme of things I had a place all my own. Bang at the bottom, as regular as amen after the praying, came my name followed by D. There was one variation - when I suddenly thought what a joke it would be to hit the other end of the scale, my name first, followed by A. I was certain I could do it, and for a week really worked. But I'd reckoned without what my father called my flair for phonetics. Even plant sections and maps were marked down due to spelling mistakes in the labelling. So that when Monday came round again it was only an unremarkable and unremarked B+ in a sandwiched position. The next week I had plummeted back to D in the depths, and I never bothered again. There were exceptions. I liked poetry. I never expended much effort on art, but then I never needed to.

Music was more than an exception, it was eccentric. To begin with I didn't take it. Instant interest was aroused by the appointment of a young and dashing music mistress. As there were others it was a bit of a gamble, but I was lucky. I had no aptitude and made minimal progress - not that I was aware of this - till one day she remarked that at least I wasn't like some, a block upon which no sort of impression could be struck. This backhanded compliment alerted me to the situation, but the subject of our assignments was to me so incidental that the remark, while it caused some wonder, was hardly a matter for concern. My problems were different. I quickly found that it was one thing to adore from a distance, quite another to decently conduct myself when alone with the loved one in a very small room with only a piano for support. I was startled to find myself suffering from shivering fits in conditions of adequate heating. The situation was not improved by near-panic in case she noticed. I discovered that the fits were worst in periods of inactivity. It was vital to be active in the shortest possible time. In fact there was no stopping me, hardly waiting for permission to enter I was inside, seated, music up and off my mark. As it turned out, in spite of the impure motive and absence of aptitude I was to find in music a very real new excitement. I enjoyed scales. Upset at not being required to do *arpeggios*, I did them on my own. Theory fascinated me. The appearance of written music with its signatures, signs and ornaments was intensely pleasurable; and as for the Italian terms, it was thought that these must surely be the finest flowering of any language. Thus it was from the beginning and in every sense, *con molto amore.* To begin with we had no piano, so I practised at school. Then one was bought for a few pounds at a local sale and it added a new dimension. My aunt played and sang the romantic music she loved, Schumann, Chopin, *Abide with Me* and *Come into the Garden, Maud*. I thumped out scales, *arpeggios, Chopsticks* and interminable earnest renderings of *The Merry Peasant*.

To the school the headmistress was known as Hippo - popularly, the 'Ip'. She was undeniably a curious shape. She had a large body that tapered to well-made calves and slender ankles, thinned out to delicate hands, and up to an unexceptional neck and face. But she was always well turned out and carried her unwieldy body well upright, sweeping smartly forward with a bouncing gait. She was amazingly light on her feet. More than once when sent to her, as I waited in the lobby outside her room, I heard someone running lightly down the long narrow corridor that led to it. The first time this happened I was sure it was one of my form, dispatched by a forgiving staff with my reprieve. Then all at once a lightly prancing Hippo, still up on her toes, was upon me - though it was a minute or two before she could speak, and she continued to pant between the questions.

Cultivation of the pleasure principle as a way of life in an institutions dedicated to different ends ensured for the dissenter a highly satisfactory limelit course of minor drama and incident. And when I look back on these years at the Grammar School its succession of staff, it is the long, enduring relationship with the headmistress that stands out. It was like a ballet, with the two of us as the principal dancers. The hours spent standing outside her door. The time spent working at a specially placed desk in the lobby of her private quarters. Our regular trials of strength, skirmishes and exchanges in all keys, all tempos, and all degrees of intensity. Yet this dance of opposing forces had a certain wayward grace, for at base there was no dislike. There was the time I'd decorated a notice put up in the gym. Some petti-fogging new regulation. A short typed line in the middle of a foolscap sheet. I even sneaked in after dinner to give it a dash of bright colour. At least now it looked interesting. The new young games staff didn't agree. She had no imagination. No sense of humour either - had once reported me for '*kicking a netball that struck a member of the staff in the face*'. (Reports had to be filled in on blue forms.) Of course the target had been accidental: I was simply returning the ball from behind the back line in the most effective way. **But the wording!** I was in exultation - could you believe it!? She now gave me a hundred lines, '*I must not deface a notice written by a member of the staff.*' The length! It wouldn't go into the width of a sheet of paper. I didn't do them. They were doubled. I still did nothing and she went on doubling till, topping a thousand, I began to lose my nerve. But then had the bright idea of doing them in school time. Maths or French would be best, we had too much of both. But Samson (maths), 'Stinking Sam' - as far as would see the only mistress indisputably and fully in league with The 'Ip, could hardly be seen as suitable. The French option was different. Indeed very possible. We had it every day, it was dead boring, and Miss Thomas was as her name implied. Think of learning French with a Welsh accent!

Better not to. I got down to work at once and was soon the proud possession of a goodly pile of paperwork. From time to time I saw her eyeing me thoughtfully, but nothing was said. She's heard about it and feels sorry for me, I thought innocently - she's decent really. I also fancied she had a soft spot for me. Why else would she be for ever keeping me in after school to hear my irregular verbs?

I was busy calculating how many periods it would take to finish the imposition, when the bell went for break and to my amazement I heard her demanding the precious sheets, *'You can bring all of that to me!'* **After watching me do them!** Not likely! A quick shuffle and they were stuffed under the clutter in my desk. I was ordered to stay where I was. She dismissed the class and charged off, not in the direction of the staffroom. By the time the 'ip' arrived the sheets were torn up and in the wastepaper basket. She took a tight-lipped look and me and the basket were summarily manhandled into the science lab. The door slammed, the key turned. I indulged in a quiet giggle. This was just the sort of new, dramatic turn of events I revelled in. What would she think up next? - handcuffs, ball and chain to the leg, perhaps? She returned with paper and paste. I heartily enjoyed that double period of imprisoned jigsawpuzzling. The sheets were soon all shapes weird and wonderful. When The 'Ip returned to let me out, I noted a flicker of amusement. *'Now take them to Miss Thomas.'* No flicker there. I was then sent to the games staff, and told she'd accept my lines on the instalment plan. In this instance, both principal players were pleased with themselves; but it wasn't usually anything like as amicable, and I was far from unaware of how near the edge my antics often came. If I didn't look out, one day I was going to wake up and find the party over.

Meanwhile, wonder of wonders, I had found a friend. Or rather, she must have found me. I would never have had the confidence, let alone presumption to entertain thoughts of such an unheard of alliance. She was a boarder. She was also form captain, on the face of it another unlikely choice as we were an unacademic jollyhockeysticking bunch, and Rachel hated games, and was always up near the top when marks were read out. The two of us were wide apart in other ways as well. But together we specialized - rather well we thought - at showing up authority as counterfeit and crazy, each reacting according to our different temperaments: fool, me; wise woman, she. In fact, she seldom played an integral part in my idiotic interludes, but would, when moved, contribute some wry aside, or set the seal on a performance with a capping remark, always in the same throw-away mutter, which somehow suggested that the insult had not so much come from her as been channelled from some exasperated, wider-ranging intelligence. And all the time looking down at her desk with a pained expression. Such weird cleverness filled me with admiration. But the low voice, the shadowed strain in Rachel was real enough, and seemed to stem from some unmentionable source, one she was only able to skirt round before suddenly drawing back from the telling. Her origin was imprinted in

Phyllis looking out of her bedroom at Woodbine Cottage

her dark good looks. She came out to the cottage one Sunday. *'She's Jewish, of course,'* said my aunt, who assessed everyone with a view to a portrait; I could see that she didn't fancy Rachel. Was it anything to do with this? It was never spoken of.

In the formroom the two of us were seated well apart. If anything, our duos were rendered more ridiculously effective. There was never the need for a glance. Like most pairs of performers each fitted the other's ticket to a turn. I, up in the air. She, earthed. Body and standing were my gains. Together we must have been surreal. As the outside examinations approached we were given a week of supervised revision. Out of this golden opportunity flowered the one time we really did work in tandem. We were promptly removed from the scene. I can't recall where Rachel went. I was back at the desk outside the head's study. We both did well. Rachel passed in all subjects, with many distinctions. I, with the required number of passes.

The village was separated from us not by distance but by precipitance. We were one of a small group of cottages at the bottom of a very steep, exceedingly rough hill, which in stormy weather became a raging torrent. These were the last years of the self-oriented village. At this time the few superimposed residents all had maids, or 'a girl', or at least a woman to come in. But none had cars. There was a village bus on market day and another bus ran once a week to the nearest city. Other than this it was taxi and train. In this small community we got to know people in a way we never had in London. People 'called'. These brief encounters, conveniently ice-breaking for the newcomer, and affording both parties uncommitted appraisal, provided my aunt with a golden opportunity to show her work. There was one snag. Our callers could never get the time right. If they called in the morning she was in the bath; if they missed the bath she was having breakfast. If they called in the afternoon she was having her midday meal. That the front door opened like the curtain going up straight on the scene, didn't appear to trouble her, but when I was home I suffered enough for us both. She made two friends. They lived near each other right in the village so that of the triangle she formed a weak far corner socially as well as topographically and this worked well. Nonetheless, friends they were; they called each other by their Christian names, and no-one lightly got this far with my aunt. They were both widows, one agnostic, the other Catholic. The Agnostic was a lone rider, a woman of strange opposites, living moderately in a tiny cottage while saving to winter in the south of France. She was spare and ascetic-looking with a high, discriminating Roman nose, even more splendid than my aunt's. She was well read, even avant-guarde. Copies of the Windham Lewis periodical, *Blast*, lay about. Her husband had been a struggling writer. After his early death from tuberculosis (the writer's disease, she explained), his place had been taken by an older man - a novelist of high repute, now also dead. I was invited to inspect an impressive row of signed volumes.

The Catholic was a war widow with a boy. She was a distinguished-looking falcon of a woman with hooded eyes and a long neck of which she took full advantage, wearing pendant earings of great length with striking effect. She had been better off, and experienced difficulty - so it appeared - in adapting to present circumstances. I was never able to puzzle out these ever-arising monetary crises. Just how was it possible to spend more than you had? There would be all this fuss and frantic rushing up to town to see the bank and solicitors and then she came home with an expensive new dress or a Bond Street handbag. Whichever way you worked it out it didn't add up. This one went to Italy, she could never afford it of course, but there was always some compelling reason, usually arising out of the ecumenical calendar. The son was three years younger than me. He was an attractive small boy, compliant and devoted. Trained from the earliest age, he already looked after his mother and a good deal of the cottage as well. He was as useful as I was useless. In every way the situation there was the opposite of ours.

At fourteen I had a low opinion of my aunt. For one thing, till the time we left London, she had been able to help me with my homework, notably French and maths, but now she was left behind and this led me to view her level of mental performance as below average. After all she couldn't even remember people's names. In fact much of the time it seemed as if she was unable to correctly take in what was going on round her. I also noted that she had plenty of vulgar curiosity but none of the intellectual kind. She never read a book. She read the paper for the postal bargains. She had no sense of proportion, and as for fair play, she could scarcely be said to know what this was. Gone for ever was the little girl who silently absorbed. I was now only too articulate. My aunt, stung and shocked, retaliated - I was intolerant, absurdly critical, spoilt and a dictator, like my father.

There was another suffering member of our household. The day before we left London I was offered a stray kitten. My aunt didn't care for animals, they only cared for her. *'Isn't it funny: I don't like them and they always come to me!'* So I was astonished when she agreed to take it, especially as at the time we had no idea what to expect. But 'he' was always 'she' to my aunt to whom only dogs were masculine. He turned out to be neutered which suggests he lost a more respectable home than I was ever able to give him. With us he was a poor relation, foraging on the outskirts. He slept in the hovel and in the cottage was restricted to the kitchen floor. To be fair, he was adequately fed. Our meals fascinated him and he would sit in silent concentration in the middle of the living-room floor, gazing at us. My aunt couldn't stand this and made it plain. He then sat in exactly the same place with his back to us, only occasionally looking longingly round over his shoulder. My aunt's way of dispatching him was to position her foot under his body and lob. This way he sailed sideways-on across the room or out of the door, and he knew better than to come back. Yet none of this treatment in any way altered his goodwill towards us. After any trouble he always returned with the same delicately-offered humble expression.. It never occurred to him to question my aunt's authority. Such pureness of heart turned a knife in mine. I fought on his behalf, but of course it was true - as my aunt was fond of pointing out - that I did nothing to provide for him. That I did nothing, anyway, while she did everything, invariably followed and this was true enough, too. I chopped wood and brought in coal, but inside only helped with the washing-up - when pressed. But this lack in me was complained of as if it was something fixed. There was no instruction, never anything precise, and since I had what amounted to a total loathing of all things domestic I could hardly be expected to take proceedings. It was also true that everything my aunt did she had to do herself as no-one else was able to do it to her satisfaction. Not only this, there was never room, you were bound to be in the way as she needed free range in all directions. As she said herself, she was born to live in a mansion, *'I have this great need of space!'*, she would cry, waving her arms accusingly at the cottage walls. The War Widow's boy was pointed to, odious comparisons made, unfortunate conclusions drawn. It was undeniable that the situation was different, he was willing and the scope was wide. There seemed to be little that he had not tackled at one time or another, in one way or another. There was the time I'd gone there for a meal when his mother was away. While he was getting this the oil cooking stove caught fire and was slung out of the window. I was far from hidebound and only too used to oddity, even so, I was pretty astounded. If he had thrown it out of the door it wouldn't have seemed quite so curious. He then shut the window with a smirk, *'To keep out the smell.'*, and lit another. How many spare stoves did they have? How many did they get through over what sort of period? It was plain that he was not domesticated in any sense acceptable in our household, where my aunt spent half the night, or so it sounded to me lying in bed, cleaning our oil cooking stove.

Although my aunt was making friends, or more probably because of this, it was painfully clear to me that she didn't really fit in. If this had been because she felt deeply in any way about conventional standards I could have gone along with it. Instead, it seemed as if she was unaware of their existence. And she was so stupid. There was no getting away from this. There was the time she sent for a half-price, lost-label collection of assorted fruit trees from an advertisement in the paper. I argued and argued, but it made no difference. She wrote, giving her choices - Cox, Blenheim, Bramley, William pear, Greengage and Victoria plums. There was the time we went to the village fête held in the manor grounds. Everyone else went in by the farm entrance and bought a ticket. We swept in through the open house to the terrace and lawn where chairs were arranged for a performer - they were all filled except the front row where we sat down. At length the county party from the manor emerged to join us in the front seats. Exchanges like, *'Does an exclamation mark go inside or outside inverted commas?'*, *'Oh, I don't think it matters, why not put it on top?'*, didn't make for companionship. It was all very well for outsiders to laugh. I had to live with it - worse, was a part of it, for how could I be sure that one day this would not be me? She had received an excellent education at one of the first girls's high schools. *'Florence, you're a fool!'*, had pronounced her headmistress of my aunt the sixth-former, and you could very well see what she meant. My aunt would tell this story with a hearty laugh. She seemed only to see herself in the context of painting. That people didn't come up to paint was also something I could understand. The trouble was that they didn't come up at all: she appeared to be blind to the concerns of others. There was also this strange anomaly that I could never work out, that although she wasn't interested in people, she had an embarrassing, almost morbid curiosity concerning them. So that if a person had some weak spot or other, she displayed a positive genius for suddenly skewering it with some terrible direct question.

In school, the misadventures continued. I was still fooling around, enjoying cheaply-gained attention and form popularity. Sometimes the 'Ip was unexpectedly kind. Being sent out of a form room was nothing to worry about, you could go and sit in the cloakroom, but being sent out of the assembly hall, used for some classes, was rather less relaxing, as it meant being exposed in a wide tiled hallway, at the junction between the school building and the private quarters of its principals. One winter afternoon I was in uneasy vigil in this area when I heard the familiar elastic step. I pressed into the shadows, willing a miraculous invisibility. She approached to view me more clearly in the half-light. I can believe that I looked pretty troubled - there'd been rather too many recent tight corners for yet another to be fitted in with any degree of confidence. But instead of the usual questions and *'follow me'*, she remarked that I'd better be getting back to my form as the place was cold and draughty and the bell about to go. At other times she was unexpectedly savage. One day I received a message to report to her after school and got a rulering. I had no idea what for. It appeared that she'd run out of punishments that could properly be applied to girls. I was 'caned' with an eighteen inch science-room ruler. It could hardly have been more of a failure. It must have hurt, but I was so intrigued by the novelty of the situation that I felt nothing at all. I went round to the school entrance and pulled my bike out of the rack and if I was at all doubled up it was with wicked glee. My two travelling companions were waiting for me, both brimming with curiosity. Their mother kept the village shop. When we got there I was taken inside, and here my hands caused something of a sensation. Though now beginning to fade, they were still good ringing tones of blue and purple. *'If it was a girl of mine, I know what **I** would do!'*, announced my school friends' mother to the customers. It was a cheap reach-me-down line that fitted nowhere. With my hands the centre of attention, I reflected on yet another demonstration of how out of touch with reality it was possible for adults to be. Not that I was unduly disheartened at the prospect before me on this account, it was just that the ones I'd met so far weren't much gifted in this field.

These two sisters from the shop were the only other grammar school girls in the village. I was lonely enough at home to have welcomed any companionship, but I had little in common with the one nearer my age, and the other girl, two forms below me, was too young. I remember the three of us pushing our bikes up the long steep hill to the village - it was always the same - the older sister forging purposefully ahead, already more than fed up with the two of us fooling together behind. I approved of the younger girl, she had a streak of what for want of a better name I called 'essential honesty', an unaccommodating quality already the cause of friction at the back of the shop where very different values flourished. I was highly excited by the discovery of this quality which seemed to me to break new ground. Certainly it had nothing to do with the neat pigeon-holing of this is right and that is wrong. It was something different and difficult, always at a tangent to the accepted and orthodox.

Meanwhile, in the cottage as I struggled to assert what I saw to be my rights, the rows had moved on again, with wrecking scenes a feature of the worst of them. Years before, as my aunt pushed me in a swing in Kensington Gardens, I'd told her I'd never get married and leave her. There were times now when I could have murdered her. She was as impervious to the need for fair play as she was unaffected by elementary reasoning. Action was all that was left to me. Whipping the cloth from the table at breakfast was one form of workout. Two seconds of racketing smash-up and it was all over and I was silently helping to pick up the pieces and mop the mess. At other times I went to work on the living-room. This took longer and my aunt usually fled upstairs. I remember on one occasion, in the silent aftermath, hearing steps over the cobblestones to the front door. A letter was pushed under it. It was seen as a sign. Certainly it was taking a series of wild scenes to win me the right to open my own letters. It was always the injustice of the matter that hit hardest, and in bed at night I cried passionately into the pillow till I fell exhausted into sleep. And in the morning I would rush to the looking-glass, expecting to find myself hollowed and anguished, marked for life. But always the same indestructible, smooth-skinned, pink-cheeked schoolgirl looked back. Other people might go white in the night and show on their faces noble lines of suffering from the pains they had to bear - but never me.

Drama Most Fiery and drama Most Tragical, but far more often drama Most Comical. My aunt whose avowed intent had always been to paint the upper crust, was an unashamed snob, though, as she observed, the lower classes didn't buy portraits, the higher you went the more they did and the royals could never stop doing it. She was slushily soft on our own royal family, and most weekends when we sat over breakfast, it was a hilarious occasion as I came up with a further instalment of my Buckingham Palace saga about smart little Hattie, the flying

Above: Phyllis's bedroom in Woodbine Cottage

Left: In a corner of the living room

Paintings, oil on canvas, by Phyllis, aged 21. Jan Gordon, reviewing student sketches at the Warren Gallery, 'Arts and Artists', the Observer, *April 1934: "...the really amazing control of texture, colour and composition in 'Chair' by Phyllis Cstle (21)."*

Hapsburg hen. Bred in the shadow of the widely-acclaimed splendid prancing horses of the old Austro-Hungarian empire, the little Hapsburg hens were relatively unknown. Yet they were more remarkable. They were that in appearance, too - satiny buff and black shot red and green, they made spectacular pets. They were also exceedingly expensive. Their owners formed a small elite group, first centred on St. Petersburg, made up of - so it was said - the wealthiest women in the Western world. At the time I speak of - the early nineteen-twenties - best known of all the Hapsburg fowl was dashing little Hattie, apple of a royal eye, who, nesting in Queen Mary's toque, went with her everywhere. To buffet lunches and ceremonial banquets when tasty morsels speared up on a fork would be washed down with enthusiastic slurpings of offered-up champagne. And should the good Queen become so absorbed in some discussion - home rule perhaps, or it might be a piece of palace gossip - as to neglect the hungry feathered favourite overhead, then an agitated chatter would arise from the toque, getting louder and louder, till finally, pecked-off pieces of brocade shot up in the air and fell down on the food. To tinkling laughter and discreet guffaws. (It was a standing court joke that the bird, not Mary, wore the crown.) But by and by the clever little Hattie played her part, laying ready-cooked, large orange-centred purple eggs of truly ambrosial flavour, stamped with the crown in gold, clunk into egg cups lined up in the palace breakfast-room. And so on, and on.

And whatever it may sound like today, at the time it had the two of us rolling around over our own breakfast table, weak from mirth, the tears streaming down aunty's face. At times like these I was told that I kept her young. We were innocent still. I now, rather less than she: one of us was changing, had changed, and it made for dissonance. But Rachel was right, rows were normal enough in family life, it was bottling up that was bad.

5

Success and Disaster

When an evening lecture on a literary subject was to take place in the small market town with the schools attending, I prompted my aunt to ask if I could stay at school overnight, and this was agreed. I only wanted to go with a view to this end, I didn't care for being a day girl, you didn't properly belong. The event proved an unqualified success on more than one level. I was rivetted by the talk itself, on opium-eater Thomas de Quincey. And after that I was transported again, prancing up and down the dormitory corridor in my pyjamas with jugs and bowls of water. A day or two afterwards I was summoned to the 'Ip's study. It appeared that I had forgotten to tell her something she had to know. I tried hard to call to mind what this could possibly be. Even when asked directly if I'd enjoyed the talk and staying over, I could only offer a guarded affirmative. Thank you for letting me stay was all she wanted. I think my aunt thought nice manners dropped as the gentle rain from heaven upon those in need beneath. Perhaps on more receptive souls they do, but none reached me. Later, quite by chance, I discovered that the 'Ip had assured my aunt that there would be no charge.

Exactly how poor were we? Well we were. Unquestionably. Yet I never felt in any way deprived. When I had to forget the needlework money three weeks running at Mayfield, aunty said, *'Ask her if **she** knows what it's like to be short of half-a-crown!'*, and we both laughed till we were exhausted. But within a village, financial levels were more clearly seen. For sure we were no better off than many genuine cottagers, but we were also an anomaly. Although it looked that way, unlike most of the residents we didn't live on unearned income. For all her protesting, I'm sure my mother - we both - enjoyed our precarious existence. We were kept women with no strings and lives of our own, and it suited us well.

It is said of the Spanish St. Teresa that she greatly enjoyed a good meal, so much so that one astonished follower had been unable to resist remarking on it. The saint wasted no words, *'When eating - **eat**, When praying - **pray**.'*, she laid down. Yes. Aunty was like that. You had only to think of the bath. It was in her nature to go to work with a will. When brushing her hair, she brushed her hair and the wonder was she had any left. It was called being thorough. *'I'm very thorough!'*, she'd announce proudly for the umpteenth time, though no-one had ever denied it. She blew her nose like a tenor horn. And, as befitted a singer, when laughing she **laughed** - from the diaphragm, in a voice of wide range and unstinted enthusiasm. *'I'm afraid I'm not very ladylike.'* she'd exclaim breathlessly, adding, *'I have too much gusto!'* On the other hand, household washing was an historic event. Sheets didn't get dirty, we bathed - weren't navvies - we didn't perspire - they got plenty of air. And she was no cook - plain, very plain - uncooked was best. Cooked food on the plate was always awash and where was the flavour? Sea salt she did sparingly use, shaved from a block with the bread knife, it stood up on a dish. But what or however it was, it was manna to her. The **first** peas, **young spinach**, induced transportation, she was lost on another plane. Like Teresa. And then at the end of the day, she, too, had her **pièce de résistance**. When painting - she **painted**.

A quite staggering realisation emerges out of this portrait of my mother. So much of it describes me as well - something I'd been on-the-spot running away from for most of my adolescence. We were two different, difficult people. Different certainly, but also in other respects astonishingly similar. In particular, and unfortunately this time not at all in accord with the saint who was self-aware, a state of expansion, we were simply self-centred, too highly concentrated in the middle, rendering peripheral consciousness misty and ragged. Inevitably, blind spots and misunderstanding abounded.

Of some social significance to us was *Plum Tree Cottage*, one of our little group, let furnished on and off all the year round. From this cottage came fleeting intimations of what it would be like to have a neighbour - not, it goes without saying, in any real sense of the word: we did not have it in our natures to be this to anyone. Of course my aunt called (with a view to doing a portrait), and of course they always returned it (and saw her work), and if nothing came of that, no more time (of ours) was wasted. Of all the *Plum Tree Cottage* tenants, my aunt got to know best an artist-writer and her friend. The Artist-writer did illustration work for magazines, and while she was with us an attractive ink and watercolour centre-spread of *Plum Tree Cottage* appeared in the *Tatler*. She had also just written a novel, which raised her higher still in my estimation. Whatever the weather or occasion she always wore the same hat - a wide, straight-brimmed black velour much in favour with the creative element, men and women at that time. They both admired my aunt's work. She had recently made a conté chalk drawing of me on tinted paper with touches of colour in pastel. The result was pleasing and a number of commissions had already resulted. She now did a head of the Hat for the friend. These two took a fancy to my aunt, she was their 'find', I gathered, but my aunt did not, fortunately. It was plain that they didn't like me. *'I'd see that one off at the earliest opportunity.'* the Hat was reported to have advised, obviously only too well filled in as to my aunt's view of the flash-fire clashes between us. Nevertheless, when they called and I was there I counted myself lucky as I hovered out in the cold, hungrily attentive. It was never

Phyllis. Drawing by Florence E. Castle with conté chalk on tinted paper with touches of colour in pastel.

conversation or discussion, but always the Hat expounding, and always too taken up by her subject to notice the blank in my aunt. In all our acquaintance I was only once directly addressed. On this memorable occasion I was standing behind the visitors as they talked to my aunt in front of the cottage. This time the Hat was enlarging on the nearness of another war. The idea of being bothered about a war that hadn't even been declared was a lost cause with my aunt, but as usual the Hat was in too deep to notice. To the rear it was different - there it was seen as an exciting prospect of stirring events. *'War - cheers!'*, I muttered, drumming my feet appreciatively on the lid of the well. I could not have hit upon a more certain way of eliciting a response had I thrown in a hand grenade. On the instant the Hat swung round and delivered a point-blank frontal attack fully three minutes long. I remained (understandably) silent! But nothing was lost, indisputable rightness was apparent from the first syllable. In those few minutes I grew up by as many years.

Sometime later my aunt asked the Hat for the head to show in the annual exhibition of the local art club. By this time it was framed. My aunt didn't care for the frame and was determined to alter it. I did my best to talk her out of it. As far as I could see the frame was all right, but this wasn't the point - it was not her property. As usual, I could make no impression. Her's was the portrait. How could she not know best? They would be delighted. They were not. She received a stiff rat-tat-tat of well-chosen words from the Hat and to my dismay the beautiful friendship was over.

As the end of term approached, the remaining days were joyously crossed off large homemade calendars pinned to the underside of desk lids. In this time of great good cheer, I became more and more despondent. Any holiday was too long for me. The summer ones always seemed as if they were never going to end.

I did have one, periodic, source of companionship in the village: the schoolmaster's family. There was a boy my age at the Boys' Grammar School and two older boys, one of them at Oxford. Sometimes the two from the shop joined us. We played tennis in the school playground where a court only just fitted in, cross-court tramline shots had to be played off walls on either side at which we became adept. But this desirable state of affairs only took place after tea and in dry weather. All day the evening was eagerly looked forward to, the sky constantly scrutinised. At these times the greatest miracle was a wet day suddenly clearing by late afternoon, with low grey clouds dispersing, newly-revealed white ones parting, blue streaks widening. And if sometimes I got there too early, the schoolmaster came out and talked while the others finished their tea. He was an understanding man. With the approach of September I took my hockey stick to a field half a mile away. This field was liberally dotted with tough, upright thistles - they must have been up to four feet high - for my purpose the opposing team and goalposts. Here I rushed up and down and in and out, dribbling, passing, shooting, even shouting instructions. These thistles were extraordinarily robust, took bulleying with hardly a quiver, and were far from inert in a tackle when to engage their hard spines was equivalent to being lanced by a porcupine.

Hearing of Confirmation classes in the village, I joined. It proved indeed a confirmation, though hardly along establishment lines. My idea of the event as something that was supposed to matter carried me through the first of the weekly meetings conducted by the Vicar. During the second, uneasy suspicion settled into inescapable conclusion, that the commentaries were an insult to intelligence. And that was that. Some weeks later, I received in the post a printed slip. The Bishop was requesting my attendance at a Ceremony of Confirmation. How entirely right I had been! It was no more than a dusty charade the sponsors themselves had long ago given up caring about. As for the Church in general, it was just the same, so I never went. It didn't seem to have to do with anything that mattered, and the sermons were idiotic. Our previous Vicar had gone very peculiar for some time before being finally removed. It didn't surprise me that you could go potty in the Church and no-one noticed.

At school there was no biology. We did botany. I enjoyed this and carefully drew many a sectioned ovary - without ever coming to any interesting conclusions. It was not the same with physics. The lesson was on the structure of matter. I can still see the form room and the exact position of the desk I occupied. I see myself standing beside this desk amid a pandemonium of banging lids after the bell had gone for break. It was probably no more than a matter of seconds before I was rushing out after the rest. But the questions that surged up then are still with me. It was the composition of the atom that did it. Hitherto thought of as the smallest particle, it was now revealed to be an entity containing a nucleus with still smaller particles revolving round it. I was immediately struck by the similarity to the solar system - and beyond. For if this kind of activity were going on right through me and my surroundings - as according to this it was - then it must work the other way as well. How small were we in a how much greater largeness? Was this whole, infinite-seeming, universe less than the merest shred of matter in something unimaginably more vast? At the time I saw this vastness in my own image, as another human being. One as fallible and ultimately helpless as I was? Could this be God? Was it simply a matter of scale? Whichever way you looked at it, it was a bit unnerving, but the fears of childhood were behind me now, what remained served to give a fine edge to the excitement and wonder of being alive. I was held by the theory. At odd times I would bring it out and look it over, but while I was never able to add to it, neither could I discover any obvious flaw.

Although I no longer went to church, I'd continued to say my prayers. They were said at night as there was never any time in the morning. I had also abandoned outside kneeling in favour of inside relaxing on the grounds that in cold and discomfort I could not give to God my undivided attention. But as I much preferred to lie stretched out and let my thoughts range, an exhausting conflict ensued. The obvious course was to pray first. It sounds simple but in practice it never happened. Invariably I gave weakly in and settled for starting off with a short excursion, which went on and on, becoming more and more marred by background interference from Thy will be not yet done. Of course there were times when I fell asleep, but more often at some point my flagging faculties were finally whipped into line. I had already noticed that my prayers were meaningless recitations, that throughout I would be busily going over more topical matters. In an attempt to beat this, the Lord's Prayer was split up and illustrated pictorially or by symbols. It was *'for ever and ever'* that I liked doing best, for this a shining circle was thrown into perspective as an ellipse and spun in space, a faultless blue sky, where it hung, lonely and beautiful for the minute, which was the longest I could hold it in my shifting mind. I also required of myself one *extempore* prayer, this was hard work and I hated it.

Another searching look was taken. This time it seemed as if plain dishonesty was the trouble. I saw that I no longer believed in God; that even the shielding belief that I ought to believe was in pieces; that I was urging myself on with unclear reasons and impure motives, instead of facing up to it; and it was felt that in the remote possibility of there really being a God, the fountain of all goodness, then it must follow that of His very nature He could not fail to affirm the rightness of my reasons. This was not say that facing up to it was altogether without anxiety, however absurd and illogical it was seen to be. Something did happen - something totally unexpected. As I discarded Him, I was at once filled with a marvellous feeling of release and lightness, in fact I felt so buoyant it was remarkable to me that I did not actually rise from the ground. The feeling was not of losing, but strongly of finding. It really did seem as if, in throwing out the letter, I had come in sight of the spirit, for Christian principles I never doubted. I also felt that my sense of right and wrong was enhanced. If I was unable to properly understand the nature of God and prayer, at least I had been able to recognize what they were not.

At school, one area where I never fooled around was in the gym or on the playing field. There, positive effort always took over. A long spell of bad weather with severe waterlogging, prompted the games staff to organise a senior-school cross-country run, using lanes and footpaths. As there hadn't been anything like this before, there was much excitement and speculation about who would win. It was thought that the agile and fleet would be shown up by someone with strength and staying power. First came a trial walk to familiarise us with the three-mile route. No-one would have been silly enough to make much of this, but a good many covered up to half the distance at a trot, and I came to the conclusion that it could be between me and another day girl, just as supple, with longer legs. She would have won, I feel sure, but when the great day came she was away ill leaving me to come in first, uncontested. So easily, that when the tape came in sight a hundred yards ahead, and no sign of anyone down the lane behind me, I dropped down to a leisurely amble. But the younger girl from the village shop beside me on her bike, became so upset that to please her I finished at a fair pace. As the others came in I was surprised to see how many were in a state of collapse, requiring attention. Someone who didn't even need to sit down was in the way, and as still more arrived and the prostrate recovered sufficiently to inquire about the result, the situation reversed with my immaculate condition giving rise to so much astonishment - even affront - that it seemed best to take up a reclining position away on a grassy bank. It was a lonely moment. It was also almost as if there'd been some mistake, and in a way I could see this myself, for although I had I felt I could win - even seen myself doing so - the established result made me wonder too, especially as I surveyed the extraordinary after-the-battle scene spread out before me. Until it crossed my mind that these stranded bodies had given up rather than out. There had been times when I could easily have done the same. But I hadn't, I'd gone on to find my third and fourth wind! The race **had** been more a test of stamina than speed. It seemed that when sufficiently roused, I had this capacity to throw everything in and hang doggedly on. And since it didn't appear to make any impression, let alone find favour, I entered into a private ceremony of congratulation in which I warmly commended myself for this - as I saw it - new, ground-breaking quality. Back at school, still no-one seemed pleased. Not even Rachel. *'What are they to think?'*, she murmured, *'Silly asses aren't winners! You were out of character. What they were hoping for was someone to look up to - a heroine. You seem to expect... oh, I don't know...'* I was given an affectionate pat. *'**Well done.** Here, help yourself to some lemon cheesecake.'*

At school, attitudes were beginning to change, sights lengthen. Peaceful intervals between trouble were already wider. I noted with amazement that I'd begun to settle down. But what seemed strongly there to me, to others would be unnoticeable: I had already some experience of this in far less subtle situations. I seemed to have created an atmosphere in which transgression never missed its mark, while anything of worth promptly faded away. Except that it arose out of calmer waters, the incident of the window pole was little different from any other minor school skirmish. It was Welsh French with poor old Tommy again. It would be. I asked to have the window open - permission granted. I was in the act of pulling it down when someone decided to feel chilly and demanded closure. Permission again granted. I was told to close the window. After a minute or two of impasse and argument I was ordered to hand over the pole to another. Instead, disgusted, I threw it back in its corner by the door against which it fell with a loud clatter. This door led to another classroom and on into the main building and, through it, with no further word, scurried the flouted mistress. She didn't return. The bell went for the end of afternoon school, and a message came for me to remain behind. Time passed. Suddenly, Rachel made a rapid entrance, duty staff in pursuit: '***Outside!*** *- you shouldn't be here, you know the rules!*', she called. *'It was Stinking Sam through the door - now stoking it up in H.Q. with Tommy in tears.'*, reported Rachel making her exit from the other side. It seemed we were into high drama.

How did she know? *'My spies!'* She suffered from regular blinding headaches, sometimes spending all day lying in a tiny room away from the main school building. There she'd made friends with Hester, a nice-looking, sharp young maid - first choice for trolleys through to the 'Ip. Some of Hester's comments were already part of our private language. '***Pay*** *- to come* ***here****?!'* however often repeated never failed to elicit Rachel's low-key chuckle and in me a fit of the giggles. The mistress on duty was the games staff. New no longer. Mellowed now, even something of a friend, I was trying to persuade her to introduce lacrosse. She inquired what I was doing on my own in the form room. Then, looking keenly at me, she remarked that it was a pity I didn't sometimes stop to think before I acted, surely it was time for me to be doing this now - didn't I agree? I did agree. I also thought I detected inside the trite words a more significant message. I had the feeling that she already knew - that we both knew - that the point had been reached where indulgence had finally run out. I experienced a moment of martyr's grandeur; but the next minute I was sure that it couldn't be true it was too ridiculous; what had I done? No, there'd be, as there's always been yet another reprieve. A message now arrived for me to go home and wait until further notice.

The end came two days later. In my opinion it was a nice letter. It stated that I had no vices; that I was likeable rather than otherwise; but that she could not run her school with me in it. I was sitting on the floor as my aunt read it out. I lay back. In silence, tears rolled down the sides of my face. Then the unbelievable happened. There took place a definite shift of viewpoint. With a neat click, like a camera shutter, the present was past, something other arising. I found myself looking at hitherto inconceivable possibilities. In the midst of disaster - and with what could only be regarded as indecent speed - it seemed that recovery was already in place. As I got to my feet I became aware of trouble from another quarter. My aunt was still going on about the 'Ip: that she had no right...in a court of law...she had a good mind...her solicitor...wicked woman...my whole career... A row followed with the unmanageable element sticking up for the school and authority.

To be fair to the school in the small market town, Mayfield had been a kind of heaven, the headmistress a saviour, her staff figures of light. After this anywhere was going to be a travesty, at best ludicrous. Yet like some awful nether playing field it had its place. At the London school I'd worked my way up effortlessly, it had seemed to arise out of where I was. I was a child in London - in London the world was magical. At the Girls' Grammar School in the small market town I became adolescent - my eyes were opening on the adult world and it looked like a sham and a con. At school I was shocked into playing a counter-character: I felt myself called to put on a show, *Whatever Kind of a Place is This?!* Up in neon lights. The need was there, the scope was wide. It was seen as an exciting breakthrough. Now, when least expected, just as the fizz was beginning to settle into something perhaps worthwhile, it had suddenly come to an end. It was Tommy's tears that had tipped the scales, I felt sure of that. I was sorry, and at the same time deeply grateful for what had been an exceedingly long run.

Outside attitudes were diverse. The War Widow thought I had got what was coming to me and it was just too bad. The Agnostic pointed out that if the headmistress couldn't run her school with me in it then perhaps she hadn't been running it as well as she should - that it was at least as much a failure on the part of authority. I was impressed by this, to some extent it was probably true, but only I knew how much she'd had to put up with, how hard she'd tried - the last straw by itself is always going to look ridiculous. The President of our Women's Institute was kind and practical as well. This was a large warm lady with plaits round her head and a cloak. Her brother was an art publisher, head of a highly-acclaimed private press; I usually went to tea when the niece came to stay. She now told my aunt that the headmistress of a high school in our nearest city was a personal friend and would be willing to give me a place, if this was what we wanted?

From my father there was no recrimination. In view of the succession of appalling reports, he was not greatly surprised. His energies were now channelled into trying to discover how best to move forward from such an unpromising position. Through it all I remained silent, willing to do what anyone thought fit. I could only supply one pointer. When asked what I wanted to do, I replied that I wanted to write. My father thumped his desk so hard the telephone jumped, as he demanded, '*What about?!*' At the time I saw this as a fair question but since it was in no way possible to draw attention to an exercise book of poems, it was also one that I couldn't answer. So the moment passed, with my father informing us that his books had been written in his spare time. To him, writing was this sort of occupation. Finally, what in heaven's name did I have to say at seventeen years that anyone would want to listen to? To my father it was clear that the pattern was now established; that it would be a waste of time and money to send me back into any orthodox educational institution. My mother wanted me to go in for art - according to her I had the ability. To him art wasn't an orthodox occupation, so it might be that in something like this lay the best chance of success. And so it was decided. As a parting shot, my father made me promise to call and apologise to the headmistress.

I waited till the new term was about to start to be sure of finding her in residence. The interview began badly, it was very evident that I wasn't welcome. I received a tight-lipped response to my apology, and the situation than showed signs of becoming, if anything, worse. I couldn't understand it, what had gone wrong? I was genuinely sorry and utterly without ill will. I was keeping off the school of art - at some point she was bound to ask about my future - it could be slipped in then. Strange that it hadn't come up...but at all costs I wished to avoid any suggestion of bouncing in with the good news. In fact so far was I from this that I actually felt uncomfortable about having a career at all. Going on the only idea to come from her, I knew I should be emigrating to Australia to do the heavy on a homestead out in the bush. As the situation deteriorated further, I found myself blocked at every turn by the recurring question, *'Is there anything else that you have to say to me?'* And I could think of nothing - but nothing, except that plainly I was never going to get it right. At least this time I was free to get up and go. By the open door at the top of the steps I got in a deprecatory reference to my future and, as if by magic, the tension fell away. Too late I was asked to stay and have tea. By this time I only wanted - desperately - to get away.

6

Ruskin Drawing School

Small is Beautiful
When my guru wanted to compliment me
he called me simple, when he wished to chide me
he called me clever.

Ram Dass

After the motley with its abrupt termination, this next movement flows forward like a muted *andante*, with the writer cut back to the child who absorbed and accepted. It was as if the school in the small market town had never been. At the same time my splendidly eccentric central character faded into the background, leaving me exposed in a world so new it could have been another planet.

There were two schools of art in Oxford. When applied to, the City School could produce no prospectus. The Principal sent us a chatty, handwritten letter outlining his courses. From the Ruskin Drawing School came an imposing prospectus on superior, deckle-edged paper and the staff included a medical man for anatomy who must have had every known qualification. For once my father and my mother were in accord. This small school, founded by John Ruskin for the study of fine art, and housing his collection of drawings and water colours, was to all appearances independent, but in fact it was answerable to the university, and undergraduates could come and work in the afternoons. The premises were open-plan in one large gallery, being the ground floor of one wing of the Ashmolean Museum. The office was unit-built of wooden filing cabinets containing the collection. In the middle area of the gallery was a long table where wood engraving went on occasionally. Beyond a curtain was the model that went on all the time. In the tiny office was a desk, a hat-and-coat stand and the Ruskin Master, and on their appointed days, his part-time assistant staff. Here, he or they went broody or talked together in an undertone before coming out to stalk the students. I was instructed to put down on paper exactly what I saw. The half imperial sheet seemed enormous - and it was so quiet. The museum was quiet. The gallery was carpeted with matting that muffled our footsteps, and the model was always with us. In this silent concentration nothing was lost of cavernous rumbling or an attack of collywobbles. I soon learnt not to rush off in the morning without swallowing something lasting or grabbing a pocketful of biscuits for the journey.

The training was straightforward. We drew from life and drew from life and drew from life, while those ahead of us painted from life and went on painting from life. I believe it was Ruskin's idea that the students should study his collection. When the university complained about the amount of electricity used, there was mild amusement, with the Ruskin Master expressing doubt as to whether the authorities were fully aware of the turn the school had taken. With regard to anatomy, not only did we never see the gentleman whose high qualifications had undoubtedly swayed my father - no-one had ever heard of him. I rather fancied some anatomy myself, so the Ruskin Master brought in a book for me to look over, pointing out that while the body for the doctor might be a matter of mechanics, the figure for the artist should be felt rather than constructed. In this, at any rate, he was in line with our founder who, in one of his more inspired moments, had described the artist as 'a seeing and a feeling creature'. The Ruskin Master at this time was Sydney Carline, a short, broad man with red-gold hair and blue eyes, sometimes to be seen emerging in that order over the tops of the cabinets, as he stood on his toes in the office to discomfit dallying students pursuing their social life after the model had gone back into the pose. He was a shy, reserved man, already a distinguished artist, but yet to make his name. As he proceeded on his rounds you could usually sense the Ruskin Master behind you. A slight ruffling of the prevailing silence followed by a concentrated stillness, then, with a sharp intake of breath as of one in pain, he would gently draw you aside and come forward to make his criticism.

The school consisted of one small group, less than twenty and never all at once - ten or twelve would be a full house. All women, with perhaps two or three undergraduates on some afternoons. It was in relation to my fellow students that I immediately stood out. Once more I was the youngest in the school. And no-one, with the exception of myself, had it in mind to do anything with their training - they didn't even think of it as such, they were following a much more basic agenda. I was also the only one who hadn't been and wasn't going to be presented at court. The first time this subject came up it drew from me a gay laugh, I couldn't believe they were serious. But they were. They'd been nannied, governessed, exclusively schooled, Continentally finished and now presented. The full treatment. They were here dutifully filling in time while waiting to get married. Everything - but everything - that made up their lives had no reality in mine. The gap in income level alone was so wide as to leave pretty well nothing in the way of common ground. They came from the residential area of North Oxford, or were the daughters of heads of colleges and others came from country houses round about. I can even name-drop. A sister of Frank, the late Lord Longford, and two of the older Hons. and Rebels.

From the outside, the situation appears fraught and embarrassing. I can only say that most emphatically it was not. They were a group of wholly delightful, confident maidens, warm and friendly in the way of the young with each other, and the particularly nice young people that they happened to be. My being younger - much younger than most - helped, and their goodwill bridged it further and I soon came to see that the difference between us worked both ways - that they were as intrigued by me as I by them. And they were **very** amusing. Certainly I was happy and contented enough to listen, absorb, admire and laugh with them.

I had to catch a train in the small market town, that arrived in Oxford an hour before the school opened. It meant getting up very early and leaving the cottage before my aunt was awake. Sometimes, in the winter, when I'd forgotten to get in water the night before and the newly-installed pump was frozen, I washed in the morning's milk. There was plenty of time for my aunt to cool off before I returned round about seven o'clock. The afternoon ended at three-thirty but my train was two hours later than this. I had a lunch and tea allowance, but I never had tea and rarely more than a gap-stopping lunch, the money went on books. Free time was spent making a tour of the bookshops, and I usually ended up in the Public Library, where my favourite reading was *The Times Literary Supplement*. It could be said that I already had some grounding in this territory. I was a great reader of reviews, a fervent sender-away after publishers' catalogues - Spring and Autumn Lists, Christmas Books - I had a boxful. And so it came about that in any discussion on some book or other that everyone was reading, I was able to make a contribution. I wouldn't have read it, but I was bound to know all about it.

And so from the Grammar School with its rules and regulations to this small free group. We were hardly taught - rather, tentatively guided and allowed to learn. It was all informal. There were no set speeches, no peddling of short cuts, no hints on how to do it. We had each to find our own way, and were then as maybe assisted along those lines. And so we grew. Every bit of art in this place was serious. We were steered by men who lived for it: artists who eschewed entirely the superficial, for them, for work to have merit, it had to have depth. At the same time we were required to keep our feet on the ground, the rather formidable term 'workmanlike' was a praiseworthy description of a drawing. A few precepts did emerge. To me by far the most important was that in any art cleverness is suspect. To learn to see this - however imperfectly - at such an early stage was a learning peak of the highest order.

'However imperfectly'. And it could only be that. This demolishing of 'the clever' - showing it up as ever ready to degenerate into slickness - while it was something I could be brought to see, at the same time I could only receive it with mixed feelings that ran deep. The one quality I so much admired and wanted to be was a hollow thing! True, I had been in obeisance, aware only of the common meaning of the word. It had never occurred to me to look into it. But it was also true that, more than anything else, I desired those qualities I had least of - polish and expertise. If my odd drawings were individual it was because that was the way **I** was, it was not the result of taking thought. Writers were clever - they had Good Brains - this was the vital requisite and ideal. Artists, as I already knew only too well, didn't need to be intellectual at all. Turning out to be like my mother was what I was really afraid of. So that this assertion, that to be clever was a hollow thing - and 'in any art', he had said - coming from Sydney whom I so much looked up to, while it was bound to take some root, could hardly of itself be expected to topple such a ramified and towering temple. But if I came to it hard, and abandoned it often, it was always there in the background waiting. It did penetrate, it did give my morale a strong boost, and all my life I have been able to call on it to get my erring self lined up again after some particularly off-course flounder or other.

At this time, the late Nineteen-Twenties, undergraduates were wearing wide, flapping Oxford bags, the new crêpe-soled shoes and horn-rimmed glasses. And these last became fixed in my mind as the mark of the intellectual. To me it was if these glasses facilitated a reciprocal exchange between eye and brain. They might be said to make up for deficiency; it was my conviction that they positively added to faculty, with one's head clasped in a pair of these the intellect was channelled in a higher concentration and flowed more freely. I recalled that my father employed a battery of such aids - one pair he wore on his nose, the other in his hair. Thus were his statements twice underlined before he opened his mouth. In my opinion I needed glasses. It was all this ceaseless sitting over a drawing board with the windows shut. My aunt wrote to my father who supplied us with the address of the Oxford Eye Hospital. I had not seen the situation as taking quite this sort of turn, but now there was no other way. They gave me the most exhaustive testing and pronounced my sight in every way perfect. I wasn't even allowed to look bright.

In addition to the Ruskin Master, there were two part-time members of staff. As the only extrovert, Gilbert Spencer was easily the most popular. He was lively, talkative and amusing in a way that the others were not - at any rate with us. And he was a great one for form. To watch Gilbert draw was an experience. He sat there and suffered, he didn't glance at the model as we did, he looked fiercely into it and the taut line of his mouth told how he sweated it out. Where we attempted copies of the model, Gilbert re-created him. I remember him making a magnificent study of a male flexed knee, and calling our attention to it - together with the fact that he had never had an anatomy lesson in his life. *'I could show this drawing to any doctor'*, he told us, *'and he would say to me, "Spencer, that knee is perfect!"'* I was delighted to hear it, it had proved surprisingly tough and been hastily dropped. But my father meant well and so it had turned out. For despite a mistaken reason drawn from erroneous information, the better school had been chosen.

John Nash was our other part-time member of staff. When a start was made in wood engraving he was in charge of this. I liked him well enough, but had intercepted the odd quizzical glance. I fancied that I was too much of an incongruous addition to the polished young ladies for John. Schoolgirl still...yes, in dress too, to begin with. Or was it in reaction to Sydney's stalwart attitude where I was concerned? To him, I knew I was in process of becoming one of them. The nearest I got to John was when he discovered me reading *Lavengro* and lent me *The Bible in Spain*. He was Romany-looking himself, small and lightly built with a swarthy complexion. Even more than Sydney he was quiet and reserved. His remarks, even when plainly strongly felt, were always offered in the same slow, thoughtful, almost inaudible tone. There was the time I went with one or two other students to tea at his cottage. Gilbert was to stay with him that weekend and came down with us in the loaded car, along with a large, exceedingly heavy suitcase. As soon as tea was over this suitcase was lugged into the sitting-room and opened. It was full of music, there was nothing else. The next minute he and John were straight-backed side by side off into their first Mozart duet. To all three men, music was the greatest of the arts, because the least representative. Painting came next. Literature, made up of words, the stuff of common exchange, was of necessity the most severely grounded.

Both our part-time staff had better-known older brothers, and both these brothers appeared in the prospectus as visiting staff. And indeed they did visit, though not usually to see us. Stanley Spencer, married to Sydney Carline's sister, appeared the more often. Gilbert loved to tell us about Stanley, both at home in Cookham and their war experiences together. We also heard about his own student days at the Slade under the proverbially caustic Tonks. The professor was apt to lay about him, leaving the ladies in tears: *'Can you knit...?'* His own work undistinguished, he was undeniably a rousing teacher - all the best English artists of that period were out of the Slade. But when Tonks did make a mark on Gilbert, it was always healed by Stanley telling how just the same or even worse had also been said to him.

At the Ruskin the longer than ever university holidays added to the familiar problem of too much solitary free time. Nonetheless, as ever incorrigibly optimistic, it was seen as just the opportunity I needed to continue my general education. Notebooks were purchased, a timetable worked out. English Literature, Geography, Botany, Psychology, Anatomy and History of Art. I actually stuck to some semblance of this timetable for a week or more, before ending up with English, English, English and English (Poetry, Shakespeare, standard works, and History of), with the Psychology now and then for a change. This last - at that time just coming into fashion - had been picked up from magazines and articles in the paper. Most used of all my textbooks was one on the elements of prosody which had presented itself to me from the bargain bookcase of a Broad Street bookshop. Scanning became a way of life. I was literally turned on by the Shakespearean measure, iambic pentameter. For a time even my thoughts jogged along in this metre. It was particularly marked when cycling, the stresses rising and falling in time to my feet on the pedals.

Of all my notebooks, the one on poetry filled fastest. Where poetry was concerned I looked up words and spent time trying to puzzle out meanings. It was hard work; often I didn't get there, and when I did I couldn't be sure I was right. Then one morning it suddenly dawned on me that it didn't matter. This was so extraordinary I couldn't believe it at first. That it literally made no difference to the pleasure I got out of the poem. Following this splendid discovery I shot ahead, content to get the drift, loving poetry for its exciting agility, immediate musical appeal and palatable qualities. Francis Thompson's *'The Hound of Heaven'* was a **banquet** of a poem to read aloud, and as for its central theme here was another marvel - I could even accept news of God in a poem. I picked up later that poetry was made up of meanings and with this revelation I felt I'd arrived. **The stuff was magical**. You couldn't miss!

Burning admiration, is how I have to describe my feeling for Shelley's Elegy on the Death of John Keats, *'Oh, weep for Adonais - he is dead!'* Death and Decay were seen as heroic Grand Themes. Swathes of Omar Khayyam were committed to memory, along with rich, resonant portions of the Old Testament. *'Remember now thy Creator in the days of thy youth...'* If I had no-one to guide me, I had no-one to inhibit me either. Across the top of one of my bedroom walls a verse from Tennyson's *In Memoriam* was lovingly lettered:

There rolls the deep where grew the tree,
O earth what changes thou has seen!
There where the long street roars hath been
The stillness of the central sea.'

The work was carried out in black paint with my aunt hammering on the door, shouting at me to stop. The room had no lock, there wasn't a door handle in the place, it was all latches, but it so happened that mine was different from the others, being made of wood. From the outside it could be raised by pushing your finger through a hole, but when fully closed from the inside it jammed secure as any lock. Thus, safe from interference - while from the hole, frantic finger alternated with outraged eye, I carried steadily on wrapped in the largeness of Lord Alfred's vision. For the only other straight-up wall, Hopkins was chosen:

"What would the world be, once bereft
Of wet and of wildness? Let them be left,
O let them be left, wildness and wet;
Long live the weeds in the wilderness yet."

Of the Tennyson I admired the perspective - again especially grandiose to a teenager still innocently set in the surety of everlasting youth. But the Hopkins touched something more real. Half a century on as I pulled weeds, and - final degradation - mowed my own lawn, a still kicking younger me was there at my shoulder, jeering.

Meanwhile, I read my way through standard fiction. Pure enjoyment. Also, at this time, in my father's household, they must have been having a turn-out for at regular intervals I received parcels of books. And so it came about that I read all of Rider Haggard. These books effectively filled in the romantic picture of my father as world traveller. *Montezuma's Daughter* was the first and for me the most thrilling, so much so that it illuminated the whole subject of Mexico. A later parcel contained *The Story of Mexico.* While reading this book in the station waiting-room my train came in and went out. I had to get back on my bike and pedal the fourteen miles to Oxford. Then the same happened at the other end and I had to hire a bike to get home. By this time, pride in my father's possible exploits had been left behind in favour of my own. I was so steeped in stepped pyramids, featherwork and floating gardens, I was certain I'd passed a previous life in ancient Central America. A very different book that made a deep impression was *John Inglesant* by J.H. Shorthouse, a nineteenth-century 'philosophical romance' set in the reign of the first Charles. What held me was the advice given to Inglesant by the Jesuit, that what you believe is of little importance, it is how you live up to it that matters. It was the first time I had come across such a view, and I found it, as put forward in this book, so much in accordance with my own ideas - or what I thought of as my own ideas - that it seemed to speak for me. I marked passages and read them often, even out loud, for the sentences rolled forth with a splendid and heroic inevitability:-

> *"This is the most important lesson that a man can learn - that all men are really alike; that all creeds and opinions are nothing but the mere result of chance and temperament; that no party is on the whole better than any other; that no creed does more than shadow imperfectly forth some one side of truth; and it is only when you begin to see this that you can feel that pity for mankind, that sympathy with its disappointments and follies, and its natural human hopes, which have such a little time of growth, and such a sure season of decay.*
>
> *"...Hereafter it will be of little importance which of these new names, Cavalier or Roundhead, you are called by, whether you turn Papist or Puritan, Jesuit or Jansenist, but it will matter very much whether you acted as became a man, and did not flinch ignobly at the moment of trial."*

'The Moment of trial'. In this respect it could be said that one great country stood out. That there is nothing new under the sun must surely be true; but to the unprepared and newly-arrived, great events will always seem to have dropped out of nowhere, as it seemed to me, when suddenly there appeared in the sky a new star, of great magnitude, and it's name was Russia. In fact it came out of that same bottomless bookcase in Broad Street - this time in the shape of Gogol and Gorki. And at once it was as if all the other books I'd read had lacked some vital ingredient. Here were people, like the rest of us but more real, for better or for worse they felt strongly and expressed freely their joys, their absurdities, their agonies. It was all with a bare breast. Above all they dared to be a little mad.

Almost on a par with Death and Decay was Madness which was seen as a fascinating wild exuberance that rang true, as against the smoothness of too much civilization. '*Great wits to madness sure are near allied/And thin partitions do their bounds divide.*' Dryden. Privately, I thought my father a little mad. It was also seen as the opposite end of the scale from my mother's shallow dottiness. But in spite of all this fervent cerebral activity, too much free time on my own still created difficulties. I'd never looked forward to the holidays, and now they often seemed like spells of long-term solitary confinement. Every summer now the War Widow let her cottage, the Agnostic had left the village, and I had lost the schoolmaster's family. Periods of social starvation were familiar enough - there were always books - but inevitably too many hopes and fears fed elaborate imaginings and unreal ideas. There were days when for lack of outside stimulation I lay inert in the garden, in the shade of a spreading fruit tree (the only one of the lost-label collection to do anything for us). I was sure I was dying of sleeping sickness, a tropical disease according to *The Home Doctor*, but I knew better. How could it not be what I had. What other explanation could there possibly be? One year this worry persisted to such an extent it became necessary to do something about it. I knew that in Samuel Butler's *Erewhon*, people who fell ill were thrown into prison. Their maladies had grown out of their transgressions. It made sense. Look at me! True, I had dispensed with God, but now that I had taken over in his place, in many ways right and wrong had become more than ever reckonable and potent (not that the burden rested heavily save in times of peril).

Just up the hill from us, living in a condemned cottage, was a young family. The father was a decent enough man but weak, he drank and couldn't keep a job. Sober, he had a kind of rare nobility born of pain and extremity. His wife was a white-faced worried-looking woman with too many small children. The oldest, a boy no more than six or seven, was to be seen about the village, never running around with others his age but always in charge of one of his sisters, hand clutching hand in a link secure as an umbilical cord. Other than this she rode in an old crate on wheels used for doing jobs, when she was dumped on top of the rubbish or goods he was carting. This inseparable pair seemed to be always around. If the boy found his sister a drag, it never showed, rather it was as if she were regarded as a more important extension of himself. He was affectionately known all over the village as Titch. He had short legs and a large head, clear blue eyes and a ready smile of out-of-the-common sweetness as if in simple wonder that any should take note of one so low.

That term, instead of buying books, I used my lunch allowance savings to buy presents for the family up the hill or, more accurately, Titch. I bought an expensive Hornby train set, with a tunnel and bridge and signal box to go with it and I bought boxes of sweets and chocolate biscuits. After dark, on Christmas Eve, I took the track that ran at a tangent off our hill to come out at the side of the condemned cottages. I had reckoned on there being no-one about, in the event I found the front door ajar and was able to push the parcels quietly inside. My aunt was sworn to secrecy. To her mind pointless. But I knew what I had to do. Only I could know how upside down my inner reason was - I had only to let my left hand in to be overdrawn on the spot. Naturally, I was thrilled at the thought of the boy getting such a present. In fact so much so that I tended to forget the object of the exercise. Though not entirely, for afterwards I was left with a feeling of gently nagging dissatisfaction tinged with guilt, over something that looked straight but wasn't. Two years later, hearing that the mystery gift had been attributed to a certain do-gooding lady who had not, it appeared, actually denied it, my aunt decided it was time to speak out. By this time it didn't seem to matter even to me. Titch duly turned up on the doorstep to stay thank-you. He was fortunately a very natural small boy. The only difference it made was an added depth to the blue eyes above the sweet smile when we saw each other in the village, matched in me by an air of connivance overlaying mine.

As time went on, the Ruskin began to expand with the intake more broadly based, and I ceased to be a lone pleb among the debs. It came at the right time. While it lasted I'd been happy and content with my little corner on rarefied ground, but by now I was as often shocked, as amused and amazed by the polished young ladies' everyday standards. Soon now I'd be moving on to London and the question arose as to where I should go. General opinion was in favour of the Central School where Bernard Meninsky was in charge of the painting. That summer term, Sydney had his first one-man show. We went up to town for the private view, piled into every available automobile. It was a fine show, well received by the critics. In fact it was a doubly festive affair as the Ruskin Master had just got married. The Central School in Southampton Row was having it's end of the year exhibition of students' work. Gilbert took me to see it. The work of the Painting School came as an unexpected surprise. At this time Meninsky was painting nudes in well-rubbed-in rhubarb reds and greens, and here were all his students doing exactly the same. Not that I felt any real concern, such obliteration was shocking to see, but I was as certain as anyone could be that no such metamorphosis would happen to me. I said nothing and Gilbert made no comment. In silence we made our way back to the others. Before splitting up for the return to Oxford, we had tea together in the West End. We were all so happy - and unsuspecting. The next school day the Ruskin Master didn't appear. Richard Carline came in to tell us that his brother was seriously ill. Then Richard came again, this time to tell us that the Ruskin Master was dead.

It was the perfect funeral. The coffin was carried from the cottage to the village church in a painted farm cart. We followed after on foot. Only his widowed mother wore black, as she always did, and for this she apologised. The young widow wore what he had liked best, scarlet and white. Afterwards, back in the cottage, the family remembered Sydney as soon and brother, bringing in his trials and tribulations over the years with affection and quiet humour. For those of us hearing it for the first time there could have been no more moving tribute - now, in death, we got to know this quiet sensitive man as we had never known him - never would have known him - in life. It was all so natural and decent. There was not a strained or false note. Not a single sentimental remark. You could feel nothing but the highest respect. At the same time it is very hard indeed for an outsider to forgive the Church of Christ, Scientist, for this almost certainly unnecessary death.

Then we went home, each to struggle with our own personal loss. And I found it the reverse of rousing. He was older than Keats, but like the poet, had it all before him. **So much** was cut off. And **why**? No other death has affected me as this one did - not even remotely. Yet I wasn't emotionally involved. I didn't really know him, except as mentor - he had been someone I could completely trust. No mean thing; in fact, arguably the most honourable of all relationships. Night after night I got into bed and, daytime restrain thrown aside, gave myself up to the unbelievably terrible finality of it.

7

Royal College of Art – Loose in London

The problem of digs, was solved for me by Madam Buttercup, a kindly middle-aged Ruskin student who collected armfuls every year in the Oxford meadows. I had a room or rather an 'unfurnished flatlet' in a club. Convenient accommodation for career women had been the idea, but almost without exception the residents were older women of modest means. It was a tall house at the end of gardens within easy walking distance of the College. My room was on the top floor, something of a crow's nest overlooking the Fulham Road. As a way of life it was difference from the primitive existence in the cottage where appearances were rarely bothered about. I had no dressing-gown. To make one for me my aunt turned her old Harris tweed coat and faced the collar and cuffs with pieces of Liberty silk. I was devoted to this rather military, and also - I privately thought - Russian-looking garment. Neither of us thought of slippers. The club was all pile-carpeting. If I hadn't needed slippers at home, what on earth would I be wanting with them here? To the other flatlet tenants I must have seemed like a visitor from an underdeveloped country. But whatever they thought never reached me as I was careful not to make their acquaintance. This had to do with previous experiences in flats and rooms with my aunt: the safest relationship was no relationship and the interpretation was literal. With one exception. Living in the splendour of the ground-floor front was a white-haired but lively lady who, upon occasion, went into determined assault and got through. Hearing me on the stairs she would emerge from her room and stand across my path to the front door. These confrontations were infrequent and brief, and she was never openly curious - it was more an exploratory probe of a barely-believable phenomenon, and as such amusing to both.

In my student days, the beginning of the Thirties, the Royal College of Art was in Exhibition Road, but that was only the entrance, a narrow door squeezed into a nether corner of the Victoria and Albert Museum. The Painting School was on the ground floor - large, lofty studios strewn about with donkeys and easels, the windows skied, gave the area the look of a derelict warehouse - delightfully casual, intriguingly ready for anything. But where were we located? I had no idea, I couldn't see, and was oddly troubled. Upstairs, design rooms overlooked shoddy institutional backs. Nowhere really. From one of the top-floor rooms, Mural Dec., I think, it was possible to climb a wall-mounted iron ladder to an area of flat roof, from which I would surely have been able to line up our position, but I never got there, for every time my legs went out of the window, I came out in such a sweat at the view of the abyss below, I had hastily to get back in again, there to watch others swarm up without a qualm. It was a popular fine-weather excursion and good for a fag. The only other door of note connected us with the Museum, where the design students often worked. This door provided us all with a splendid bolt-hole. The school day was morning, short afternoon, and then an evening session, but apart from freshers not many of us bothered with this last, we walked in, signed on, and straightway walked out again through the Museum. Another form of escape was into the Museum reference library where it was possible to see all known art journals, and in the matter of books the interpretation of art was wide. It was an imposing, book-lined salon, heavily Victorian and smelling richly of polish, with spacious, well-equipped desks. Over all lay an impressive blanket of silent concentration broken only by turning pages, chairs squeaking on waxed lino and the muted passage of attendants with trolleys conveying the heavier volumes and piles of books. It was usually possible to recognize one or two other students. I remember spending an afternoon next to a young man in fierce concentration over an enormous volume of unrelieved print that turned out to be a book on ethics. When I returned after tea, he was still there, only the page number had changed.

I needn't have worried about the choice of art school. I was formed, and now had to find my own way. The College afforded a convenient environment for this. Confidence and conceit were now such that professors of painting were so many appurtenances to be put up with. The College Principal, Sir William Rothenstein, was head of the Painting School. We saw little of him, and I can only now imagine how much he must have hated coming among us. He favoured the use of a plumb-line and believed that a drawing should have construction. We all knew better than this. No-one stooped to the first, and most cared nothing for the other, either. We were feeling creatures, not surveyors.

My allowance for living, artists' materials and spare pocket money was adequate enough and doled out weekly by post. But, like my aunt before me, I experienced difficulty living within my means. And so we come to Zelda. It was kind of her to offer, and, having accepted, I found myself into the bargain committed to her company. Gradually it became the regular thing for us to spend the evening together, sometimes in her digs, sometimes in mine. Zelda was pale and dark, with upslanted narrow eyes that gave her a faintly Slav appearance. As it came to light, she was something of a *femme fatale*, though still very much the beginner with only one in the bag. This was an artist with a tickly beard up in the industrial Midlands from which she came, and typically he was a married man. It seemed that she needed not only to attract, but the additional thrill of abduction. Nonetheless, where feeling was concerned, she was direct and generous. We made an unlikely couple but in fact she was a splendid source of much needed education. My almost total innocence astounded her and was the cause of much hilarity. To move from the hot-house of the emotions to the rough airs of the open field, Zelda had a passion for potatoes. Of all my remembrances of her, the time I saw her from a bus going down the Fulham Road was the most moving. She was sailing purposefully towards my digs, bearing aloft, like a votive offering, a white pudding basin covered with a cloth from which a light steam rose. I was there before her and quickly prepared the table. The basin was full of boiled potatoes. Nothing else. But I knew that she had brought me of her finest. That Christmas holiday I was moved to make a cake to take back with me. I used half the flour and twice the fruit, with lashings of cherries and chopped nuts: it was a very splendid cake. Unnecessarily so, according to my aunt who was quite upset by the lavishness of it. I got back to find that Zelda had returned with home-made mince pies and shortcake, so it was quite some time before I was able with any effect to lift my treasure from its tin. But when I did, we both agreed it was the finest cake we'd ever tasted.

A minute or two away from the College was the students' common room, where facilities were provided for pretty well everything short of sleeping. You crossed Exhibition Road and carried on straight ahead between the backs of more museums, and outcrops of permanent temporary buildings, including our own Pottery and Sculpture Schools. The common room was at the Queen's Gate end, its shed-like appearance broken by a patch of grass and shrubs from the stony gaze of the heavily superior colonnade opposite. But whatever the common room may have looked like, it served us well. Inside was divided in two: on one side a canteen, and - as the common room was run by the students everything was unbelievably cheap - the other side was the lounge area, a long row of assorted armchairs in varying degrees of dilapidation, divans, ping-pong and shove-ha'penny tables, the stage and a piano. Outside of this there was provision for laundry work and dressmaking. First-rate, easy-going accommodation. Unfortunately, a cold hard stare wasn't all we drew from Queen's Gate. It detested everything about us. In nice weather we picnicked on the grassy patch and left thick white cups and plates about. And, although they could hardly complain of our personal appearance, I don't suppose they were much cheered by this either. Finally, most Saturday nights there was a 'hop', when nasty-minded spies noted mutually-interested couples rolling round joyously under the bushes. The Pillars complained and went on complaining and, in the end, they got through, and while I was at the college the common room lost its independence with the appointment of an outsider to organize and run it.

The students of the Royal College of Art came from a wide, cross-section of the community with the emphasis on scholars from state art schools all over the country. It was an altogether more bracing society than that of the Ruskin. All the same, the two of us soon found ourselves part of a small group of painters and designers who lunched together in the common room under the leadership of a dominant girl with a neon-lit personality. She was notable rather than good looking, large but compact, and brimful of dash and flair. Educated at a well-known south-coast girls' boarding school, she was very sure of herself - at any rate with us - and as for the rest of the community it was hilariously seen as a menagerie in a dump, though it was obvious that she would have applied the same mordant analysis to pretty well any other establishment. She never bothered with people's rightful names, so that individual students came to be known to us as Hair, Teeth, Feet (a poor dancer this one), Hot Hands and Plum Suit, and among the girls a pair of flashy maidens always together were Tarty 1 and Tarty 2. Not original, not subtle, but always dead on. To me it was wholly admirable and highly catching. She was my Great Figure.

All through lunch we were treated to a sharp-witted, supremely funny running commentary on our fellow students, and this would be followed by the latest instalment of her own off-the-premises adventures which were usually every bit as searchingly ridiculous. I can still summon a fascinating picture of the Great Figure, madly bracing an insecurely crowned front tooth with her tongue while being passionately kissed by a hungry taxi-tiger. And if her own behaviour and vicissitudes were grist for the mill, so were ours, and there were times when we were not so kindly treated. Nothing and no-one was sacred. But her sudden cuts were clean and salutary, and as far as I was concerned instantaneously healed in the warmth of my unbounded admiration. Great Figures, I was sure, were by nature unpredictable - they made their own laws. To me it was simply a liability of the privilege of acceptance as one of her train. She came from Northumberland, but we heard little of that or of her parents. It was all 'My Younger Sister'. At that time still at the south-coast boarding school. She could do no wrong. According to the Great Figure she was born with a soaring intelligence, writing fluent prose and poetry at five years. She was wildly attractive to look at as well as being good, kind and generous. *'Everything I'm not!'*, paraded the Great Figure. She sounded satisfied. It sometimes crossed my mind that perhaps we were knocked down in exasperation and disappointment for falling so far short of this paragon. *'When I finish my training and leave this place you'll not hear of me again.'*, the Great Figure pronounced over us, as if reading a tablet prior to setting off with her rod and staff for the North Pole. *'But you will hear of* ***her****!'*

And we did. I fancy I heard of her first when I had a piece about being a land girl printed in a wartime paperback*, which also featured a neat poem by 'My Younger Sister' who'd become a Wren. Later she emerged as a journalist with a taste for interviewing celebrities. Beyond doubt she could have done better than this; but 'having fun' was a way of life after the war, and, given the talent and opportunity, having fun in public - in the popular press, on radio and later television - would have been irresistible. High-spirited and daring, she was soon a distinctive, hilarious presence on top shows. Sometimes rashly persistent, she made mistakes. Having the temerity to tangle with Evelyn Waugh was her most intriguing disaster. And all this, while pursuing a decidedly alternative private life as if it were the most natural thing in the world. Variously described as boy, gypsy, pirate, she was all of these and more. She still wrote verse - stowing it away in a folder marked 'To please myself'. Meanwhile, ignoring all exhortations to come south and have fun, the Great Figure held resolutely to the north and married into the peerage. Different the two girls certainly were, but they did have one outstanding quality in common. Verve. **Unlimited** verve. Then, in early middle age, just as she was beginning to slow down and look around, newsworthy to the end, 'My Younger Sister' was killed in a plane crash.

As our first College year advanced into the third term the pattern of our social life loosened and started to break up. Zelda began to adventure elsewhere, in fact in two directions - adroitly holding one in reserve in case the main interest should fall short of expectation. Neither man was lightweight in character, both were talented, and both had regular girls. The Great Figure, too, became restive. She slapped us down with more than usual vigour, and Zelda came in for real venom. So much so that she ceased to attend the High Table. I was already seeing less of her, I now hardly saw her at all. Yet it had been a good year. Despite wide differences we had got on well. Some would say too well. But the note had been right and lightly struck, the resonance was mine. I missed her badly, the pain was astonishing. But it had to end, I saw that and regretted nothing.

While I received an ever-lengthening training in one art, I was all the more surprised at how much excitement and satisfaction could be had from another - one in which I was poorly-equipped and incompetent. As ever it look me a long time to learn a piece of music well enough to reproduce it at all, let alone at any sort of level. But help was on the way. It all began when I was lent a portable gramophone and three or four records to take home one holiday. It was an inferior gramophone and of the records only one side of one of them found favour - a Russian orchestra playing Mozart's '*Turkish March*'. I played this by the hour, day after day, without tiring - the wonder and excitement went on growing. After this I quickly saw to it that I had a gramophone of my own. In those days you could buy almost anything in Oxford without paying for it, at any rate in full, the desires of youth are mesmerising, the spirit innocently willing, I always meant to pay up - at some ever-advancing future date.

In common with all the other ignorant enthusiasts, I knew what I liked; and most of all I liked singing. I also liked to sing myself and now, thanks to an apparently bottomless tolerance of repetition, I became acquainted with a number of songs, out of which I was able to build a repertoire of my own, culminating in the *Messiah* aria, *'Rejoice Greatly'* complete with runs. When quite small, I'd been deeply wounded by my aunt's reaction to a rendering of *'While Shepherds Watched'* learnt at a nursery school. She burst out laughing. I was quick to tell her there were five more verses - I was word perfect. But you have no **tune,** she informed me, wiping her eyes. Not till years later at Mayfield did I loosen up sufficiently to open my mouth and begin to enjoy singing again. I now made up for lost time. The urge was strong. As once I had been a secret versifier, I now became a secret singer. There wasn't much scope for this in London, but at home it was different. There I could sing to my heart's content in bed at night. Because it was so still it was taken for granted that no-one was conscious. True, I was horizontal, the window was small and overhung by foot-thick thatch, but it looked out over four other cottages. My voice was higher than my aunt's and I sang vigorously, you didn't get the same satisfaction if you tried to keep it down, besides where was the need? In any case at the time the pure enjoyment was such that I didn't see how - if there were anyone awake - they could possibly fail to congratulate themselves on their good fortune. Today, I'm astounded. If proof is needed, here it is - that I could be every bit as quaintly innocent as my mother. At least it was a respectable programme. Arias from the oratorios. Schubert's *'Ave Maria'* was always included, so was a melancholy song of Handel's, *'Hear Thou My Weeping'* (as lone I wander). More cheerfully, when really wound up, a transposed rendering of Bach's robust baritone aria, *'How Jovial is My Laughter'*. The recitals usually ended with *'What Is This feeling?'* (Mozart's 'Voi Che Sapete'), and the song I liked best of all, Purcell's, *'I Attempt From Love's Sickness to Fly* (in vain, for I am myself my own sickness and pain').

That my aunt never heard me wasn't surprising. There was the landing and another bedroom between us, and her window was in a different wall. There were also her sleeping habits. Having slept with her so long, I knew them well. Sinking into her carefully-moulded downy trough she pulled up the bedclothes and disappeared from view, no more than a stray puff of grey hair would be visible. At least this muffled her snores to which the bed would soon be strongly vibrating. At some point during the night there usually arose an acute oxygen crisis, when she woke as one drowning, with a sudden agonised intake of breath, she shot up and flung back the covers. Then, after deep restoring gulps of cool fresh air, she sank once more from sight.

One afternoon, window-shopping along the Fulham Road, on impulse I bought an antique flute. It was a fine-looking instrument with yellowed ivory bands at the intersections, a scribed ivory head and eight tarnished silver keys that looked like ancient salt spoons. I tried blowing down the large hole in the thick end but could only produce a ghostly soughing. In the end I took it to the College common room and in a matter of minutes a student came across and, breathing softly into it, produced a most ravishing *'Drink to me Only'*. I had given up the piano. After leaving school, for a time I'd had lessons in the village, but my new teacher hadn't been critical and chose drippy pieces. I had also arrived at a point where even I could see that no progress was being made. The piano is a complex instrument demanding wide-ranging concentration. One note at a time, as with the flute, was more within my grasp, and I admired the instrument's agility and liquid tone. So if I was inhibited from indulging in singing sessions in town, now at least I could play the flute. No so fine, no, but a lot less naked.

I was now going to church again, this time from choice though not for the usual reasons. Most frequently to High Mass at Westminster Cathedral, but anywhere where the singing was good. One Easter holiday I remained in London for Holy Week. Most of my friends and acquaintances were understanding enough of this rather odd aberration of mine, but the daughter of a Scottish Presbyterian missionary, misnamed Charity, taxed me with, *'This has nothing to do with religion, you know!'* It had never occurred to me that it had. Where other students were balletomanes, I had this passion for singing. At the same time the overtone of self-congratulation was annoying enough to stir up the feeling that perhaps in some way it did, though I could find no ready reply. One answer I could have given was definite enough. I went out of my way to hear good singing. With equal fervour I avoided sermons. A church service could elevate and religious music fell into the same vital category as Madness, Death and Decay. But all of this could be wiped out by the Address. The extraordinary thing about sermons was that, in so far as they were about anything, to me it seldom seemed to be Christian. And they were so stupid - any idiot was allowed to stand up there and drivel on and on. Whenever I could, I avoided the Address, but there were times when I found myself inescapably trapped. On these occasions I ran rapidly through boredom and disgust into outrage. By the end, all pleasure worse than wrecked, I was left tingling with frustration and filled with an exceedingly strong dislike for all men of God.

Meanwhile, at the club, two other art students had come to share a large room on a lower floor, one of them was also from the Ruskin, the other, an engraver. Few two people could have been more different. The Engraver was a submerged girl whose eyes never rested but slid away or turned inward. She was equally tangential in posture, being out of the straight with her head on one side. It seemed that a severe mastoid as a child had left her forever presenting one ear and shielding the other. She was also a heavy girl who found it hard to get off the ground physically, and difficult to get down to it by any other route; but where the funny side of things was concerned she possessed wildly waving antennae: a supple sense of the absurd had grown out of a genius for landing herself in preposterous situations. What made the Engraver something of an endurance test was verbal incontinence. Any loose association of thought that happened to flicker across her mind was forthwith thrown up, undigested; she seemed unable to distinguish between this and an acceptable contribution. Within a group it was hardly noticeable, there was less scope and the effect was spread; on the other hand to be alone with her could add up to a refined torture approaching dispossession of consciousness.

In complete contrast to her room-mate, the Ruskinite spoke little. She never chattered and she never expanded and exaggerated as we usually did, but on those occasions when her interest was caught by some worthwhile new prospect or possibility, she came suddenly alight and left us all behind. Most mornings, if the Ruskinite was with us we were routed through the common room, at that time deserted except for one or two staff. She spread the daily papers over the ping-pong table and was apt to strike up a discussion with the pale elderly man patiently sweeping scattered tea leaves with a wide broom. You had to admire the Ruskinite. She was strongly responsible. Her interests were varied and broad-based. She appeared to have purpose. She attended political meetings and leaned left. She read the *New Statesman*. She already lived in two worlds, commuting smoothly back and forth across the Atlantic. But under such circumstances we didn't really get to know her. Chance crumbs of information came our way. I was reading an Everyman edition of a Russian classic. She picked up the book and checked the title page. The translation was by her mother.

One night the Ruskinite came back from a meeting where two opposing speakers had each given such a good account of their side of the argument, she'd been obliged to agree with them both, and was genuinely at a loss. Of course, we laughed. But I treasured these sudden flashes of awkward honesty. She went out bravely to meet life. To me it seemed that she was real, the rest of us only copies, and 'To please myself' I wrote a poem about it. This sporadic, desultory, one-sided relationship went deep and was influential. Occasional passing signals of acknowledgement did come my way, and on these notes of grace I was nourished and warmed. Curiously, Zelda was interested. She had it in mind to paint a portrait and asked the Ruskinite to sit. On being smartly disabused of any such - in the Ruskinite's view - time-wasting procedure, she went ahead and painted one anyway, calling it '*Madam*'!

It was the Ruskinite's habit of going away most weekends that let in the problem of the Engraver. In the end I learned to spin round my head a light resilient dome off which the blather softly bounced. Occasional mono-syllabic soothing noises created a reasonable reception illusion; this way it was possible to keep a skeleton service of basic faculties gently ticking over. There was what came to be known as the Silent Sunday, the weekend the Ruskiniste didn't go away and parried the other's verbal rumination by behaving as it its source didn't exist - nothing the Engraver said or did elicited the least response. By the end of the morning, feeling that things had gone far enough, the Engraver decided that two could play at this and for the rest of the day she waited eagerly, under cover of the silence, to cap an unwary comment with a telling non-remark. But the Ruskinite pottered busily on, went out, came in, and finally got to bed and turned to the wall. I never heard the other side of these episodes from the robust Ruskinite, I always had it from the Engraver, who as soon as she had cooled off came up to share the fun.

It wasn't only the Engraver who came up against the Ruskinite's strong sense of destination. One morning I was again waylaid by the lady from the ground-floor front. A new term had started without the Ruskinite. *'What has happened to your friend up there?'*, inquired my acquaintance, *'Isn't she coming back?'* I could only suppose that she was. *'Is she a particular friend of yours?'*, pursued the white-haired lady. With the Ruskinite it wasn't easy to say. *'She's the sort of person who'd trample your dead body to get where she wanted to go.'*, observed the ground-floor front with what sounded like the conviction of first-hand experience.

While the Ruskinite was away, and following a visit to Sadler's Wells, the Engraver was inspired to take up ballet, beginning that very night on our return, with two other students, to the club. It was such good fun, and must surely be so slimming, it was decided to make a regular feature of it. This wasn't possible, though, due to the arrival the next day of a strongly-worded note demanding that the two of them vacate their accommodation by the end of the month. Once we'd recovered from shock it was action stations. The principal dancer found a vacancy in a hostel. The plight of the absent Ruskinite was complicated by furniture. Something needed to be done, but the Engraver seemed unable to move, so I led a snap search for digs, and soon we had a collection of possibilities, with costs and comments, for the Ruskinite to go and see. As the time for the Ruskinite's return approached, the Engraver became even more acutely angled with emotion. The thought of her room-mate's justifiable reaction hung over all of us - it was felt that on this occasion she would surely speak. As indeed she did. I don't quite know what I'd expected - a number of possibilities had passed through my mind - but simple acceptance hadn't been one of them. There was not a word of rebuke and she was touchingly grateful for our thoughtfulness in the matter of the addresses, in one of which she settled down with such promptness and aplomb, it seemed to more than one of us that it had to be exactly what she wanted.

Following the Diploma, I was awarded an exhibition for a fourth year. I had already been a student far too long, but the opportunity was there and put off the disquieting prospect of having to earn a living. Almost at once there was a sinking into mild neurosis. I suffered from inertia, couldn't sleep, was affected by noise and prey to formless fears. I found reasons. The Fulham Road traffic kept me awake.

There was now a bus stop over the road, and instead of a smooth roar past we had stopping and starting. Odd nights I slept on the floor in other students' digs, but although this was quieter it made little difference, the sleeplessness and fears persisted, now thriving on the discomfort and unfamiliar surroundings. There were other reasons. I wasn't doing what I really wanted to do. I could paint well enough. A painting in a show of students' work held in a West-End gallery had been mentioned in the press, a drawing had been accepted by the London Group, at the College I had just won the Principal's Prize. It was gratifying, but it also served to confuse the issue. Deep down I knew I had no true vocation - that the undeviating interest that passionately mattered lay elsewhere. It had become simply a question of plodding on and getting on; that I'd fail to arrive was inconceivable. How boring it all was! The choice of career, reasonable and well-intentioned, generous too under the exceptional circumstances, had never been my own. The future I wanted could have no being. But we were now in the position where the future I had failed to hold me.

Another facet of the situation was this upholding of failure over success. Success was seen as unreal and hollow, degrading and coarsening to the finer sensibilities. If some of this was a bit of a pose, the armature was genuine enough. It was a line of thought that had been maturing for some time, nurtured on Borrow's *Lavengro*, the poet W.H. Davies's *The Autobiography of a Super-Tramp*, and now I had Gorki's appealing down-and-outs. It also found expression in a favourite verse by Whitman that begins, '*I think I could turn and live with animals*', and ends, '*Not one is respectable or industrious over the whole earth.*'

At last one of the college staff hearing of an opening at the B.B.C. suggested that this might suit or, at any rate, tide me over, seeing that I didn't want to teach and had to get a job. Assistant art editor of the *Radio Times*? It appeared that there was some dis-satisfaction over the appearance of the paper. It was felt that the infiltration of someone from outside and unconnected with journalism might be worth trying, and a woman was seen to be in a particularly favourable position to influence. Anyone more completely unsuitable would have been hard to find. I was interviewed by the head of the Public Relations Department, a suave, middle-aged gentleman, charming of course, but in a mild state of shock from his encounter with the Daisy Ashford spelling mistakes in my application before him on his desk. And it wasn't only the spelling he couldn't believe. As I was passing through the door on my way out, he was unable to resist remarking, '*You need not have given your age as in the twenties - you'd still have got the job!*'

I left college mid-term. I was launched. What's more, industry was to prove my salvation for, as if by magic from the very first day, the inertia vanished, the fears faded and once more I slept out the nights.

I went home for the last time. There was break-up here, too. My aunt was by now summer-letting the cottage and once more looking round in London. I arrived late. By the time I got down from the bus, the village square was deserted and in bright moonlight with the dipping roofline of a row of cottages thrown across in sharp-edged shadow. As the rumble of the bus died away it was completely still. I stood with my own cut-out shadow, an island in the moonlight, a part of the stillness, and was filled with thankfulness for being me, here in this place, at this moment in time, and back over the years - Eleven years. Gradually, I became aware of muted light through drawn curtains, and in the distance a dog barked. I crossed the square, passed the manor and carried on down the rough stony hill to where the lane flattened out with permanently wet, froggy ditches. The stone steps, the cobblestones, the honeysuckle, that **enormous** key. Home! And home it had been - the flats mere perches. But now it was over, it had played its part, time now for another family to be lying in bed, listening to the starlings scrabbling round under the thatch, and in the spring, puzzling over their habit of dropping blue eggs on the newly-turned garden.

8

B.B.C. What is Work?

"The vulgarity of the Radio Times
makes me sorry I ever started it."
Reith Diaries, 7 September 1963

I remained with the BBC almost four years. For one thing it took this time for me to fully realise I was no longer in the school situation - that I was free to leave at any time. Not that it was so dreadful. As office jobs went it must have been better than most; and as image went it was second to none. And I enjoyed the travelling: leaping into buses, squeezing into tubes, racing up moving staircases and in and out of the West-End traffic. City-street sport. Finally (when early enough), striding it out with the tides of humanity converging on their various places of business. This last was epic - like being in a Russian film. It was also entirely novel - I was a world's worker just like everyone else! And right to the end it never lost its thrill.

In the morning, with an arrival time of 9.30 and an actual entry of up to two minutes to ten, the main surge was usually over. It was more a matter of split-second timing. I fell out of bed at the last minute and thereafter the journey was similar to the Mayfield one, with tube instead of tram. I stopped running only in Lower Regent Street as Broadcasting House came in view, and my only awkward moment was the actual entry - getting past the majestic figure of the commissionaire. Whenever I could, I blotted myself out behind some black-coated dispatch case-carrying gentleman. Then up the stairs in multiple leaps. I never bothered with the lift. And all the time I'd be willing the clock not to strike. If I wasn't there by ten, there'd be words, and this would mean having to make an effort for at least the rest of the week. The art editor was only a year or two older than me and easy enough, I don't think he really minded, rather he felt it not the done thing for his assistant to be arriving after him. But usually I just made it, dropping into my swivel chair with a sigh of relief as the clock struck. I then shook off my shoes (hot feet), lit a cigarette and sent the office boy down to the canteen for coffee and bourbon biscuits (breakfast).

The transition from art student to office worker was not so much uncomfortable as unsatisfying. The work was not uninteresting and easy enough; the typography didn't present problems there wasn't the scope, and although all I ever wrote were captions, I enjoyed the idea of being a journalist. The art editor was a lively character who fancied himself as a funny man. It was a light-hearted department and I liked that, too. But since I was in no way fully engaged it hardly seemed like an occupation, and all too soon there emerged that well-known syndrome: an emotional fixation on the end of the afternoon together with the longer-term goal of Friday as the 'Gateway to Freedom'.

Tall, straight, stiff, hair shaved short, and never without his umbrella, the editor-in-chief was very different from the art editor. And at his desk he was just as unbending, given to grinding his teeth over undotted 'i's. He had long boney fingers with black wires shooting out of them. I would watch these gruesome digits running like tarantulas over the galleys and make-up. Between him and me there was less than no communication; we met all ways on except the right way round. It seemed this couldn't fail. Fortunately, it was only at those times when the art editor was away that I had anything to do with the editor-in-chief. Sometimes it was just a straight misunderstanding. He would suddenly fling open the door, drop a depth charge, toss in a hand grenade and storm off. He was Irish. At other times there might be a degree of justification for some little thing anyone else would have got away with. But it did also seem as if he himself was partly responsible. I got the impression that he didn't care for artists - was determined to find them unprincipled and crooked - and the onus of proof fell on me. At the same time it didn't occur to me that a good deal of this could have been a projection of the discomposure experienced over an astounding appointment foisted on him from above. Finally, although on the rim of middle-age, he was unmarried and possessed, it was said, by a phantom woman, wholly feminine, totally sweet. Not that I worried much, and on his return the art editor was delighted. The last thing anyone wants to find after absence is a more successful or popular stand-in.

However, being exposed to the Irish commander was the least of my troubles when the art editor went on holiday. At these times, for two or three days a week, I was liable to find myself still in Broadcasting House at 7 or 8 o'clock, or even later. I didn't care for this - as I saw it - violation of personal freedom. Although one year it did have a good side too, when the art editor and editor were away at the same time, and someone in the deputy editor's family suddenly became mortally ill. In this free situation I got away with a piece of typography that earned praise from the elect Publications Department, and on his return, a sharp reprimand from the editor. You would have thought that there might have been some reciprocation or exchange between the Publications Department and ourselves, but here, too, there was a hiatus. Without doubt the sight of our product made them shrink.

It was my job to call in photographic material. The very good B.B.C.

Photographic Section supplied us with pictures of entertainers and shots of shows. For material other than this it was necessary to ring up outside agencies and professional photographers. I enjoyed this. As a disembodied voice I found myself relaxed to a degree that wouldn't otherwise have been possible and I soon had a circle of equally unseen acquaintances to whom I became warmly attached. With one exception. This was a bloody-minded gentleman whose photographs of certain parts of Africa were unfortunately the best available. On Saturday mornings one editorial staff had to be on duty. It meant going in for a few hours something like every six weeks. But it was quiet and peaceful - enough to lull one into feeling more private person than public servant. It was on one such sunny Saturday morning that I told the said photographer where he could go. Some weeks later his complaint finally filtered through to the department and the editor paid me a visit. Not at all in the manner I had every reason to expect, but quietly, thoughtfully, it could almost be said, with deference. As for the rest of the department, I enjoyed a period of popular notoriety. The man was widely known: I received tokens of appreciation from other departments. Someone from outside rang up. I had to apologise, but here, too, there was a bonus in store, for the photographer now became charm itself, and from then on we had better, larger, more promptly despatched selections of prints than had ever come our way in the past.

The one thing that annoyed the art editor was if he should happen to see me glance in the direction of the clock towards the end of the afternoon. He was proud of his job and put his whole self into it, and because I recognised the value of this it made me feel pretty poor too. What was I doing in this place? It was surely time for me to be taking some initiative of my own. Meanwhile, it was the end of the afternoon that held the promise, with rush-hour travelling at its most zestful and exciting, when I became one joyous drop in the tidal-wave racing back to personal freedom. It was as if for most of the day we had all been holding our breath and were now coasting home on a great gust of relief.

Up to this time I had been one person. Now that I had to earn a living I became two people. There was this other me waiting like a relay runner to take over the minute I stepped out of Broadcasting House. On the face of it this one would seem to have less value than the young woman who worked to keep her, except that the working girl was held in position by economic pressures. It was the kept woman, lazy and pleasure-loving, restless and mistake-prone, who was seen as the more real. Ideas of work are strongly held. From the beginning I'd been brought up to regard work as something created by oneself. The other, so-called, whether hard or horrible, or fun, or worthwhile, or whatever else it might be, was merely employment.

But soon it was plain that there was an impoverishment, a falling-off in this untethered self. Being squeezed into a peripheral existence weakened her vitality.

She didn't paint, she didn't write, while a passion for the cinema began to assume the proportions of drug addiction. Yet still the only recognised employer was this self, the conviction persisted that promise and possibilities remained, and if this was so then it had to be here. There was no conflict between these two; each recognised her place, the cheerful drifter, scornful of hire, floated confidently out on top - 'that paid slave at Broadcasting House' knew she was counterfeit. But it wasn't easy. The familiar specialised setting gone, I was as out of my element as oil on water and a magnet to mines. Only too well I knew myself to be different from ordinary people. That I considered myself their superior was far from being the passport I thought it was, and this led to an alternating situation like picking petals off a daisy. I loved them, I loved them not. One minute nice, ordinary people were the salt of the earth, the next I was hating them, sure that the truth was that ordinary people were never nice. And though at odd intervals I would find myself sensing that they were as unnerved by me as I was lacking in understanding of them, it never at any time occurred to me that the least effort on my part would be required - where was the need when I was so far above them? Nonetheless so much novelty did this new workaday world appear to have that each jolt was followed by an instant refill of joyful expectation. In any case the present was seen as introductory, a scanning of possibilities, the real thing yet to come. That it never seemed to get any nearer wasn't worrying because there was so much time - unlimited time in endless youth. It was easier to imagine oneself ceasing to be than middle-aged or old.

There were solaces. Smoking helped. I had first taken to it on an unfamiliar social occasion, and at once felt less cut-off. It was like a small miracle, and after that I soon discovered further applications of its usefulness. Not that I smoked a lot. In fact I didn't genuinely care for it and never learnt to inhale. It was the image that was important, and in this respect it took on much the same role as I'd imagined for myself in horn-rimmed glasses. It could widen the horizon or focus the faculties. It was the anticipatory movements that had the charging effect - extracting the cigarette from the packet and setting it in position, the scratch and fizz of the match. After that - especially in the office - it tended to become a nuisance. I was so bad at it. Left in my mouth, smoke got in my eyes; cast on one side, it burnt the furniture; while absent-mindedly discarded matches ignited the contents of my waste-paper basket. Sometimes, though, the preliminaries were so efficacious, the release of ideas so immediate and urgent, that I quite forgot to complete the ritual. This was altogether more satisfactory, being cleaner, safer and cheaper.

Not long after joining the B.B.C. I left the club to share a flat with the Engraver in a block of mansions in Chelsea. In fact we shared two flats. The first was furnished and belonged to a friend of a friend of the Engraver. It seemed this lady wanted it lived in while she was away and thought of needy students, we were charged only a nominal rent. It was a nice little flat, comfortably furnished - two rooms and a

The 'Engraver' with Phyllis at Woodbine Cottage

kitchenette. No bath, but by this time my aunt had left the cottage and was living in Hampstead. The arrangement worked well, being convenient for us both. We didn't see too much of each other as there were two students of the Engraver's year already in the mansions. At those times, when we were both in the flat together, we usually kept to our rooms, and any remarks we wished to make were bellowed across. The flat was on the ground floor and faced the street. In warm weather with the windows wide open it was not unusual for a discussion to be broken into from the pavement, and some of our questions received interesting answers. At the top of the building we discovered a trapdoor leaving up to an area of flat roof good for sunbathing, and in really hot weather there were occasions when the four of us slept out, with the Engraver (something of a somnambulist) tied to a chimney.

At the end of our tenancy we heard of an unfurnished flat at the top of our block - if we didn't mind the state it was in. For redecoration, we would have to sign a three-year agreement; but there was nothing to stop us doing it up ourselves if we wanted to. We each decorated our own rooms. I even went so far as to do the kitchenette and make a start on the hall, but the paint ran out halfway down the front door and thus it remained for our tenancy. We continued to enjoy a relaxed way of life still yelling across and chatting contentedly in the kitchen, really only listening to ourselves. What I appreciated in the Engraver as flat-mate was her lack of definition, she was there and yet she was not there. It was companionship with a unique degree of privacy. When now and again she suddenly surfaced and made some discerning remark or hard statement of fact I got quite a shock. On Sundays we took it in turn to do the coffee and toast (breakfast in bed), and the midday greasy meal. The Engraver insisted on the milk and water in separate saucepans for the coffee - sheer waste of time in my opinion. Invariably I made it in one and hotly denied it and she never knew the difference. Or perhaps she did, for the odd Sunday, when feeling spiteful, she'd make the supreme effort and get out of bed to come in and check. I was also accused of not pulling my weight in the matter of the midday cook-ups. This usually occurred because she couldn't wait and I wasn't hungry yet.

But we were happy enough. Although I could show such acute temper at home, outside of this I was as easy-going as ever, and never seemed to become irritated. In fact the Engraver only achieved this once - on top of a bus coming home one night from the flicks. It had been a warm film about fighter pilots, full of handsome young men being splendidly heroic in their living and their dying. I was sitting silent, the marvel of it still working in me like a yeast, when I heard, *'Well, aren't you going to say something?!'*, and on the instant I became wildly incensed at this violation of a holy place.

As soon as I had some real money I bought a professional flute, a fine, silvery rod studded with keys, costing as much as a piano. I was to find that a musical instrument could be put to good use in the flat for those times when the Engraver did rather impinge. On such occasions I was able to blow my way clear with a spirited recital. One day I was given proof that the Engraver did sometimes listen to whatever it was I was currently going on about - even to the point of becoming well and truly fed up with it. To yet another highflown dissertation on the subject of failure, she replied with a needling, *'Well, you are one - aren't you?!'* I was astounded. I never expected to be taken literally. Such was **my** success that I could afford to dispense with it - this was the point, the epitome of conceit, well-deserving of a knock; and when you looked into it, it wasn't even the thing itself, only the promise of it that I appeared to be so keen to jettison. Nonetheless, the remark had its effect, the subject as a topic of conversation abruptly ceased..

But all this was by the way; it didn't touch the tangle of feelings and reasonings - serious, indulgent, idiotic - that made up this obsession. Nothing was going to shake that central conviction of the highest virtue in the lowest places - innocent virtue of genuine dignity, with even a touch of splendour along the lines of losing your life to find it. The despised and rejected, the tramp, the outsider, these were the heros I recognized - the poets of living. At this time a generation was emerging from middle-class insulation into a climate of working-class unrest, cracks in a rigidly-held social system were exposing injustice and suffering. For many, indignation settled into socialism; for some it became a crusade, replacing bankrupt religion. It was an element in the very air.

Periods of restlessness became more acute. I was beginning to feel walled-in by full employment. I gazed hungrily out of the office window at the narrow strip of sky. I was a prisoner! One sunny Sunday while the Engraver was on holiday, I went off on my own to Kew Gardens and found it appealing. I ate a sandwich under a tree and was struck by the thought - why not live out here? It was green and fresh. So few people. Of London not a hint. And it **was** a garden, paradise even, compared with poor trampled-on Kensington Gardens and Hyde Park. When the Engraver returned I put it to her and she agreed. We looked at a few flats and finally decided on one of them. Hardly had the decision been made than I came to my senses. I was sure that it wasn't at all what I was looking for. My aunt had suggested my joining her in a larger Hampstead flat, and I now felt strongly that this would be the better course, especially as it would give more time for the cultivation of that naggingly important, difficult, treasured **ME**.

It remained to tell the Engraver - an unenviable task as I knew my flatmate to be sensitive of slight. In both our flats I'd been careful to give her the choice of room. I also fully recognized our sharing arrangements in terms of convenience, and while I was sure it was the same for her - as to whether she was fully aware of it, of this I was less certain. Her reaction was as I'd feared. I was reproved in a typically roundabout fashion through a friend of hers, an earnest young woman doing social studies or some such at London University.

So I moved again. And the more important, difficult me did have extra time - to laze and dream, read and go to the pictures. But 'doing nothing' was also seen as a necessary regenerative state, capable of throwing up ideas and fostering inspiration. For certain it was a state out of which, by taking thought, you could shape an infinitely desirable future where anything and everything was possible. For these few years, films surpassed books. The cinema had been an ever-ready source of excitement and glamour for some time. At the Royal College most of us went to the flicks at least once a week. At that time - the early Thirties - the near-by tiny Boltons Repertory Cinema was still silent and showing a selection of the more interesting films, most of them from the Continent, where Germany was then in the ascendant. I'd already seen Fritz Lang's *Metropolis* at Oxford. I now saw marvels like *The White Hell of Pitz Palu* with Leni Reifenstahl on skis, and her own Bavarian peasant idyll, *The Blue Light*. And with the coming of sound, finest of all, Pabst's powerful masterpiece, *Kameradschaft*. This film made a deep impression. Set in the coal-mining area of Alsace-Lorraine on the Franco-German border, with the two peoples hostile to each other, it effectively contrasts the French and German characters, unjudgementally showing them as simply different. It opens with a French boy and German lad playing together, squabbling, then fighting, and runs on to end on a double climax. First the mine disaster - a collapsed tunnel entombs the shift. The deafening clamour of the alarm alerts the district. Frantic young women in aprons, clutching babies, rush out of poor dwellings, bitter mothers of working sons, and lamenting old women in shawls, who have seen it all before, bring up the rear, thronging the mine gates. But now the film delivers its counter-climax as nationality forgotten, danger disregarded, the men from over the border, hauling their more advanced equipment, stream in to rescue their trapped comrades. *Kameradschaft.*

But the Thirties were also the great years of Hollywood. And now the cinema became little short of an alternative for living.. It could supply all the things I didn't have, give entrée into all grades of society in at least two countries, one still something of an empire, the other a continent. Here at last was an adult world where I was always certain of admission and couldn't put a foot wrong. All the same it wasn't only fiction that held me. There was also location. I had seen a fine documentary on the dust bowl and *The River* dramatised the problem of the flooding Mississippi. These were specialist films, but in fact America - the country itself - was splendidly bound up in so many popular productions: it flickered through, or thundered in the background, or simply lay there mute and glorious. At other times it took over from the players, the story might be feeble - something the country could never be. From the fertile farms of Wisconsin to the moss-dripping oaks of the deep south, from picture-book New England to the arid south-western deserts, it was all there.

Books, too, played their part. I was now on a course of paperbacks about victims of chronically appalling circumstances - misfits and rejects, the weak, the trampled on, fending for themselves in the world's backwaters. It was an irresistible theme to which other, more solid works, also contributed: Liam O'Flaherty's *Two Years*, William Robinson's *Deep Water and Shoal*, Orwell's *Down and Out in Paris and London*. *Adventures of a Wanderer*, *Half a Million Tramps*. Belfrage's *Away From it All* and Jack Jones's *Unfinished Journey* also made their mark. Borrow, Gorki, Whitman and W.H. Davies had gone before.

It all contributed to the belief that those in extremity, along with the few who chose to live marginal lives, were the most valuable, that there was more real living in them than in the whole body of surrounding conformity. Out of this potent mixture of influences there arose a strongly-growing desire to be uprooted, to disappear. At the back of my mind was a purifying experience as near as possible to rebirth. In a recurring fantasy I saw myself, memory wiped out, washed up on the deserted shore of some far-away continent.

At this point I saw a British film, *The Edge of the World*, made on Foula, an isolated Shetland island. While there was a story, it was as much a documentary, showing the last families being taken off for re-settlement on the mainland. It was all surging sea and gale-force winds and I was swept off my feet, deciding there and then to go and live in the Hebrides. It was a measure of how serious I was that I could accept such a compromise. Mull, Tiree or Coll? Muck, Eigg or Rum! Or even an outer island? Highland and Island Tourist Board information was collected, books and maps came out of the library and soon I had a pretty good idea of the varying flora and fauna, approximate populations, ports - even steamer-service timetables. Following all this paper-work and study I was prudent enough to choose Mull. I'd take over a crofter's cottage and adopt the simple life, live from the soil, drink from a spring, dig peat, fish, perhaps keep a goat. I'd be taking an easel, my flute and a box of fat notebooks. Alone on an island of rock and heather, lashed by the wind and waves, sea birds mewing, with any luck a golden eagle or two - there surely I could get myself together and see the way clear.

I was now in my fourth year at the B.B.C. and full of the seeds of escape, and this bracing imaginative excursion was the first to germinate. If not exactly original, it was a nice enough idea, pleasingly poetic, and I had every intention of carrying it out. Absurd? Well yes, obviously the original high-flown synopsis would have had to be more than somewhat modified. But why, oh why, didn't I at least take a holiday up there and explore the island, which after all does include St. Columba's Iona? And somewhat further over the water, the volcanic architectural wonders of Staffa - for those hopeful enough to set out and lucky enough to be able to land, though Turner and Mendelssohn, even Keats, appeared to have managed all right. To have lived in the Hebrides if only for a year or two would surely have been a most refreshing experience, and I might even have elected to stay.

But it wasn't to be. In the end the idea gradually faded before what was for me then a much more novel and exciting project - to tramp America, or rather, seeing that distances in that country made it virtually untrampable, to hitch-hike, over there already an accepted way of getting about. More books came out of the library. Not a single radio relay from the States was missed; and as I listened the world became a larger place with myself extended across it. This plan persisted. It filled out and took shape, till, finally, I was working on a large map, plotting a detailed course from coast to coast, and from the Canadian border to the Gulf of Mexico. The whole thing was so obvious and ridiculously simple I couldn't think why everyone else wasn't doing it, too. Cash? It was laid on. The Corporation's pension scheme had saved it all up for me.

It was jokingly said that only one employee had voluntarily given up a career in the B.B.C., an office boy to become steward on an ocean-going liner, and the Corporation was reputed to be still smarting from the slight. Certainly great kindness and consideration came my way. Jobs in other, possibly more congenial departments hung in the air - discreet soundings were taken. It looked like an instance of an often-noted tendency of the B.B.C. at that time, to promote from within rather than recruit from without - its strong, familial loyalty to its staff, at any rate under John Reith. I was even taken out to lunch by one of the Director-General's favourite polished young ladies. Finally, I was summoned for an interview. Up till this point I'd never even seen the Director-General, John Reith, according to popular hear-say a God-Almighty fanatic son of the manse, strong on all-day Sabbath observance, and never a drinkie in sight. So I hadn't much idea what to expect - except something different. I was right there. The usual reactions of amusement and condescension were absent. He asked questions, listened intently and wished the enterprise well. He did more than that. To my astonishment, he added a remarkable degree of understanding. He spoke of an Australian book about a middle-aged man who had suddenly faced about from the familiar and known; saying nothing and carrying nothing, and for no reason fathomable to family or friends, he ad simply got up and walked away - and gone on walking right out of his previous life.

What I didn't know then, and would never have dreamt, was that he, too, felt the need to be moving on - was struggling to discover some other way forward. He had raised up an institution, of its kind the finest in the world. But the mountains had moved, the construction over, he was sitting pretty and it didn't suit. His faculties cried out for use - exercise, challenges. In his own graphic words, he needed to be **stretched**.

II

THE U.S.A.: TRAVELLING LIGHTLY
a 14,000 miles hitchhike
1938-1939

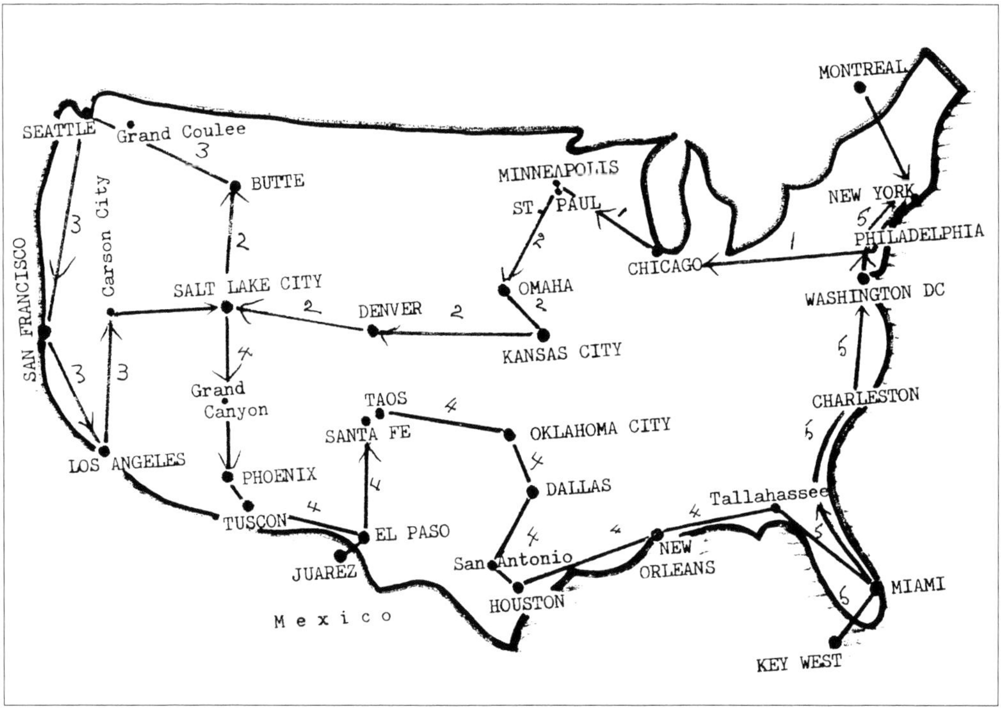

MONTREAL
SEATTLE
Grand Coulee
BUTTE
MINNEAPOLIS
ST. PAUL
NEW YORK
PHILADELPHIA
CHICAGO
Carson City
SAN FRANCISCO
SALT LAKE CITY
DENVER
OMAHA
KANSAS CITY
WASHINGTON DC
Grand Canyon
TAOS
SANTA FE
OKLAHOMA CITY
CHARLESTON
LOS ANGELES
PHOENIX
DALLAS
Tallahassee
TUSCON
EL PASO
JUAREZ
San Antonio
NEW ORLEANS
HOUSTON
MIAMI
Mexico
KEY WEST

9

Not the Niagara Falls

New England to Minnesota – agreeable emptiness -Tourist Homes - New England scenic - sleep out - Paul and the old man - Greasy and the Latin - jellied donuts - bed bugs - brother and sister in Wisconsin - a date with a peach - Swedish girls - falls.

It was with an agreeable feeling of emptiness that I walked out of Montreal. The sleepless nights, the threshing around in a fever of excited planning had long ago been left behind. I was so worked out and wound up it seemed as if I was doing the most natural thing in the world.

In the residential outskirts of a small town I accepted a lift from a French Canadian on his way to Lake Champlayne to inspect land for a summer cottage. If I wouldn't mind going with him, he would afterwards take me on to the U.S. border. We walked through the bracken and trees to the water's edge. I had heard of the beauty of this lake. It came up to expectation. But not the Frenchman. I had yet to learn that to pick up a ride in a built-up area is never a good idea; genuine travellers don't stop, while any citizen at a loose end who may happen to spot you hopefully takes to the car. The customs officer who checked my passport was just going off duty. *'Take care how you pick up rides'* he said as we drove along, *'Don't be afraid to look people over, and, if you don't like the look of them, wave them on. There're ruffians around any place. Most folks are pretty nice though.'* He spoke for himself; most people did, I was to find.

The first real ride came from three ragged youths in a two-seater that just about held together. They were on a forty-mile detour to avoid a rough secondary road; taking it in turn they'd been driving all night. There was much shouting and laughter. I sat in the dicky seat with a pale fleshless boy who joined in, but on his face in repose was a look of singular gentleness. They put me down to turn off for home. There was a town half a mile down the road, but before I could reach it they re-appeared to take me through and out on the open highway again, the better to pick up the next ride. I had hardly spoken. But now I saw how I had been accepted and considered.

Historic New England is tourist territory. First nights were spent in Tourist Homes (bed without breakfast). The trouble was involvement with the family. I should have welcomed it. But American hospitality is strong and I was powerless before it. To be fair, an English girl crossing the continent on her feet was something of a novelty. There was plainly the need for cover. It was also necessary to conceal opinions. On learning that, no, I wouldn't be visiting the Niagara Falls, I didn't much care for sight-seeing, people were affronted or thought me out of my mind. And who could blame them? And the nicer and more helpful they were trying to be, the more upsetting it was.

Ed had short hair that stuck up and was driving barefoot. He was a laid-off motor mechanic from Milwaukee, like me experiencing New England for the first time; and we were both heading for New York. What luck! Listening to him, I thought so, too. It was his first car-trip holiday. Previous to this his spare time had been spent bumming around and riding the rods. He'd been all over. I was enthralled. He, too. He was unable to tell of his travels at home as his stay-at-home older brother got mad and rushed out, slamming the door fit to shatter the windows.

We stayed in Portland, Maine, that night, in a reasonable but quite superior guest house, where no sooner had the good lady left us, than Ed came charging in to my room, ripped open the bed and plucked up the lower sheet to examine the mattress. He even scraped down a seam with his finger-nail. We could not have done better at the best hotel, I was informed.

Ed's idea of catering matched mine. Bottles of milk, cheese and crackers, bags of fruit and bananas, eaten in the car, on a seat or some shady grass, backed up by drug-store coffee and 'burgers (he), ice-cream soda and pumpkin pie (me). Neither of us smoked or drank.

From the White Mountains of Vermont to the Green Mountains of New Hampshire, sanctified by a golden sun and unfailing clear sky. New England, bright and clean and neat like pictures by a Sunday painter was easy to love. Particularly appealing were the white steepled churches, often as simple and direct as a child's toy. Some were so lightweight in construction it seemed they could once have sprung into being round a kneeling community. Even the trees were special - looked somehow more handsome and shapely than ours. But then so they should, I thought, with so much more space to express themselves in. Which by this time was something I needed myself - I felt terrible. The trouble was motion sickness, too many hours on four wheels. Ed kept saying, it's nothing, it'll soon pass. But it didn't.

When we came to some more than usually historic church, Ed put on a pair of tatty tennis shoes and got out his camera. I remained firmly seated, scanning the map for somewhere to get out and die. Boston was next but I didn't fancy it. Ed returned, determined to have me in a picture. I was somehow propped up in a suitable position and we were off again.

Into Boston we stopped at some ornamental water where children were paddling, and Ed had to get in with them to cool off his feet. Then came a mini-museum up on a grassy bank, complete with pyramids of cannon balls. Inside were mostly photographs, accompanied by sheets of closely-packed small print and it was obvious that Ed was going to read every word. I got back in the car and picked up the map, and then I saw it: Providence! Providentially on our route. That was where I'd get out and recover. Ed came back; he was tickled that the place was a monument to how the Yanks had seen off the Brits, - **naturally**, I hadn't wanted to read all about it! He was a nice lad, hugely enjoying himself; as always the pleasure is twofold with a friend, and a girl, too! We made an odd couple, I suppose, but for its short run it didn't feel that way. We had like interests and shared a sort of daft innocence that made for an easy relationship. I'd be missing him, too. It seemed a shame, but would have to come. We were nearing New York, and he was looking forward to Coney Island, just about the last place I wanted to visit. So I went to bed in Providence and woke up, cured.

Out of Providence, it was still tourist territory - lifts were few and walking good - which was what I wanted; but by the time it began to get dark I was out in the country, so far as I knew near to nowhere. At this early juncture in the proceedings, I was still carrying an elementary home-made sleeping bag, believe it or not nothing more than a long laundry bag with a drawstring, as useless as it was unnecessary; but I didn't know that then. Then, everything pointed to its use. Filled with this fine resolve, with springing steps I turned down a lane that led to a wood. Inside though, the wood seemed less well designed for sleeping in, everywhere was a tangle of wiry undergrowth. I stopped for a minute and was covered by a brigade of mosquitoes. An open field, perhaps, might be a wiser choice? It was dark enough now to be private anywhere. I came to the edge of the wood and climbed over a low wall under a spreading evergreen; my feet sank in soft turf, I knocked my knee against a stone - upon examination, a tombstone. I got back over the wall. There were fireflies everywhere, their incandescence hung fire and went out, pricking the darkness with a continuously changing pattern of tiny lights.

Without realizing it, I must have regained the road, for suddenly a beam of blinding light swung round, as it seemed out of nowhere, and a huge truck came to a racketing halt. High over my head a door opened. This wasn't at all what I had in mind, though what I did have hardly seemed to be working for me. Needless to say, hitch-hiking after dark had nothing to recommend it; but true to what was rapidly becoming established form, far from picking my rides, I was putty in the hands of whatever turned up.

'Hallo there, whereya going?' sang out a voice from the cab... *Well come on up then - I can't hang around all night! ... Holy mackerel, look what's here! - an' I thought you was someone's kid brother!'*

Paul asked me where I was from and I said Montreal. I then discovered he'd been born there - but that was all fortunately. He had an expressive way of opening a hand, palm upwards, together with a lift of the brows and tilt of the head. He was a man with a problem. I learned about his job - it was the hours. Yes, you could stop and sleep, but you preferred to get the journey over to have the extra time. He didn't see enough of his little girl. His wife complained he was never home; but when he was, she went out. They were living separate lives. And when they quarrelled the child cried to them to stop. What could he do? The hand, the brows, the head. The truck made such a racket we had to shout and soon my voice began to give out. Paul said, repeatedly, *'Make yourself at home. Get some sleep.'* Sensible advice I was too self-conscious to take. In the early hours of the morning we arrived at the edge of the Bronx, New York. Paul's destination was New Jersey, his route wasn't through but round Manhattan Island, and he felt quite certain that I couldn't just get out and walk off, as I would have been happy enough to do. It appeared that his father lived a few miles out on the other side of the city. We would be passing through this place. *'Why not let me leave you there? You could bed down on the sofa. My old man wouldn't mind, and you'd be perfectly all right.'* The hand came up and out. Once more, at the dictation of circumstance, I agreed and Paul went off to ring up. It was just beginning to get light as we crossed the George Washington Bridge into New Jersey.

The old man wasn't at all like his son, but he, too, had a problem. He was lonely. He drew up a chair and unburdened himself while I sat on the sofa, waiting. His wife was in hospital, she might never be home again. He was out of work at the wrong age. The days, the nights, seemed endless... And despite the promise, what was left of this one was no better.

Over breakfast, I learned that he used to sing. His wife was a music teacher; they'd belonged to the same Montreal choral society. If I was again apprehensive of questions about Canada, once more I needn't have worried. It wasn't my history that interested him. What did interest him were the dangers of a girl - on her own - on the road - in New York - for that matter, anywhere. And this was followed by the sort of advice you feel the giver is hoping you will need rather than heed; under cover he is busy, happily plotting a course of pit-falls. The cumulative effect was debilitating. I got up to go.

New York

It was not a pretty scene. Miscellaneous grimy buildings, here and there odd stores, wayside stands, gas stations, and patches of coarse metropolitan grass have of every kind of debris, the slops of a great city. The prospect for lifts could hardly have been worse. I went forward, noting the highway numbers and constantly consulting a map, but turnings were numerous and confusing. I had little idea where I was.

A couple of toughs in a pioneer Ford kept riding by, potting remarks. After a bit, convinced I was completely lost, I stopped and the toughs drew up. I observed their grinning faces; they were an unsavoury enough pair. I needed help but it hardly seemed possible that it would come from them. It appeared that the road I should be on was a mile or two over. *'We'll putcha there.'*

Following **pick your ride** and **do not travel after dark**, the next cautionary rule for a girl on the road is **avoid more than one man**. But I'd already exploded this one, too. I got in. No sensible girl would have done so. But then no sensible girl would have found herself in my circumstances. On the side-walk two girls were giggling and nudging each other, suggesting that other categories of girls would not have got in, either.

I hadn't much voice. I gave the toughs to understand that this was due to sleeping out. I was heading for New York to find a job, I said. The driver was youngish and Latin-looking with a pasty complexion and gappy teeth. The other man was older. From under a mucky cap hung ratty tails of adhesive hair. His oily, sunken cheeks were unhealthily red. He asked what work I did. I said I was looking for a job in a restaurant or perhaps a hotel.

'Yeah, sure, thas the sorta work you wanna do; only look, this ain't the place - no one around, see? Atlantic City - thas where you wanna go. Long lina hoe tells, full now, plentya dough - season, git me? I bin a waiter, see?' I quickly put forward that I had no previous experience. *'Thassall right, thas O.K. Listen, I know the head water in wunna them hoe tells. He doan care, likes to break 'em in hisself, see? Swell guy, too. Atlantic City, kid, thas where you wanna go.'* But my mind, I said was fixed on New York. *'Sure, I know; well, thassall right - you pick the wrong time, see? I bin up'ere'n down Miami, so I know. Lemme write down that add dress. Look - thas him'n the place; thisis me, see? He'll remember. Swell guy. And you'll be all right. Thas where you wanna go, kid, sure - I know, see?'*

We arrived at the banks of the Hudson and drew up. From this place there was a ferry, or underground tunnel through to Manhattan. *'We gitcha ride, see?'* The scene was much the same as before. Rusting iron girders lay around on a patch of soiled grass. There was a popular wayside eats stand with one or two trucks drawn up alongside. The two got going on these, but without any luck. Greasy came back with a plate of pie and a bottle of milk. At length a small delivery van drew up and the two pounced with some success. A tall, slim lad hesitated. They brought him across between them, both talking at once. *'Do you wanna go wit this guy?'* asked Greasy. Compared with them, he looked like the prince in the fairy tale. But whatever his conduct, it was unlikely to better theirs. Once again I had taken the first opening. I couldn't pretend I was out to prove anything, though perhaps I had, if only how deceptive appearances could be.

Len's driver, a good-looking Jewish boy, arranged a cushion for me to sit between them and we dived under the Hudson, one in a ceaseless stream of roaring traffic. I had the address of a YWCA. *'You stick with us'*, said Len, *'We deliver right by there.'* As the van ran forward and stopped up and down the streets, he pointed out the tallest skyscrapers and well-known squares. At one of the stops the Jewish boy bought a paper-covered column of lozenges, *'For the throat.'*

I told them something about myself - once more as coming from Canada. They wanted to know how I'd made out for rides, and wondered how I'd come to be on the Jersey side of the river. I explained. Len looked alarmed. *'The old boy was over fifty'*, I said. He laughed; *'You want to remember that old boys in this country run to young ideas!'*

When we reached my destination, Len tore a page from his order book and wrote down where they could be found. *'This place'*, he said, indicating the billhead, *'owns a chain of cafés, so maybe we can get you a job.'* Before going into the Y, I looked back. The little van was darting forward again; its rear doors carrying the vital reminder *J E L L I E D D O N U T S*, was quickly swallowed in the stream of traffic.

I should have been more grateful for the Tourist Homes in smiling New England. Not far from Chicago I was put down at dusk in a small town. I was tired, and a nearby bungalow displayed a Tourist Home sign. Madam was peacefully rocking on the porch. As I approached, she half rose, then, properly taking me in, promptly sat down again, now rocking furiously. No one spoke, there wasn't the need. Girls on the road weren't highly thought of, except by gentlemen in cars. And I must have looked the part. I'd been given a lift by the driver of a van who wasn't supposed to carry passengers, so every time we passed through a town I'd been obliged to climb in the back and mingle with the clutter.

In fact, as a learning situation, the refusal was doubly enlightening, for as I carried on down the street I came to another sign, *'Rooms 50c'* So cheap! The room was tiny and basic but no more was required. While undressing I noticed on the wall a minute pencil signature, *'Iron Trail Kid coast to coast 43 states'*, and got into bed transported. I had no more than one minute of this high state before it was punctured by a bed bug. It was easily caught, being large, black, slow and sheet-bound. I dabbed my swelling eye, already beginning to turn dark red. Despite this palpable evidence, it was a situation I couldn't altogether believe in. I lay down again and was at once bitten, this time on the leg and neck. The rest of the night was spent on the floor, as far as possible from the bed. At first light I was out on the road and soon up in a truck.

On a particularly fresh and sparkling morning in Wisconsin I was picked up by a brother and sister. They were on their way north to the lakes for a vacation. I sat in the back, surrounded by fishing tackle, shot guns and bathing gear. The girl, a pretty blond, was a happy, friendly person. We stopped to eat in a small town. The brother asked about roads - there had been an unusual amount of rain locally and parts of the state were said to be flooded. We collected all we needed to know and more from a full-belted prosperous-looking individual at one of the tables, who finally went so far as to rise up from his beer to lead the way. All this attention plainly worried the brother, a reserved young man, but our self-appointed guide was already impatiently tooting the horn, beckoning and pointing the way. At the end of the detour we were obliged to have a drink with him at a place he knew of. Reminiscence - equally obligatory - followed. He was German, he told us. Fifty years ago his family had come to America not knowing a word of the language. They were fine folks; and it was a fine country they'd come to, none finer. It belonged to the people, not the President, always remember that! With ambition and energy you could get yourself someplace. And you could say what you wanted, speak out what was on your mind - you were free. He was mindful, I suppose, of what was going on in Nazi Germany. It was 1938. He spoke rapidly, chewing on the end of a cigar, breathing hard and belching freely.

The fact that I wasn't one of the family was soon laid bare. I was heading for St. Paul. A few miles further on the road branches; although not the more direct route I was going on with the brother and sister as, ultimately, this would land me not many miles from my destination. But now our masterful acquaintance waved this aside. It was quite unnecessary for me to go out of my way as he, himself, was going to St. Paul.

'Feel all right about him', asked the brother, looking uncertain. But I was as helpless as a canoe on the rapids. Of a silent film seen many years before, one short sequence had been vividly retained. This was a full-length close-up of a plump, middle-aged gentleman all slicked up, with spats, silk hat and carnation in buttonhole, rolling his eyes and twiddling the ends of a wicked-looking waxed moustache. The caption flash revealed that he *'had a date with a peach'* - pictured by me as an ice-cream sundae. The middle-aged moneyed one called to mind the gentleman in the film, and it wasn't fruit ice-cream this time, either. But it was, as he had said, a free country. In fact I was much indebted to the forceful gentleman. But for his intervention, I would have missed the road up by the river.

I had felt no particular anticipation, formed no preconceived idea of the upper Mississippi. Now, looking down on it, broad and full, plopping with fish and turtle and flanked by a deep lush undergrowth, it was love at first sight. Of all the more familiar country I passed through, this upper Mississippi valley ranks easily first. It was large and abundant, peaceful and deeply satisfying. The farmsteads were far enough apart to be welcome events: the farmhouse, a clump of trees, a windmill, and huge sun-baked barns, red-maroon colour and usually finished off with a tower or steeple. In the background, low pleated hills followed along the river

That evening, just as it was beginning to get dark, feeling more than usually happy and satisfied I arrived in a small town. Not caring for the looks of the other accommodation, I fixed myself up in a Tourist Home on the outskirts. After tidying up, I sat on the verandah in the inevitable rocking chair and talked to the lady of the house. By now, I had a quite respectable line in conversation of interest to the average American, but this evening the listener was different, neither pressing nor curious, and so it came about that on this occasion it was really me speaking. A fourteen-year-old daughter sat opposite us, swinging on a hanging seat. It was almost dark; apart from a pair of well-made legs that caught the light in the foreground, she was just a shadowy figure who never spoke.

The lady of the house kindly offered to get supper for me. The home-cooked food was delicious. I ate with enthusiasm, and was just about to begin on the appetising-looking dessert, when I heard my hostess calling from above. *'You really should be in bed, now, honey - it's school tomorrow, remember!'* I turned round. The bungalow was split-level, I was in a roomy kitchen-dining room, half a dozen wide wooden steps led down to it. Seated on these was a hunched, absorbed, pyjama-clad figure. No notice was taken of mother, the concentration never wavered. Neither of us spoke. I should have, but, sadly, I could rise no higher than embarrassment, nervously wondering if I'd shovelled in the lettuce somewhat unceremoniously. The meal was continued with a shade more elegance. By the time I got up from the table the pyjama'd presence was gone.

The next morning the lady of the house said in tones half-amused, half-uncertain, *'My daughter says she's going to see the country, hitch-hiking like you, as soon as she's free of school!'* As I walked away, it was with the feeling that there could be no greater compliment than this. It also occurred to me that the hunched figure could have been a reflection of myself.

Due to the failing light, I hadn't properly seen the little town the evening before. Now I saw that it was almost entirely surrounded by the table-topped hills, so much a feature of the area. At one point on the perimeter stood a single, curiously-shaped, prophetic-looking rock. It was a dramatic setting. I was soon once more along by the river. Where it broadened into Lake Pepin, 'the lake of the tears', the weather abruptly changed to fit the name; there was a sudden hailstorm with thunder.

Later in the day I reached St. Paul, Minnesota. Most Y's have separate accommodation for transients, but in this one I was in a dormitory with residents. It meant becoming the latest novelty. London, England, here it had to be, I could never have sustained anything else; and I could hardly expect to be mistaken for Swedish - as often happened - in a community where so many really were. I decided to take a break in St. Paul. It felt comfortable and jobs needed to be done.

I made friends with two Swedish girls. They wanted to know if I'd seen the Court House. Firmly secured between the two I was marched downtown. They seemed to regard my lack of enthusiasm for sights as an unfortunate defect, someone had better be doing something about. Before disappearing into the tall building where both worked, my two friends reeled off a list of other places I should see. Instead, I walked to the Mississippi Boulevard and leaped over the parapet to watch the boats. And so bemused was I by the glory of this river, that I thought of disregarding my itinerary to follow it up to its source in the lakes of northern Minnesota. Today there is no doubt in my mind. The person I am now is upset that the young woman I was then could have rejected such a fine inclination.

I was a bit astonished to find myself having bed-bug trouble in a Y. Though they were nothing like so vicious as the ones down Chicago way. These were unseen, humble, domesticated little creatures who knew their place - well below the salt at the bottom of the bed. Toothless, too, I wasn't aware of being bitten, or did they wait for me to fall asleep? Someone less charitable suggested semi-anaesthesia due to massive application of flea powder when the bed was made up. However that may be, these sorry mites proved cumulatively more destructive than their murderous cousins. Every night my ankles suffered and I must have scratched. To get off my socks without stripping my ankles it was necessary to bandage both.

I said nothing to my Swedish friends, and they said nothing to me, but dormitories are open-plan living. I was touched when I learned how ashamed they were, and how they'd complained to the management, and for the last two days they found accommodation for me in the pretty bungalow of a friend. Which was fine, and so kind except that she was desperate to call the local paper - to me a form of rubbishing far worse than any bugs. It never ceased to come as a surprise that Americans, so seeming language-wise the same as us, could also be so dis-similar. This wasn't the first or last time my horror of publicity caused problems. And no attempt at an explanation to otherwise intelligent and reasonable people got anywhere; on this score we remained solidly incomprehensible to each other.

Twin to German-built St. Paul, on the opposite side of the river, is Minneapolis founded by the Swedes. My two friends were determined that I should see it, and in a fitting manner. They cast around for someone with a car. On Sunday afternoon the car arrived, driven by a girl pleasingly called Fern. Fern had been to a party the night before, and not to bed; she was short on a proper concentration, but we always managed to bring her round in time to avert disaster. Fern then, being diverted from running us into a Minneapolis bank, we turned down Hiawatha Avenue into a green shady park 'Where the falls of Minnehaha, Flash and gleam among the oak trees, Laugh and leap into the valley'. There were many people. It appeared that for once the waterfall was unassisted. However, after viewing with concern the sad thin trickle which was all that it could manage, it was generally agreed that the state had better have continued to man the pumps. But however poor the spectacle, it was lavish in associations. Here, once again, I met my younger self. I had loved the poem at school, even gone so far as to compose one of my own modelled on it. I hadn't bothered with the Niagara, and had no regrets. Now by some miracle, I found myself by this little fall, one I would never knowingly have missed. And it was still a lovely place - if by an effort of will you banished the paved road, the statue of the poet, the neatly-mown lawn and rustic railings. 'Minnehaha, Laughing Water'. Rather it seemed like gentle weeping now.

10

Attitude and Altitude

Plain and Mountain - Travelling salesmen - across the wide Missouri - Kansas city - the 'Rubens' - the hoppers - the accident - Denver - steam truck to Salt Lake City - Pocatello - with miners to Butte

Like anything else, much of hitch-hiking was ordinary enough when you got used to it. People were met in number, but lightly encountered, sometimes not encountered at all. Nonetheless, there were also times when recognition played a part, the language understood. I took to giving en route destinations to break up the journey, to make sure of exercise and give time to myself; but these were only rough guide lines, no rules could be made, it had to be open - this was the joy of it.

The Great Plain was the territory of the travelling salesman and the statistical questionnaire. The white collar approach. All the same there were bound to be misunderstandings. To most, being on the road meant only one thing. And if it didn't, then it should. To me, as I never saw myself as a tourist and the last thing I wanted was to be thought one, it could have been worse. You could be put down at a state border. There was a still operable law against carrying a girl from one state to another - 'for immoral purposes'- having in mind the days of slave trafficking. The trouble was different now: unscrupulous roving young women made a living blackmailing obliging drivers. On the way to Omaha and Kansas City I was picked up by a travelling salesman in a spotless panama. He asked a great many questions, and turned the answers carefully over in his mind, sucking his teeth in thought. *'Live in London!... Got any brothers or sisters?... What does your father do?... Married?... Ever bin married?... Binta college, have you?'* Age, height and weight followed with a period for digestion. Then, *'Cigarette?... What, don't smoke? What's the matter? - drink, dontcha?... Don't drink, either!... The girls in England don't drink beer! My God, I'm telling you, they just about have the men beat over here! Don't lacquer your nails, I see; don't the girls in England do that, either?'* When he learned that I had no camera the mileage slipped as if even the automobile was aghast. It was excessively hot and the travelling man wasn't having a cool time assessing such an unlikely character. The spotless panama was by now way out on the back of his head. He drove fast; we were making for the heart of the continent. At Blue Earth the road branched and we parted.

Travelling Salesman II was an older man with an imposing beltline, and again the spotless panama. He drove fast, too - the faster, the cooler - and by early evening we arrived at his destination, a small town, where regarding accommodation he came up with a suggestion. He could, he said, over-ruling my refusal, face a medical any day. Once more I declined and thanked him politely, and he was very civil about it; we could have been a pair of honourable bowing Chinese.

The next day I was conveyed to Omaha by an unsmiling character in a cloth cap who knew all about girls on the road and wasted no time. Staring in disbelief at my rucksack, he inquired how business was. As impersonally as I could - though it wasn't possible to entirely exclude a hint of apology - I explained the situation, clearly less and less credible as we approached the middle of middle America. He was pretty amazed. *'Well, I'm going to Omaha anyways, see?'* You can work that out for yourself. He went on to describe other girls he'd picked up, peaches of girls, pretty as pictures, who made packets. I was asked if I'd been in Omaha before. No, well there were more pretty girls in Omaha than in any other city in the country. Yes, it was well-known. It was certainly a popular pre-occupation: I was to hear the same glad tidings of other middle-western urban areas. He got back at me, though. Omaha is in Nebraska, just inside the border, the Missouri River. *'I can't take a girl over a state line'* he pointed out, suddenly coming over all upright, *'So I'll let you down here, see? All you have to do is cross the river.'*

'Away, I'm bound to go, 'cross the wide Missouri'. Wide is right, and all the time the heat was becoming more intense. I took frequent rests gazing down at the water which was so opaque and sandy red it could have been an expanse of wind-rippled desert. And when the bridge did finally end, the road into town was uphill. It was in more than one sense gruelling. Cars drew up at the curb alongside, and anyone with time to spare fell in beside me to try his luck. I wanted to ask where the Y was but lacked the nerve. In the end I went into a shop where a startled husky tough looked it up in the telephone directory.

At the Y my room had closed windows 'To keep out the heat.' I got in a bath of cold water. Back in the room I put on a soaked towel like a turban, it was all I wore till evening. Outside, a buffeting wind was hotter than the still air. I appeared to be the only inmate in the Y. Towels were borrowed from empty rooms and I got into bed freshly turbaned, between charged bath sheets.

I told myself I'd be up early - beat the sun to it. I did get up early, but travelling wasn't good, and by the time it was beginning to get dark I'd only reached St. Joseph. The St. Jo Y was a modern building, a considerable flight of wide shallow steps led up to it. Intimate clusters of twittering St. Jo young women, typical American teenagers, in spruce print frocks, were dotted about the steps. *'Look - girl scout!'*, I overheard, as, blushing, I wound my way upward. At the desk my request for a room elicited a barely perceptible twitch, and as I waited so the rigidity hardened. It was only too obvious that the management didn't think me a girl scout. I was a little shaken, it was the first time I'd come up against this sort of reception at a Y. But as it turned out, it was all for the best. I found excellent accommodation in a modest hotel with fans in all the rooms.

The next day my one concern was to reach Kansas City before the banks closed. I was picked up by yet another travelling salesman. *'Where to, little lady?... Kansas City! - you're practically there.'* Then, *'Ever been in Kansas City?... No, well it's quite a place, and I'll tell you one thing, there are more pretty girls in that city than anywhere else in the States!'*

In the Kansas City Y the misunderstanding was healthily different. As I was hesitating, more than a little uncertain after what had gone before, a tall imposing woman in a hat of some span and draped to the ground in something softly floral and loosely flowing - surely she must be on her way to a garden party? - swept in and waved me with wide gesture to the appropriate office, and herself sat down behind the desk. I learned that the Y had no residence, but there was a reasonable hostel for women not far away. *'You'll get a bed there for fifty cents.'* She wrote out an introduction. At this point she suddenly rose, and, splicing into the discourse a neat *'Pardon me, so loose'* yanked up a voluminous pair of knickers. My own get-up came next. *'What is in that pack? Is there a dress? No employer will look at you twice in trousers.'* Who had said anything about employment? A large cardboard box was dragged out; it was stuffed with cast-off clothing. *'Help yourself. Take three.'* I began to protest but was cut short. It was the only way. She favoured black, decorated with glass beads - *'So serviceable'* But after I'd gone the good lady continued to busy herself on my behalf. From a group of young Christians came an invitation to supper. Girl scout? Black with glass beads! I shook out a clean Liberty-printed silk shirt - one of two and they lasted well. I brushed my slacks. At least for this encounter I wouldn't have to compete with an attention-hogging backpack.

It was the subjects they wanted to talk about, these Middle-Western young women - that came as such a surprise. T.S. Eliot, Auden, Spender and Co., the Oxford Group and peace campaigns. They also wanted to know what had made me set out and why the States. Good questions. Very good questions. It was the first and only time that anything of this nature arose. And **here**, smack in the middle of the Great Plain - **hick** America! At least I wasn't found wanting on the literary front. It was exciting discovering how deep in some places, shallow in others, the Atlantic could be. They had never heard of the Sitwells, I had never heard of Thomas Wolfe.

I met one of them again the next day. Unlike the others, this one was gentle and tentative, saying little; but alone together - that was a different matter. She was slim and narrow, not colourful, but as intriguing to look at as a drawing by Modigliani.

Her people had come as immigrants from the old Austria-Hungary, scene of those breakfast-time, upper-crust episodes back in the cottage. But there were no hens, and nothing comical in the story she had to tell. It had me recalling with shame my own wild reactions to insignificant troubles. And as I listened to her quiet unemotional voice and my own responses and offerings, I became aware of something that usually escaped my notice - the way I sang buoyantly out, confidently underlining everything. (When talking to people I felt comfortable with, that is.) I finished on a prize contribution. That she'd never been to New York filled me with amazement (only 1,300 miles!). Marvellous place - mincemeat to London's tame spotted dick, I assured her blithely. I quite forgot that America was a continent; and anyway, though considerably older, where had I been in my own tight little island? Next to nowhere. But what of that? It was valid enough to us, then, happily sharing.

Out of Kansas City, I was relieved to find myself picked up by a family instead of yet another travelling salesman. The young couple were going some two hundred miles in my direction, but were breaking the journey to visit the girl's mother. If I cared to go along with them, they would take me on afterwards. It was just about lunchtime when we left the road to raise the dust on a track through the corn, and drew up at a small farm alone in the flat country. Before we could get out, the car was surrounded by a flock of excited squawking hens.

Inside, attention was at once rivetted on the mother, a character very much in the round and highly vibrant, with large black eyes, shining black waving hair and curvaceous bare feet. A brightly-patterned straight-down dress covered a huge body splendidly independent of support. Her voice was strong, her laugh rocked the flimsy building. When I learnt that the community round about was Dutch it was plain that here was a Rubens masterpiece. For the rest, there was the farmer, his mother and a hired woman. The man, her second husband, was grey and lined and never spoke. His mother was a skinny bent old lady well up in the nineties, past recognising anyone but still physically active. She shook violently, muttered to herself, and either dropped suddenly off to sleep on her appointed couch - taking to it like an animal to its basket - or went briskly about some business or other known only to herself, but always under the watchful eye of the hired woman who lived with them and slept by her for this purpose.

Fried chicken and pie appeared. The children sprawled on the floor, eating one piece of chicken after another, sucking and licking the bits and leaving half-eaten relics under chairs, in corners and stuck to the rug. And after that they lathered their faced with pie. A few enterprising hens entered and fluttered excitedly over morsels of their kind left stuck to the floor by the children.

When the meal was over they wanted to know about England. I experienced some difficulty as no-one had much idea where it was. Different from New England? Where was London, then? (My amazement equalled theirs.) The hired woman was of help here. She knew about Europe and performed as interpreter. On the home front there was gossip concerning a neighbouring farm blown off its site by a tornado. Pieces of wreckage had been found over a mile away. The people? All the farms had dugouts or cellars. The old woman suddenly left off muttering at the window and hurried out, the hired woman close behind. The son and daughter, on the point of leaving, began to haggle over the price of eggs and a couple of chickens. By this time the children were fast asleep on the floor. The Rubens swept them up, shook them out, and stuffed them in the back of the car, and we were away.

I stayed the night with the young couple and was out on the road early the next day. One or two short rides followed and then I stuck. Nothing came, and it began to look as if nothing ever would. I was in the middle of nowhere. I didn't mind, except perhaps for the 'hoppers, not at all like the bright little nippers that lark about in the green fields at home: these were monsters with yellow bellies, and wings, and when they flew they rattled.

At least flattened 'hoppers showed the road was used, Then, suddenly, as if someone had thrown a switch, everything changed. The most extraordinary thing happened. **It began to rain. Enormous** drops fell. Partially-sighted and deafened, I wasn't aware of the car till it drew up beside me. A man and a boy were in front, I slipped gratefully into the back. It appeared that the boy, like me, was a hitch-hiker, picked up by the inevitable travelling salesman; and for once I was glad, at least he'd be going somewhere, I'd not end up at the next farm. He drove fast, there was no other traffic, rain drummed on the car. We were now well into the Corn Belt, a tall fringe of waving sunflowers grew on either side of the road; there were no hedges, nothing else.

I lay back, comfortable and contented. But the boy twisted round in his seat, he wanted to talk. *'She's English!'*, he cried excitedly. We were at a junction. As the man turned the car I just had time to take in a large warning notice: THIS ROAD IS SLIPPERY WHEN WET. As if acting on cue, the car promptly swung round to one side and then the other, the screeching front-wheel tyres rubbing dry arcs on the streaming road, there followed a split-second interval as it locked into full power and shot like a mad projectile into the sunflowers and corn. I hit one door and was then thrown against the other; it didn't hurt and I felt no fear - like a ping-pong ball, I remember thinking!

I came to, hearing this terrible screaming. I then heard a man's voice saying,

'Where does it hurt - where does it hurt most?' ***'My back! My back! My back!'*** *yelled the screamer.* I had no idea it was me. As soon as I did I shut up, aghast. I felt no pain, consciously. I was given an injection and realised I was in a doctor's surgery. *'Do you have any money?'* he asked... *'Good. It's nothing serious - you're lucky. There's a hotel opposite, you can lie up there for a week. Can you stand up?'* I did so, and promptly sat down again, feeling sick. *'No - well it doesn't matter, I'll go over and fix it up and we'll give you a chair lift across.'*

The proprietress was waiting for us in the vestibule, lips pursed, eyes flashing outrage and horror. I must have looked pretty terrible, but at my most pristine I couldn't imagine that this one would have fancied me. I was put in a double room with a bath on the ground floor.

After a short rest, I tried to clean up. My face was splodged with blood and mud but sound enough underneath. As I combed my hair, glass tinkled onto the floor. I put on a clean top - I had no pyjamas - and got carefully into bed. Sleep came fitfully. I found that I needed to keep my head still or the ceiling tilted at alarming angles. Towards morning the injection wore off, which didn't help - the previous day's excitement abated, I experienced only too acutely what my shocked body had been yelling about. It now took - I was genuinely sure of this - at least two hours to turn over, millimetre by millimetre, with adequate rests between. But obviously it can't really have been anything like that.

When the doctor came the next morning I was advised to soak myself in hot water. I asked him about the man and the boy. They were unhurt, he said. Was he sure I'd be all right in only a week? Given the difficulty and the time it took to move about - to move at all - it didn't seem possible. I would have appreciated another injection, but it wasn't offered and I was determined not to ask, so I went without.

I saw the proprietress every day, she brought in my meals herself, never failing to tell me how many dollars and cents she was adding to my ticket, or to pause, gazing in disbelief at the rucksack on a chair beside the wardrobe. I may have been forced to take in this tramp, her look clearly implied, but at least I can show she in no way fools **me**, The rucksack, unknown to untravelled Americans, seemed destined to rank as a potent symbol according to their bent.

So I lay in the steaming tub, watching shining fingers of running water slide down the bathroom wall. Or I sat up in bed and examined again the state of the backyard weeds, which was all I could see out of the window. I still had no idea where I was. The name of the little town appeared on the hotel regulations, glued to the door, but was on no map. I had nothing to read. But I wasn't bored; everything I did took a very long time, and without the experience I would never have credited how much artless coaxing, backed up by continuous reassurance, encouragement and congratulation, would be required to bring about the simplest movements. In fact I was talking to myself - or rather, chatting-up my body, most of the time. I told it how much I loved it, what I knew it could do, had done in the past and how grateful I was. We both enjoyed this, and by the fifth day I could walk back and forth across the bedroom naturally enough. I wasn't able to hurry or run, but short of that no-one would have dreamt there had ever been anything wrong.

Once more I was in need of money. There were two women in the first car. The second was filled with the family, but forty yards up the road it halted. I watched, idly. Then the driver got out and shouted. *'I guess it's kinda hot out on the road'* he remarked as he stowed the rucksack, without a second glance, and ushered me into the back with two teenage girls. Mindful of the bank, I watched the clock on the dashboard and spread out the map. With luck I'd just do it. The next time I looked up it was to find the snow-capped Rocky Mountains, misty with distance, lying clear across the horizon.

I reached the bank on time; but Colorado Springs proved to be a small place, full of Indian souvenirs, mock cowboy hats and coach trips. Even the Y was touristy. No-one could understand why I didn't want to go up Pike's Peak. The idea had been to stay a day or two and rest. But now I changed my mind and decided to go on to Denver.

Appropriately enough, I was conveyed to Denver in a wrecking service truck. It was a bit of a wreck itself, coughing and spitting up front and exploding behind. Twice it gave out; but each time the quiet mechanic went patiently to work. He had no business downtown Denver, but insisted on taking me in and finding the Y.

The mile-high city of Denver more than fulfilled expectation: the place was big enough to be decently lost in, the evenings deliciously cool. There was even therapy at hand. In the Indian Section of a museum I fell in love with a crooked-face mask. One side of the long thin visage was black, the other earthy red; the nose was kinked, the eyes pierced tin, and the skinny mouth grinned craftily up at one side with comic ripples of flesh round the top corner. From the crown of the head hung down two long grey wisps. Its wicked air of shocking good cheer was marvellously refreshing to the spirit.

Leaving Denver, with Salt Lake City as my destination, I couldn't make up my mind whether to cross the Rockies over the more obvious and spectacular route, or to take the lower road through Wyoming. I was under the impression that this lower road ran through the sort of wilderness that would have greater personal appeal. However, after travelling some fifty miles north I came to an unexpected junction where a road ran due west through Rocky Mountain National Park, and after further deliberation I suddenly shot down this turning.

I stayed the night in a cabin at the gate of the Rocky Mountain National Park, and in the early morning sun of the next day set off over the back of the Rockies. Traffic was intermittent and mostly tourist. After a peaceful hour or two I got a lift in a light truck carrying cherries to Steamboat Springs. The driver usually travelled the older, more frequented, highway, but he'd never carried fruit before and this newer road was less rough, or so he'd heard. This turned out to be anything but the case, and our progress was marked by much cursing and many stops to see how the cherries were making out under the battering. Over the worst parts of the road I found it a good plan to insert my clenched fist between me and the back of the seat where it acted as shock-absorber.

We passed through thick dark green forests, followed by terrible devastation, mile after mile of black tree trunks and prone grey logs. Nothing breathed, a little white ash rose. Patches of snow came next. Finally, a grim row of craggy peaks, massive granite spurs, partly snow-covered, emerged. It had become cold, my ears sang and popped. And at each turn of the road we came on some fresh view of the jagged summits - or it might be a drop - sheer cliffs of mountain down to a valley so far away below it seemed to belong to a different world, one where not only conditions but attitudes and values must be different, too.

The next morning I was still in Colorado, three hundred miles from Salt Lake City. It was hot again, and there was not much traffic. In the end I got a ride in an unlikely-looking flashy saloon with three people in it. I sat in front with the two men. In the back, by herself, was a girl and so stunning were her looks, so perfect her complexion, so immaculate her get-up that it was hard to believe she was real. She was surrounded by glossy magazines, boxes of expensive candy, bunches of grapes and several smart hats. Oblivious to it all, she gazed out of the window with a far-away expression. From time to time she fingered a ukulele that hung over her shoulder on pink and green ribbons. And it appeared that I owed the lift to this American dream girl. Gravely, gently, I was asked questions - only one or two - and they were well spaced out. I felt like a tender chicken being carved with a silver knife and fork. At last, after a longer than usual interval and just as I was about to get out, she remarked, '*I went hitch-hiking myself once - just for the fun of it. It was swell, I don't think I ever enjoyed anything so much!*'

They turned off down a track to a ranch, and I was alone in the flat country. There was no shade - not a building in sight. With the exception of a few cattle it was all unfamiliar. Sagebrush and cactus grew spot-patternwise off the dusty soil. Skeletal tumbleweed, caught in the barbed wire at the side of the road, twitched in the wind. I was rescued by three youths in an open car. There were more miles of sage and cactus, with here and their weird formations of uneroded striped rock. By the time I was put down I was painfully windblown and sore from the sun.

On the outskirts of a small town I found a patch of shade and prepared to wait. One or two automobiles passed, I didn't bother with them nor they with me. Then peace was suddenly shattered by a row like an avalanche of scrap metal, as a huge truck crashed past. I was amazed to note a slim smoke-stack with steam shooting out of it. Up the road it came to a halt and a man leant out of the cab. His, '*Where do you think you're going?'* was hardly an invitation.

My reply was a grudging admission.

'You're in luck!' The door swung open. Then I saw the other man. It was a long journey of which quite a stretch would be by night; it was also a noisy truck, I'd lose my voice if nothing else. But the door was open. The way made plain? I got in.

The driver was a youngish Irishman with a long boney face and ruffled hair. He was easy company. The other man was a colourless German with small features; he lay lazily back over by the window, to all appearances immersed in a blanket of surly bad temper. Now and again he fired a question - but always with the air of one resigned to the worst. My replies were treated to protracted periods of what appeared to be painful thought.

It was still flat desert territory with outcrops of rock and the occasional giant boulder. A large bird with an astonishing wing-span sailed by. Long-eared jack rabbits shot across the road. It was an event to encounter other traffic, for the most part we were thundering over the country alone. Meanwhile, I was becoming interested in the German. He had got round to making sardonic remarks in a tired voice that made me laugh. We stopped at a gas station. The German went inside and came out with a coke apiece and then disappeared again. The Irishman told me they were from Indianapolis. *'He's my boss'*, he said. *'I like to have a real drink, myself'*, he went on, gazing with long-suffering resignation at the bottle of sody-pop, *'But he won't allow it - not while I'm driving anyway. Non-drinker, see? Keen on it. Good churchman, too.'* Then with a surge of reassurance, *'Aw, he's all right, really. A man might do worse'n him for a boss at that!'* I understood then why I'd been so oddly received to begin with. The good churchman came back and we drove off.

As it began to get dark the country changed. Soon we were travelling along the bottom of a canyon; there were trees now, and a flashing mountain creek. Roadside notices, 'Caution Deer' and 'Caution Prairie Grouse', were sad reminders of what was being missed, while 'Danger, Falling Rocks' which we could have done without was amply demonstrated as we came to a part of the road where several tons of mountain had fallen across it. Clearing was being carried out by the light of powerful arc lamps; rock, bush and creek were lit like a stage set. A narrow way through had been hastily levelled, but it was no more than a bed of loose rocks over which, rattling and shaking, we bumped forward at a crawl. We came on Salt Lake City from above - a pattern of pinpricks of yellow light. The two were spending the night in a cabin outside the city, but steamed into town to put me down at the Y.

It was a residential house. The manageress appeared in a dressing gown (it was past midnight), and I was given a bed on the porch which had been made into a small dormitory. I was heartened to note that it was well screened, a climbing plant grew over the netting at the head of my bed. The night was filled with the insistent shrill scissoring of crickets, a luxuriously foreign sound. I lay back and let it lap over me, hearing it still in sleep.

The next day was Sunday and intensely hot. It was said to be 115° in the city streets, but it wasn't oppressive as in Omaha. I flopped out flat in the lounge, along with others, all in loose wraps. The manageress, likewise robed, came in with an electric fan. The manageress could have been English. She was lightly conversational and that was all. She asked no questions, and the Salt Lake young Christians were likewise reserved.

Following a collection of short rides in farm trucks, I finally wound up in one going to Pocatello, Idaho. The front was jammed tight with the family, Ma and Pa farmer and three little girls. The back of the truck was open with the sides down. I climbed up and lay stretched out on the earthy boards. All day long it had been like this, rides offered as a matter of course by working people, ready to lend a hand and think nothing of it. I was left alone. No-one was interested in my personal statistics or legal status. It was bliss, lying effortlessly back on the jolting platform. The country wasn't rushing at me; for once it was lingering lovingly. In the dusk, the irrigated fields and small farmhouses - the whole scene - seemed full of peace and inner satisfaction, and so was I.

In the Pocatello Y a bed was made up for me in the art room along with stacked scenery and pots of paint. The manageress was out when I arrived, but came in soon afterwards. *'You want a free bed for tonight'*, she put forward, the tone was business-like but friendly. It was misunderstanding again, but with a refreshingly new response. I gladly paid fifty cents and got into the snugly-arranged bed.

The next morning I was standing at the corner of a block, wondering which road was mine, when a trio of not-so-young but cheerful down-and-outs, propping up a store behind me, called out a greeting. *'Lookinfa work?'* asked one sympathetically, coming forward. *'Nice little town. Nice people. F'we can make out we're gonna stay. How's travelling'?... Yeah, well it's cleaner by road, I guess. Not certain enough f'rus. We jus come off a freight.'* The matter of fact tone, he might have been telling me that they couldn't stop to mess about with the car, was full of appeal. I said the town seemed pretty nice to me, too, as indeed it did.

Up in yet another farm truck, we passed a billboard displaying DON'T DRINK AND DRIVE. It was still Mormon territory. Small irrigated farms claimed from the dusty prairie by hard-working people, most of them by American standards poorly off, who yet gave 10% of their earnings to the Church. Not a farm truck passed me by, there was no need to signal. They even seemed surprised by gratitude. *'You're welcome'* or *'You bet'*, and we were off on our separate ways.

It was just beginning to get dark when a modest truck passed, struggling slowly uphill. The back was open and piled with bedding, suitcases and miscellaneous effects, and surmounted by a tousled youth asleep under a blanket. At the top of the hill the outfit drew up and waited. Inside were two young men. *'I guess we can make room'*, said the driver.

They were miners. They'd been working in California and run on thin times and decided to try their luck back in Montana. They were travelling to Butte, a mining centre. The two in the cab were natives of the state and had worked there before; the boy on the back was from Louisiana. After a bit there was a change round; the southerner who had never been so far north was shivering with cold. Unshaven and champion spitters, they couldn't have been nicer; they were easy and good-natured, even courteous, especially Dave and Woody, the two from Montana. There were no questions; it was taken for granted that I was as decent and regular as they were. I was given to understand that what I was doing on the road was my own business; I was going to Butte and so were they - it was a piece of good fortune all round.

It was night before their long journey came to an end. There was general excitement as we passed the Butte city limits. Dave: *Boy, we're home - you know it?* Woody with satisfaction: ***'I know it!'*** And from Louisiana: *'Jeez, it's cold!'*

The truck was put up downtown, and Louis and Woody at once went off for a drink and to have a game. Dave, saying he'd be with them shortly, shouldered my rucksack and began inquiring around for the Y. I assured him that I could find it myself, but this was waved aside. It turned out that there wasn't one, but a reasonable hotel was recommended. *'This is a wide-open town'*, explained Dave, *'You don't want to be out on your own after dark in a place like this.'* He was apprehensive of his other charges, too. He was plainly very fond of Woody, *'He's the swellest guy I know, the kindest hearted cuss - but gets rid of his money like that! - he can't hold it a minute; I got to get back while there's still some left in his pocket.'*

'You'll find', he went on, *'that Montana people are the kindest and most generous in the States. It's a fact!'* Some of them certainly were. It also made another refreshing change. In the flat Mid-Western Corn Belt, the percentage of pretty girls. In the upper airs of the mountain states, kindness and consideration. Different worlds.

11

The Pacific Seaboard

Interior ride-about - Scenic Washington - peaches - Coulee Dam - Seattle with spuds - a fishy tale - wild and foggy - night ride to 'Frisco - the Trial - horse box to L.A. - 3 gentlemen - Mohave desert - Mort and Norm - Salt Lake City again.

On a glorious day of golden sun and gentian sky, I was crossing over the Bitterroot Mountains into northern Idaho, through dark green forests, by still blue lakes like polished mirrors, past tracts of floating logs and waterside match factories. A long private car with two women in it stopped. I sat in the back with a tray of ripe peaches. *'Help yourself!'* They were happy and laughing. It was like being on holiday. But over the border in the state of Washington they could talk of nothing but the Grand Coulee Dam under construction at a point on the Columbia River. It was to be the biggest in the world. *'Here's your chance - you wouldn't pass up the Great Pyramid in Egypt?'* cried a scandalised Washingtonian. *'This dam is going to be three times as big!'* The greatest project undertaken by man, was another assessment. Here, pretty girls were nowhere, it didn't matter who the driver was, when he opened his mouth it was always the same.

The dam was only some thirty odd miles from civilization, but it seemed more like three hundred, being on no sort of road with hardly any traffic. Gone was the picture-postcard scenery. The country was flat and fast turning into desert: dust and wind, wind and dust - in the eyes, in the teeth, granulated hair. Isolated farms, then simply sage. On the horizon, what looked like wandering bonfires were 'twisters', miniature whirlwinds. Buzzards soundlessly drifting on the air were the only sign of life. But in the end I got a good ride right into the project. And as for the dam itself, to me it was just a big building site.

It was the return journey, over a different road, that proved so unforgettable. I got a lift along the Upper Grand Coulee from one of the workers. The road ran like a fine scratch along the bottom of a broad, shallow trench, an extensive flat sagebrush area a mile or more wide, walled by scored cliffs with red and sulphur markings. *'You should seem them in the spring when the snow melts and they're one continuous waterfall from end to end'*, said the worker. It was thought, he went on, that towards the end of the Ice Age, when melting began, that the whole area had been filled with cascading water.

It was silent enough now - the polar opposite of the upper Mississippi, 'Wildness and Wet' - life. This bare-bones of a place was a kind of death, but it had a haunting beauty of its own. It was like some metaphysical hinterland, imbued with cold meaning, giving hints, perhaps, of a between-the-lines reality at least as valid as our own familiar animated world of the quick. At the very least the bare-bones wilderness exemplified that other cottage-wall quotation, Tennyson's *'Oh earth, what changes thou hast seen!'*

Later, once more on my feet, I was joined by two youths going to Wenatchee for the fruit picking. They, like me, were out of their way to view the wonder, but whatever they thought of it, again like me, they kept it to themselves. That they were fascinated by my rucksack there could be no doubting. They took turns trying it out and wanted to know where I got it. I said I thought they'd have trouble finding one as it was usually greeted with, *'What the heck you got there?'* (The final comment was to come from a black hotel porter in Oklahoma who, astonished to the whites of his eyes, inquired in a high squeak how I came to be travelling by parachute.)

We were picked up out of the dust by the first car to come along. The driver was surly and monosyllabic. We were travelling along the Lower Coulee now, a curious alkaline territory of departed rivers and ancient long-dried waterfalls. The man drove at a furious pace, there was no other traffic, even so we glanced at each other. Soap Lake appeared and was gone, but sure enough there were soft white woolly suds at the water's edge; bits whipped free by the wind blew gently about the bank.

The man was going to Seattle and so was I. After the boys had gone it was soon dark and the speed began to get on my nerves. The country had again changed, once more we were travelling over mountain passes, through forests, by moonlit lakes. It was the smiling Washington of the holiday brochures; but we were also doing ninety and passing trucks on corners. At the first promising-looking small town

I got out. In the morning I found my window looked down on a garden filled with roses. An hour or two later, along with a load of potatoes, I arrived in Seattle. Coast to coast.

I was sitting on my bed in the Y dormitory when a tall girl was brought in and allotted the bed next to mine. She at once collected round her everyone in the room to hear her life story. It appeared that she'd just run away from her second husband. He had attacked her. I stayed several days in the cool, airy city of Seattle, and so I saw - whether I liked it or not - quite a bit of the Trial, and there were times when I could have attacked her, too. It was a relief when she got a job.

The road turned south and ran along the coast. My first view of the Pacific was far from blue and inviting. It could have been the Atlantic from anywhere in England: leaden and icy cold. It was even raining and foggy. I was rescued by two nice people in an automobile full of fishing tackle. Nicky and Joanna were on their way to a cottage they'd taken for the summer. It was fishing all day, they said. Nicky's wife and some friends were there already. I was invited to meet them and try a fresh fish supper. Nicky was spare and narrow, with light hair and eyes, and cheeks so hollow that when he smiled the flesh folded back like a concertina. He was as quiet as Joanna was noisy.

The cottage was already full of fishing tackle, with the freshly-caught fish in a basket on the table. Nicky's wife was preparing it, and the fire was being stoked by a powerful Scandinavian whose wife and baby completed the party. As soon as the introductions were over, an enthusiastic reunion broke loose with Joanna roaring over all the others.

I ended by staying the night. A spare camp bed was found and fixed up. There were no bedclothes but everyone contributed a warm coat or jacket. I slept in the large livingroom with Nicky and his wife and little girl, and with Joanna in another camp bed over in the opposite corner. The Scandinavian and his wife slept in the only bedroom. Nicky was up at six, making a roaring fire for heating the water and cooking breakfast. And after that the table was once more covered with tackle and so deep was the concentration that hardly a word was spoken; then, with everything assembled and ready, the trip up the river before them, their faces took on an extra radiance.

Much of the coast was vigorously forested right to the sea. I was picked up by a man who had just spent a month in the interior, fighting a forest fire. As if in illustration of this we passed through a burnt-out town. It had happened a year ago, the fire-fighter said, and so suddenly that almost nothing of personal property was saved. Chimneys stood off the seared earth like tall gravestones. The concrete foundations of the school and a bank remained. Charred stumps in the river showed where the wharf had been. And all round for miles, rising out of a tangled white undergrowth was a rigid, lifeless forest: these trees still stood, their out-stretched ash grey branches still in place right down to the delicate tracery of the smallest twig.

What followed was more like hiking than hitching. The main highway between cities was inland, but I stuck faithfully to the coast road that ran along the edge of high rugged cliffs. White fog still rolled around below, randomly obscuring the water, rubbing out trees, sometimes billowing onto the road. (I was still having trouble with a fixed idea of the Pacific as unfailingly warm, unalterably sapphire.) I got a short lift into California and after that I thought I was going to walk for ever. Till a neat coupé drew up, and a good-looking, tastefully-dressed young man pushed open the door.

'Where to?'

'San Francisco.'

'Fine. We'll be there sometime today - or tomorrow!'

The tastefully-dressed young man was quiet and serious, even reserved. But after an interval he began to talk and I learnt that he'd been in the lumber business, saved some cash, and was now going out to New Zealand. He planned to get a job on a boat and see something of the South Seas. To our mutual satisfaction we found we'd been reading much the same sort of books, in my case centred on the United States, in his on parts of the British Empire. But I'd read books about sailing round the world, too, and we discussed the merits and demerits and degrees of exploitation of the various Pacific islands with some expertise. It was as well we had this common interest as it was soon night and the tastefully-dressed young man had been driving since dawn. As midnight passed it wasn't easy to keep awake. Once he did drop off, and I must have, too. Luckily the car bumped over a stone at the side of the road - we were heading for the trunk of a giant redwood. An hour short of sunrise we drove over the Golden Gate into San Francisco.

At first I thought I must be the only inmate of the 'Frisco Y under the age of fifty, so that it was actually with a feeling almost of relief that I came across - of all people - the Trial. It appeared that her job hadn't come up to expectations, so she and another girl had decided to try their luck further down the coast. Since they had less than a dollar between them they decided to hitch-hike, and taking the more direct inland highway they'd made it in two days. *'We had only to buy ourselves one meal'*, paraded the Trial, *'and we never got up in trucks - too dirty and uncomfortable. Travelling salesmen brought us all the way; one of them paid for our night's lodging. The men you meet up with on the road will do most anything for a girl, especially if she's a blond!'*

All the same they hadn't been brought right into town. And since by that time they were without even the price of a streetcar ticket, they had had to walk. After some miles of this the friend sat down and couldn't get up: she was ill. With help from the police they reached the Y, where the Trial insisted that her friend should be in hospital. The manageress didn't agree, but in the end for the sake of peace she did ring up. *'No vacant beds'* was the result. The Trial wasn't being fobbed off with this, she fetched a priest (the girl was Catholic). She was now in hospital.

The next evening I accompanied the triumphant Trial to the hospital. The patient was a dark handsome girl with a soft southern drawl. She'd been a model, and was interested in economics.

The following day I visited the hospital on my own. I'd found a small library at the Y - several bookcases in one of the lounges. It looked as if no-one had touched them in years. A glance across the titles told why. But the Model wanted something to read, so I persevered and found two: George Eliot's lovely *Scenes from Clerical Life* and *Basic Principles of Scientific Socialism*. I had no idea what scientific socialism was but it sounded promising. As it turned out the Model was a little quizzical with me over the *Scenes*, but exhibited a healthy interest in the *Scientific Socialism*. I thought her a fine person. Had she wished, she could have lost the baby. Nor would she name the father.

South of 'Frisco, still keeping to the coast, the road turned into not much more than a country lane with little traffic. Further south again, without meaning to, I left the coast and ended up in Santa Maria. The next day I determined that come what might - or might not - I was going to reach Los Angeles. To begin with all went well - or so I thought - forgetting how early and rapidly the light goes in the south. By the time I was clear of Santa Barbara it was dark. I came to a pleasant place high up overlooking the water, and climbed on to a wooden rail. Down below in the gloom I could just see long silver lines of ocean curling in, hear the forward boom and tinkling, shingly retreat. When eventually something pulled up I thought it was a bus and took no notice - till it struck up a hearty honking and an arm waves out of the side. In fact it was a horse box going to San Diego. It was only skirting Los Angeles, but I was put down, complete with detailed instructions, at a bus stop. But no bus came and after looking at the map I didn't see the need. I was approaching L.A. from the north and Hollywood was a northern suburb. By one o'clock miles of pavement walking had begun to affect my feet. I was now in a residential district planted with palms and pepper trees. I tried walking along the edges of front lawns but the sprinklers had worked to such good effect my shoes filled with water. Presently the district became more urban. As I stopped at yet another intersection to look at the map, a truck drew up and the driver leant out to ask if I was lost. He was able to take me a few miles further in. A large hotel showed signs of life; they were suction-sweeping the reception hall carpets. A helpful young man explained how to get to the Y. *'But you'd best shake down here on one of the settees till morning'*, he added. It was now three o'clock. But I was set on my destination, which turned out to be a small informal bungalow with the usual porch and rockers. There was also a hanging seat on which I arranged my rucksack as a pillow. But this Y didn't take transients. The manageress recommended a small hotel.

Hollywood was a pleasing place, high, airy and clean, and as pyjama suits and slacks were common women's wear, I fitted unnoticeably in. But also in this tourist Mecca I was exposed for what I was. Here then, for a short spell, I was on holiday, free from misunderstanding and cross purposes. It was plain sailing, and, although I would have been loathe to admit it at the time, it made a welcome break.

As I already knew, the illustrious no longer lived in Hollywood; and by this time most of the studios had moved out, too. Yet stars were still to be seen. At a preview in Westwood Village I joined the crowd and saw Gary Cooper and Jeanette Macdonald arrive. Cowboy Cooper in horn-rimmed glasses, tightly reserved and plainly disapproving of what was, for us, such a joyous encounter, could have been the author of several serious books. One long arm protected his wife, the other waved off autograph hounds. Jeanette, very dainty and surprisingly petite, emerged from an extraordinarily long, monogrammed automobile and rewarded us all with smiles. I had a glimpse of Constance Bennett in the courtyard of Grauman's Chinese Theatre, and later, in the Los Angeles Labour Day Parade, Melvin Douglas rode at the head of the float representing the Screen Actor's Guild. It was more than I ever expected. In fact, as I'd never really expected to see anything at all of such high luminaries, it was sheer bonus.

All the same, it wasn't only film stars that I wished to see. All this time in California and I hadn't yet caught sight of a growing orange. So I worked out a day trip of only 180 miles. What could be more simple? That day I saw all I wanted of oranges, and as for olives, I stood under a tree for an hour. As usual in farming areas, the rides were sweet, but short. I had reckoned without this, I also again forgot how early and rapidly it got dark, but most stupid of all I took no account of the urban sprawl of Los Angeles itself. The L.A. city limits were playfully said to extend up to Oakland and down to San Diego. The place has also been described as fifty suburbs in search of a city. In fact, at that time, the built-up area was near enough fifty miles across. It can't have been far off the worst city in the world from the point of view of a hitch-hiker.

It was almost dark before I got a lift going anywhere worthwhile. It came from Gentleman Jake. A two-seater pulled up and a broad dark face was thrust out. *'I'll be very glad to give you a lift, little lady'*, said the face earnestly, *'but before you get in I think I ought to tell you that I'm coloured. But you can set your mind at rest'*, he went on, still blocking entry determined to say his piece, *'you'll be perfectly all right with me because I'm a gentleman!'* I was sure of it I said as I got in. I was told that California was a good state to live in, that there was comparative equality. But although it was nearly dark, he kept the sun visor down. He also wanted to give me money to take my supper in one place, while he took his another. I didn't care for this, so we went without.

I parted from him at a cross-roads near San Bernardino. It was really dark now and moonless, and there was still a considerable distance to be covered. The road must have run through a Mexican settlement. I was picked up by a handsome young workman with solid black eyes. He wasn't going far, but before he left I was motioned into a wayside eats and we had pie and coffee, though I don't think he was hungry himself. He then drove past his destination to take me way out on the road, and left with a nod and a smile. All without a word. Another gentleman.

I walked further down the road, but it wasn't a good idea. I passed a lighted gas station and was spotted by a group of little Mexican boys, who rushed up and clustered round, their solemn faces full of unswerving interest. As I moved on, so did they, chattering excitedly. Suddenly, there was a flash of lightening and roll of thunder, followed immediately by torrential rain. It effectively scattered the boys, and obliged me to wave to attract attention.

I was rescued by a pale young man going to Pomona. This wasn't far, and he appeared to be worried about it. I was presented with a large handkerchief to use as a towel. A restful silence followed with only the hum of the engine and the lashing rain, and this went on unbroken till we arrived at the Los Angeles city limits. Without a word, he'd gone straight through Pomona. Then this serious young man put me down where I could shelter from the rain, pointed out where the streetcar stopped, slipped the fare in my pocket and was turned about before I had time to thank him. Gentleman number three.

According to plan, I was now routed through Arizona and New Mexico. But I still felt I hadn't seen enough of California. Coast, cities, film stars, fruit; but nothing of mountains and desert. I therefore decided to go up through eastern California and across Nevada to Salt Lake City again, and from there drop down into Arizona.

Once more I left Los Angeles, this time for good. At length I was up in a truck going to Reno. A long ride. But the driver had hoped for a different type of hitch-hiker and seemed unable to adjust to the luck of the draw. He came over glum and exchanges between us ceased. It left me free to take in the beginning of the Mohave Desert with its strange, half-palm, half-cactus Joshua trees. I got down in Mohave itself, a small desert town.

The next morning I had hardly left the town behind when an Inland Stage bus passed and drew up. I took no notice as all I'd had from buses so far was a layer of dust; but then the driver climbed down and gave me a shout. *'I can take you to Bishop anyway'*, he said as I got in. There were only two people in the bus. The woman remarked, smiling, *'On the chance a good-looking driver picks me up, I think I'll attempt to walk it myself next time!'* I looked up Bishop on the map, it was 170 odd miles. The seat was well sprung, the running was smooth and there was a notable absence of racket; the driver now concentrated on his job, the woman said no more and the other passenger looked out of the window. In splendid silence we travelled across the Mohave Desert and into the Sierra Nevadas. It was late September now, and in places the desert was prettily overlaid with flowers in pastel shades of mauve and pink and yellow. It was a quiet, even-tempered desert.

When we reached Bishop, the driver explained that this was where he left the bus. He didn't yet know who the new driver would be, but with any luck he'd be able to fix it for me to travel on a piece, which he did.

The next day, I'd just made myself comfortable on the parapet of a bridge near a cross-roads where I'd been put down, when a car passed, not going in my direction. In the distance I happened to notice it turn and come back. In view of this - as I thought - rather fishy proceeding, I was careful to remain uninterested; but when it drew up I saw that there was a woman with two men. I got in the back with the suitcases, crocks, cooking gear and boxes of food.

Mort and Norm were agents for a railroad insurance company, and M'ree was Mort's wife. The reason they'd turned back had nothing to do with me; they were having trouble finding one of their clients. Further on, we turned off the road to cross the Carson Sink, following a rutted track to an isolated railroad halt kept by Mexicans. It was weird territory. The earth was a white alkaline crust with smooth swellings like bubbles that crumbled when you trod on them. It was nearly dark when we reached the second railroad halt. As before, it was Mort who conducted the business. He was a big man, far from good-looking, but humorous, gentle and kind. He got back in the car and told us he thought they must all be deaf - the radio was on so loud he'd had to roar. He added that there was a baby in there no more than a day old, if that, and he reckoned it must be punch-drunk from the racket. We all enjoyed this, Norm so much that he went off into sudden bursts of merriment at odd intervals for the rest of the journey. By the time we were back on the road it was late. We found an auto-court and decided to take two cabins. Then the old man in charge offered us his cottage for a dollar less. Mort came in to kiss his wife goodnight and shortly afterwards the cottage was vibrating with King-Kong snores.

Still in Nevada, I was picked up by three youths in a pioneer two-seater. It could have been a good lift - they were really travelling - but there wasn't the room. I was seated on a lap and had to hold on to the window frame to keep in position, and I tried not to be too heavy. So in the middle of nowhere, I got out in the first reasonable-looking village.

The next morning I was having breakfast in a drugstore when a middle-aged woman came in. She began a spirited conversation with the girl behind the counter and skilfully netted me in. My origin and object were soon revealed, but it was done with such genuine interest and enthusiasm it was impossible not to go along with it. Instead of being laid bare, I found myself sheltered and warmed. One of the reasons I'd chosen to get down in this small town was its attractive wooden church. My new friend lived right by it. I was taken in and introduced to her tall, quizzically-amused husband, the Episcopalian minister.

It occurred to Mrs. Minister that I might need a break - why not stay with them for a day or two? But I said I had to be going on. She then sat down at the bureau, put on her glasses and began writing letters of introduction. I assured her that I didn't need them, but it made no difference: she seemed to see it as being as much for the recipient's benefit as mine. While she was writing, a little girl came in, a child about seven. I was mildly surprised as somehow Mrs. Minister didn't seem like a family woman. It was a distinctive child, unlike either of them, a pale slim changeling-like little creature with a serious pointed face, clear of any thought of self two bright eyes looked out with unswerving directness.

Mrs. Minister now took over planning my route. She wanted me to leave out the Petrified Forest which she assured me would be a waste of time and take me out of my way. To this end she fetched a souvenir of her own of petrified oak and a heavy hammer, and took them out on the sidewalk to smash off a piece for me. Now, definitely, I need not bother!

As I was leaving, Mrs. Minister turned to the little girl. *'This young lady from England has hitch-hiked right across the continent'*, she said, *'and I hope that when you grow up you'll do the same. It's a wonderful thing to do; and if you know you will be all right, you* ***will*** *be all right.'*

It was the Minnesota schoolgirl again, with a switch-round of roles, but the unspoiled young are naturally pure in heart and ardent for adventure. She was a rare person, this middle-aged woman, still hungry for goodness and miracles, and quite unaware that the wonder was herself, not me.

This time I was approaching Salt Lake City from the west. Almost without my realising it, the Great Salt Lake Desert began: long lines of white with smudged and lacy edges like the tide of some vast inland ocean. Then for miles we were travelling over a dense white waste. Not a bush, not a weed, not a bird, just the road and adjacent railroad track.

It was 1938. I arrived in the city a day or two short of Munich. I was in need of money, but with the possibility of a European war the exchange was falling so rapidly no bank would accept my letter of credit. Luckily it was all right at the Y. Once more I stayed a few days, once more I slept out on the porch to the shrilling of the crickets, and still the Salt Lake young Christians' reserve matched mine. Though this time one did speak. Under cover of the relay of a ranting speech from the German Chancellor, she leaned across and breathed the burning question, *'Are you a girl scout'*

12

Fast and Slow

South-Western and Southern States - Grand Canyon - a hot truck - 3 more gentlemen - Tucson - a virtue preserved - root beer - sage, dust devils, desert - El Paso - Santa Fé - ochre desert - following advice at last - Texas - Oklahoma - Dallas - Wild Cat Jo - Louisiana

After a walk in the sun and one or two short lifts, I was put down at Jacob Lake, Arizona, a touristy place on the approach road to the Grand Canyon's north rim. A cowboy with suitcases was squatting at the side of the road. He came across to tell me we were in luck as he'd just found out there was a truck through to Phoenix on this particular afternoon. It was mid-morning. As bad as that! Noting my look of disbelief, he added that it was a waste of time to bother with tourists. All the same I determined to try. I walked further out and signalled every car. True, there were hardly any. Five hours later, still there, I had worked up a warm interest in the truck.

But then at last a car did slow down. The driver was a travelling man. An unusual one. As the car still moved slowly forward, he rolled down the window and shot one or two test questions, watching me closely as I walked alongside, answering him. Following a final, measuring look, he drew up and opened the door. By now I knew that this sort of approach meant an absence of problems for me, too. And so it proved. It was a pity the journey began so late. The road ran along by a Navajo Indian Reservation. There were mud huts and crackling fires, laughing children and old Indians in wooden carts. There was an Indian Trading Post full of weaving and silverware, with a row of huts attached for the convenience of travellers who'd come a day's ride from their village. Then latitude brought down the curtain: early and suddenly, it was dark.

The next day my objective was the Grand Canyon. I reached Williams easily enough. Here again the traffic was infrequent and tourist; but the reasonable temperature made it good for walking, till a sudden hailstorm blew up. Fortunately, I was just coming to a gas station. As I was making a dash for it, a car with three tourists passed me. They pulled in and we entered at the same time, laughing together, as under the porch I shook myself like a dog to get rid of the worst of the wet ice before entering the little refreshment room. I sat down at the table next to theirs. Pleasantries were exchanged and I was offered a lift.

We coasted along the canyon in rain, hail, thunder and sun. Areas of bright sunlight and navy-blue shadows swept across the red and purple rock. Through frayed openings in shifting cloud below the rim, the river could be seen a mile below as a muddy snake and all the time heard in a low dull roar. We were out walking when yet another downpour came so suddenly we were soaked. The three then decided to stay overnight in the expensive cabins, and I - somewhat crazed by the wonder of it all - decided to walk back.

I was soon out in the Kaibab Forest It was dark now, but the unsettled day had turned into a splendidly clear night with a full moon and rain had brought out the smell of the pines. I went forward with springing steps. There was no traffic. Cattle and deer regarded me with surprise. It was cold - good clean fine cold that was just right. But everything was right: I was full of a marvellous elation. It was fifty-seven miles to a useful road; I divided this by twelve and there was nothing to it. I was sure I could walk for ever; I saw myself still fresh and elastic-limbed hitting the road at dawn.

I must have covered four or five miles when a small car passed and then drew up, and, strongly protesting, I was 'rescued' by a park employee and his family who lived in a shack in the forest. They refused to take no for an answer: *'There'll be nothing else on this road; you can't walk all night!'* The shack was untidy and tumbled but cosy and lived-in. A huge iron stove was lit and I soon dried through. We had a fine hot supper of soup and beans, and then the employee fetched an armful of blankets for me to doss down on the sofa and I was glad enough to get under them.

The next morning, at the main road I got a lift in a huge truck so heavily loaded it could only crawl up hills, and so hot I was sure I must be sitting on top of the engine. Well, believe it or not, the driver's mate was hanging his feet out of the window. The racket was shattering, but, even worse, the two kept up an unceasing cross-fire of fatuous funny remarks till I thought I'd go mad. It was all harmless enough: they were decent fellows, enjoying themselves and, as they thought, entertaining me. But I knew I had to get out. I felt bad about it. And when we arrived in Prescott and they pulled in the truck and I was invited to pie and coffee, I felt even worse. But I looked at my red, sore fist which had been on duty as a shock absorber and it gave me additional strength. I said the cab was too hot; I explained about my back. They couldn't quite credit it at first but just stood, bewildered. Then without a word, my pack was handed down. The dignity was theirs. I remembered the Trial, *'We never got up in trucks - too dirty and uncomfortable.'* I had reached the bottom.

Soon enough I was picked up by a rancher, and then it was a matter for congratulation that I was free of heavy transport, for it was a winding, uphill road.

The rancher knew it like a part of himself, and his high-powered car swept effortlessly upward while the upholstery eased my aching back. And when he turned off to his ranch, as if laid on, a car with three men in it stopped.

The three were quiet, courteous and uninquisitive. Even more unusual, they were interesting-looking. My companion in the back looked like an explorer; there was a youthful earnestness about his middle-aged intelligent face. He spoke rapidly, following long pauses, as though from a reserve of concentrated thought. It was rugged country. When we came to some sort of vantage-point we drew up. The view was dramatic - there down below for as far as the eye could see - lay a vast expanse of mixed Arizona desert. I'd already noticed that in Arizona the desert was again different; it had become lively and exciting. There was much more and varied growth and it was peppered with stones, some high as a standing man. The automobile engine was turned off as in suitable silence we took this in, with on their part it seemed to me a high degree of understanding and appreciation, something as fine in its way as the splendid desert wilderness itself, and once more unusual. Surely these men's work must be directly concerned with the physical world, geologists, perhaps? We got going again and some miles further on turned off the road down a trail right into the desert. *'This won't take long, you'll be in Wickenburg before dark'*, the driver said. The track ran between huge, smooth boulders, prickly pear, agave and the usual wiry shrubs, with towering over all like signposts to the universe, the giant, stub-fingered saguaro. It was a richly ornamental, busy, worldly desert. All too quickly we reached a group of sheds which turned out to be a small gold mill.

As promised, I was put down in Wickenburg before dark. It was now necessary to get a lift to Phoenix without delay, and again I was lucky. Dark fell, but didn't matter as far from taking away it added to the scene. This part of the journey continued through the desert, now dramatically transformed under a heavily silver-plated southern moon.

The Phoenix Y was Spanish-looking with a colonnade and palm trees. I was allotted a bed on the roof which had been made into a dormitory. Rain? O no! although two years ago... Now October, it was hot, very hot. Once more nudity wasn't enough, I was sleeping between soaked towels.

Leaving Tucson I was picked up by a railroad worker who spoke of riding the rods: that was the way to travel! He could smuggle me into a freight car - it was easy, he said - and launched into technicalities. Since to travel that way would be travelling blind, it wasn't really what I wanted; at the same time it was an opportunity I'd never expected to come my way, and now that it had it was tempting. I was also a challenge: he could hardly have brought up any subject more calculated to take my mind off where we were going. Till all at once I became aware that we were no longer on any sort of road.

The result was the kind of situation most people would have expected to come up long before this, and all the other would-be deflowerers had taken time off to warn me about. I suppose a young woman can fight for worse things than a state of virginity. Today it hardly seems to matter. It did to me then, though - no question! Following a brief kerfuffle in which he got bitten and I lost some buttons, his interest suddenly flagged. Like a flash, I was through the door and out in the dust. My rucksack was flung after me. He'd chosen well, a featureless waste - worse than the moon, not even a crater! The car started up, but instead of driving off he leant out of the window and tried to persuade me to get back in, or at least stand on the running-board back to the road, which at such a juncture was decidedly decent and thoughtful, and which I regret to say I spitefully refused. All in all, not exactly a victory a person can look back on with any pride.

So after all 'virtue' was preserved. But we had both been swayed by cupidity: I for a train at the mouth-watering prospect of becoming, if only for a short stretch, a lady Super Tramp, he by a more mature appetite. It was a long, hard, dusty, boring walk back and I reached some sort of road in no good humour. Worse than death had been averted; but now of my own making, worse than worse than death was not. For the first time, I refused a lift.

It was an old dilapidated open truck with a sideways roll, piled high and wide with basic possessions - sticks of poor furniture, pots and pans and a cooking stove; a worn mattress spilling out rusty springs was died on top, and a chicken coop full of squawking hens was secured to the running board. The driver was an old man with a thin, weathered face, creased and kind. His blue eyes lighted up as he took me in, '*Wanna ride, little lady?*' Once more I explained about my back. (Bare boards were all he had to offer.) He nodded - too quickly for comfort. With spits and explosions the motor started again and I watched the overloaded truck sway down the road and out of sight.

Shame and regret are useless now. I did feel concern. What sort of hitch-hiker had I become. Disordered temper declined into low spirits. The poor situation threw up unpromising prospects; I even fleetingly wondered if this 'tour' had gone on long enough. But in the interval that followed, when no car came and nothing happened, the weakness passed; the lengthy wait on the silent road proved restorative. I recollected myself. After all, when you looked into it, with the exception of the odd incident harmful to no-one, it had been straightforward to an extent that few would believe possible. And this was no sooner thought than put to the proof.

A car finally appeared and there was room for one. The driver was cheerful and talkative; the other two, the woman sitting in the back with me and the girl in front with him, were mother and daughter and also hitch-hiking. When we arrived at his destination, the driver bought us drinks - mine tasted odd, I thought. He then took us a mile or two out of town.

We sat together at the side of the road. The girl talked of her home in

California, her husband and baby. She seemed regular enough. The mother was different. Her language was the worst I'd heard, the simplest utterance was obscene. She enjoyed this sort of travelling, she said. Suddenly the girl remarked, *'Fancy that guy getting us root beers!'*

*'I **thought** it was queer-tasting coke'*, I put in chattily, *'Imagine - my first beer and I didn't even know!'* I became aware of my merriment echoing in a void; and then I saw that the two were frozen motionless, and so filled with amazement their faces appeared to be swollen. Up to that point I'd been suffered. This was now at an end. It was time to be leaving them, three together was no good for getting lifts; but before I could get up I received a broadside-on hint from mother.

There was little traffic and suddenly it was dark. In the end I got a lift from a Mexican in a sombrero; he was crossing the border, but went out of his way to take me to a small town with a hotel.

Out of Rodeo, I found an accommodating railroad bridge that provided good seating. It was just as well, as the traffic on this very secondary road was almost non-existent. *'Hallo, there!'*, the call came from a railroad worker on the line below; *'Like a drink of water?'* I shook my head and moved along, as I hoped, out of view. *'It's all right - you don't need to be skeered of me'*, he was up on the embankment now, *'I'm jest a plain working man. Where you going to, anyways? ... Well, there's a truck along sometime - allus goes out today. Hungry? ... No! Had any breakfast? - I bet you ain't'* He disappeared and came back with a packet of sandwiches. *'Thas all right - goo on. I c'n easy git me more. Well, good luck.'* He disappeared again, this time for good.

On one side rugged, sage-pocked mountains, on the other, mile upon mile of open desert. Large birds rose and wheeled. Dust devils rocked slowly across the distance. Tumble weed rolled restlessly over and over or slid in fits and starts in the loose dust. My hair was splayed by the wind. But it was peaceful and pleasant enough, occasional clouds kept it from being too hot. Hours passed. At one point a private car with a man and woman in it slowed down, then the woman turned to the man and it started up again.

It was afternoon before I was picked up by two cowboys travelling to Lordsburg. The vehicle was a unique blend of age and accident. They were kind-hearted, happy boys, grateful that the wheels still went round and delighted to be helping me on my way. *'Waal, we had this wreck'n I guess there ain't much lefta this ool cab, but she do still jest about goo.'* The back was full of bottles and cans of water required to replenish the radiator. The back of the seat was exposed springs, we sat on coats. The smashed windscreen was clamped in place with two lengths of wood screwed together through a hole. A crude wooden hook held the door roughly in the closed position. Water from the open radiator spattered the screen and us; when this ceased it was time to be filling up.

Unfortunately, I was put down right in Lordsburg. The sight of me and my rucksack passing through on a Saturday afternoon all but brought the little desert town to a halt. People stopped dead in their tracks and then turned round. Children ceased playing. Old men shuffled to the edge of the sidewalk right out in the sun for a longer-lasting look. And when I finally got clear of the place it was to find other hitch-hikers strung out along the road, eager for weekend transport. So I wasn't optimistic, forgetting - believe it or not - that at the sight of a girl alone hope springs eternal. I was soon up in a truck and into the familiar questionnaire.

'Where you from, then?'

'San Francisco.'

'Fine place, 'Frisco. Have a good time there?' Age and weight came next. *'Hmm. Cigarette? ... Don't smoke!'*, the beginnings of concern. Then, *'Like your beer, huh?'* At yet another negative the concern rapidly spread now, mixed with naked astonishment. But after a pause he gathered himself together and pressed manfully on, *'Like to neck, though, doncha!'* At the final dashing of high hopes there was no more: I was driven over the desert to Deeming - he in baffled silence, I host to a state of mild apology, troubled by a familiar nagging feeling of being engaged in some sort of deceit.

It was a hundred miles to El Paso and there was an hour of light. My next lift came from a quiet, slow-spoken man who owned a gold mine in the mountains; with pride he showed me a piece of ore. The road was now running adjacent to the Rio Grande. When we reached El Paso I was taken to a high place from which to view the illuminated twin cities: El Paso, U.S.A.; Ciudad Juarez, Mexico.

The next day I took a streetcar over the Rio Grande into Mexico. It could be no more than a fleeting glance at a country which here seemed rich in atmosphere if nothing else. Poverty and dirty were everywhere. Old men with thin criss-crossed sunbaked faces, wearing sprouting straw hats, women in torn black head scarves, barefoot children. Even the fruit and vegetables in the market looked puny. By crossing this river I was in a foreign country in the sense that in crossing the Atlantic I had never been. In London I'd tried to get a Mexican visa but the time wasn't right. It had to do with the ownership of oil wells. It was plain to see that theirs was the need.

In Santa Fé it would have been impossible not to check in at the Hotel Montezuma. New Mexico's small state capital had attractive adobe buildings, even an art gallery. It also had a fine background of snow-capped mountains, and marvellously cold nights. Only two days before I'd been sweating it out in El Paso where, as they proudly put it, the mosquitoes settle on the automobiles. Now, at night in Santa Fé, it was heating stoves and blankets.

North to Taos, with a nice young man in a well-sprung light truck. The road soon turned into a twisting trail with plenty of loose stones and pot-holes. It was a joyous ride - more off than on the seat - through a fine ochre desert occasionally broken by Indian dwellings, mud blocks with chilli peppers hanging out to dry in the sun. Taos, entirely adobe, was good-looking and aware of it.

That afternoon I walked the two miles to the Indian pueblo. There was little traffic; one car passed but it traversed a different world. Here, walking put me on a level with the natives. Soft-stepping young Indians, older men in blankets, elders usually mounted on an ambling horse, nodded and grunted as they passed. One young Indian wished me a courteous 'Good afternoon', an unheard of form of address on the road. Following the *National Monument Visitors Welcome* signs, I came suddenly on the communal dwellings. I also came upon lines of washing, a scramble of children and frisking dogs, with squaws in and out, up and down ladders, and busy cooking at the beehive ovens. None of the reproductions and postcards I'd seen had prepared me for this; in all of them the unique, five-storey dwellings were deserted. O course I knew that the place was a present-day Indian village, but what I hadn't realised was that the flats themselves were still lived in. I'd come so quietly round the corner that no-one noticed me. I stood still, a privileged spectator, watching the happy, natural scene.

On the way back I met again the same ebony-faced old man on pony-back I'd passed on the way in. He pronounced gravely over me, *'You go then - hallo! You come back now - goodbye!'*

It was also goodbye to northern New Mexico. A hot sun and desert, a prospect of snow-capped mountains, fine cold nights, and a stirring encounter with a monument.

Texas and Oklahoma next. Back to reality. I was unable to shake off a guilty feeling of having indulged myself in Arizona and New Mexico, in California, too. All this sightseeing. Back now to the real America. I got it. Perhaps predictably, this next part of the journey somewhat resembled the Corn Belt, that other America plain, land of the long questionnaire. Except that here it wasn't long. With the minimum waste of time we were down to the bare proposition known as 'filling a date'. Whether it was some bouncing middle-ager or decrepit old man with two sticks, it made no difference. All were mad keen for dates, and my light-footed, side-stepping practice met shocked disbelief. What was I **doing** then!

Yet this district was no worse than many others. There were good rides here, too, as there were propositioners who were neither fast nor insistent; and to further confound me, the long slow quiet ride - of all time, I should think - was in this area. So that probably it was simply the cumulative effect that here came to a head. Certainly my outlook shifted. There were times when my heart sank at the sight of a car. I began to adopt a more protective technique; it was essential to find out where the driver was going, and I continued to turn down unpromising-looking lifts.

In other words, I now followed the advice I was always being given. Yet I'd done so well for so long without following that advice, and anyway it was impossible to predict when repeatedly the most unlikely lifts turned out so well. Up to this point it had seemed as if out on the road, exposed as I was, defensive measures were out of place, and it occurs to me now, perhaps even likely to attract what they were put up to defend. In any case, this was the only bad patch that lasted, and it was soon enough gone.

I got a lift in northern Texas from a nice young truck driver who came out from east and didn't think much of his new situation. There was this strong insistent wind blowing over the plains and it never let up. Back home he'd had curly hair and look at it now - all blown out! Or so he reckoned. This struck me as highly humorous - till I got out into it. I could believe anything then, as I struggled through a little town against wind and dust - fine dust that quickly found the eyes and mouth and lay rippled in the gutters. I took cover in a café where I sat with a cup of coffee watching the torn awning flap as animated by perpetual motion. Suddenly, it came to me: The Dust Bowl! *The Grapes of Wrath*. I remembered how moved I'd been by the book and the film. Raped earth. This place must be on the edge of it - a vast, unmarked, unwelcoming monument to greed.

Out of Oklahoma City, on the way to Dallas, a pioneer Ford drew up. The driver was a skinny old man wearing a dusty encrusted hat that could have been rooted to his head, and along with the jalopy made up the perfect ensemble. I asked where he was going: this seemed all right, so I got in. He said nothing and I said nothing and we travelled at a speed of twenty miles an hour. There was unbelievable play on the steering wheel, but the driver had obviously grown old with his auto and knew it like the back of his worn brown hand. On we went. Everything passed us. We existed in a different world where time seemed less to stand still as go retrograde. I had to fight down an ever-mounting impulse to get out and push. The afternoon wore on, and still he said nothing and I said nothing, and I could only hope that he was really going somewhere, because if not he was wasting a whole lot of irrecoverable time. More than once I was on the point of making a remark to this effect, but it seemed so discourteous and anyway I couldn't bear to break the beautiful silence. So I still said nothing and he said nothing, and now the sun was halfway down the sky. When we reached his destination my sagging spirits rose - and then subsided as he drove straight through. Could it possibly be that he had it in mind to take me to Dallas? If so, for goodness sake what day of the week would we be arriving there? Then a mile or so further on, out of the fading blue, a development - he half-turned and a hand like an autumn leaf fluttered down on my knee. I quickly brushed it off; he said nothing and I said nothing and we rolled steadily on. When we arrived at the Red River, the Texas state line, he pulled in to the side of the road and I nipped smartly out. I shouldered my rucksack and thanked him politely. Once more he half-turned and this time he opened his mouth, though nothing came out. As I crossed the bridge, I looked back. He hadn't moved. Over the bridge and some way on, I looked back again. In the misty distance the old Ford was still standing there.

The next day I was invited up into a truck by a homespun middle-aged body, who had first taken the precaution of finding out about me. *'Well isn't that just fine'*, he exclaimed on learning my destination, *'I'll be glad to take you ninety miles. You just get right in.'* I revealed that I was going to relations in San Antonio to get a job, and there followed a splendid silence. The truck was heavily loaded but well-sprung and decently speedy. The driver looked so like Vaughan Williams that it was on the tip of my tongue to ask if he was fond of music, but - once again - the quiet was too precious to be put at risk.

At length mention was made of a packet of sandwiches and cookies. There was plenty for two, and if I'd agree to share them with him we could stop at a place he knew of, where there was a bench and a table under some trees. But if I didn't like the idea I wasn't to worry - we'd carry right on... I would - well that was fine. He liked to stop at this place, the scenery was pretty and the near-by house - he would dearly love to have a cottage like that himself, a little place in the country - but it didn't seem as if he ever would. While we were eating, he inquired if my parents were alive and knew what I was doing. I don't think he believed the second affirmative, but he said, *'Well, that's fine'* and we went on eating. At another point, he remarked, *'Well now you look such a baby to be on the road.'* I knocked off eight and told him I was twenty, hoping it would satisfy. After the meal we picked up pocketfuls of pecan nuts from under the trees, and then got back in the truck, and the beautiful silence continued till we reached his home town. He took me through and out on the highway again and gave me his address. *'Now if you don't get a lift, I want you to come right back into town and find me - don't hesitate, because I'll take care of you - you'll see how I'll take care of you!'* And no-one will ever persuade me that he would not have done just that.

Out of San Antonio I refused a number of, as I thought, suspicious looking characters before getting in with Wildcat Joe. Joe was a baseball referee, but now the season had ended and he was on his way to Houston to drive for a strictly off-the-level form of passenger transport, known as wildcatting. This was a racket with centres in most of the big cities, where you could fix up to travel by car at less than half the cost of the fare by bus or train. I discovered afterwards that the cars used were commonly substandard, unpaid for, uninsured and without a carrier's licence, and the driver's hours were nobody else's business.

Joe turned out to be one of the best, kindness itself and full of lively good humour. He assured me that even if Houston supplied him with a full load to New Orleans, he'd manage to squeeze me in somewhere - there was always a way if you'd a will to put behind it! He stopped to get out and pick some cotton for me to see; and again further on to pull down silvery strands of Spanish moss, a curious Old Father Time's beard effect, found hanging off trees and even telegraph wires in the deep south.

He asked if I intended to stay the night in Houston. I said I had in mind somewhere on the outskirts as getting out of the larger cities could be such a problem. He said he knew of a tourist court out of town on the New Orleans road. The cabins were reasonable and well-equipped; he'd often stayed there and knew which ones to ask for. It was dark by the time we reached Houston. Joe took me down the main street to see the town; then on to the auto court where he saw to it that I was given one of the better cabins. He then went away to ring up and came back to tell me it was all arranged.

The next morning I waited half an hour before setting off on my own. I hoped he hadn't come up against a bus company spotter or alerted police. I was sorry not to see him again, but relieved to be free of the sweltering prospect of being squeezed into an already loaded car.

Louisiana was full of plantations of robust bamboo waving palm-like crowns. Truck-load after truck-load passed. The driver of the car I was in was horrified by such ignorance. *'**Bamboo** - that's sugar cane!'* and to prove it he stopped the car and plunged into the crop to break off a ripe piece for me to suck. When he turned off for home, I was left on a road that ran like a channel through the sugar; there was nothing else bar the tops of two slim refinery chimneys smoking moderately into the clear blue sky. Then two small black children appeared and approached as near as they dared in O-mouthed amazement.

The road followed round the Gulf of Mexico. Stretched out into the quiet water were wooden fishing piers with shacks mounted on them like lake dwellings. It was appealing country. Life was leisurely, and my progress matched this with short rides and long walks. But there was something else. Here lived America's failures, the ones who hadn't made it. They'd lost the Civil War and now their manhood. Poor whites - the lowest of the low. A faint, sad climate of rejection pervaded - something I felt I should have been able to connect with, and in an odd unexpected way I did, absorbing the sadness and experiencing the rejection. I must have got in with quite a number of local drivers, but nothing remains. Little was spoken, but instead of a living silence, a cold, dead one. There hadn't been anything quite like this before. It was as if hope had withered to the bone. Imagination? To some extent, but most of all I think it had to do with my low meeting theirs.

Then, as always on the road, came sudden change. The dolorous air evaporated, releasing full-strength sun as I was swept from the deep south by a travelling salesman going to Tallahassee. *'A Limey, by God!'* he cried. He'd been in England as a serviceman at the end of the First World War. He thought he was in luck, but soon discovered that he wasn't, or not precisely as originally envisaged. But he took it well, congratulated me on being smart, switched to his loving wife and rewarding children, and finished with a resounding selection of songs of the University of Georgia.

13

The Commercial Coast

Riding with 5 boxers - wildly happy - Miami Beach - a wait at a gas station - dawn in St. Augustine - rain and more rain - Savannah - Charleston - Washington - Traveller's Aid - peeling off a fleshy youth - New York

Trailing moss; bronze water; the cough and whistle of birds; a deep blue sky and heat: the end of October in northern Florida. It was also Sunday morning with cars few and filled with the family. In the end I got a ride from a young couple in a light truck. The boy drove at a brisk pace. Herons rose as we rattled by. The hazard was a type of small black hog, rooting at the sides of the road, quite unconcerned. We came on two trotting sedately side by side along the sidewalk of a village main street. Only the hats were missing.

Further south, as I was resting in the shade of a clump of feathery trees, a car with five people in it drew up. *'Plenty of room'*, said the driver as he stowed my rucksack, and when I inquired where he was going I was once more promptly and accurately identified. The driver turned out to be a boxers' manager accompanied by his girl 'wife'. The two young men, whose appearance and character respectively came to suggest The Nose and Gluey Ron, were boxers. The surprise came when I learnt that the other, older man, quiet civilized Ray, who looked and sounded such an evolutionary advance on the others, was like me hitch-hiking. He looked Jewish, he appeared to be intelligent, yet he had less than two dollars to his name. The driver had just bought him a meal. It seemed out of character.

The road ran through a sub-tropical swamp, in some places nothing but water, in others profusely overgrown. There were no towns, just occasional gas stations and Seminole Indian villages. We stopped to take a closer look at one of these. The houses were palm-thatched, South Sea Island fashion. These Indians had particularly neat, decorative features as well as the usual dignified expressions. I wondered what they thought of me. In my view they looked the more advance - me a jumped-up barbarian. My accent caused a good deal of diversion; at one point an *'Oh rather!'* nearly put us in the water. When we reached Miami, Ray and I got out. The others were booked in at Miami Beach. Ray, who had once lived in Miami, led the way to a place he knew of where he wangled us dollar rooms for seventy-five cents.

The next day I was mooching around when I heard, *'Hey, English!'* It was the boxing trio held up at a road junction. Once more I got in. After being weighed at the City Hall, the boys came out with Ray, who hadn't yet got a job. We ended up at a very large empty hotel and here the men went off, leaving me with the 'wife', who was keen to bathe.

While she was in the water I relaxed on the sand. To begin with she was the only one out there and it was plain that she was unacquainted with surf: she tried to swim and got a ducking and was then knocked flat by a breaker. But in no time at all a handsome young man with a splendid brown torso sprang out of the hotel to her rescue. She came out of the water in a state about her hair - we were going to the boxing later. She dashed in to fix it.

I remained on the beach. I was by myself now and it was rapidly getting dark. I went down to the water's edge and stood among the freshly washed up shells and glistening seaweed. Behind me coconut palms threshed in the wind. I was suddenly wildly happy, thinking of all the people I cared about - had ever been fond of - and as it welled up I sang at the top of my voice into the covering roar of the pounding surf. It was a splendid experience, something of which remained with me through the evening as I watched The Nose knocked out and Ron the Bond withdrawn with a cut eye.

Miami is exceedingly hot out of season. Walking over the shadeless Venetian Way I was obliged to keep shaking my head to re-focus dissolving faculties. Even after dark the sheerest silk was too much. At night I lay in damp nudity. It would have been impossible not to form a strong attachment to the local drinks: frothy, chilled coconut milk, and a mixture of this with pineapple juice and iced papaya.

It was now November, I'd been in America five months. A careful look at my letter of credit revealed that I should be on the move again, especially as before making for New York and home I was keen to go down the Florida Keys, a string of coral islands bridged together between the Gulf of Mexico and the Atlantic. In times gone by a railroad had linked mainland Florida to America's land's end, Key West, but this had been smashed by a hurricane. The new overseas highway, 150 miles long, had just been built.

I got up early and took a streetcar out of town. A young couple went out of their way to take me to the mainland outpost. The boy insisted. It was hard to tell whether he was more fascinated or appalled by my project. As I set off he called after me, *'Hey! - you can't go* ***walking*** *down there!'*

I could think of nothing nicer, but as usual it was out of my hands. I'd hardly gone fifty yards when I was picked up by a dark silky gentleman who had already noted me around town, and greeted me as a long-lost friend: *'Well! Do you believe in fate?!'* which I didn't fancy augured well for mine. He was a salesman of holiday hats, caps and souvenirs. He assured me that I'd never make it there and back in one day, and at the pace he seemed determined to travel it was obvious that I wouldn't. According to him you ran the risk of a seabird in your windscreen at any sort of speed. But worst of all was his never-ending, irrepressible line in quips and jokes of the kind that fitted in with the hats and caps, the punch lines of which were emphasised with enthusiastic slaps liable to land anywhere and linger till brushed off; and this further slowed us down. Finally, when we came on two cars at the side of the road, one with the bonnet up, we had to stop as well. Hats and Caps waffled round, making useless suggestions and getting in the way. Suddenly, I saw my opportunity. Unnoticed, I slipped aside and walked smartly off. The road snaked over the water bridging the gaps between the islands, it was like walking a tight-rope out to sea. I was surprised to find the coral white; I'd imagined it was always pink like necklaces I'd seen. In due course Fate came sailing by, point taken, passing me up. But I got a lift from one of the other cars. The driver observed that Hats and Caps looked like a foreigner to him; and after that he concentrated on the driving.

That to travel hopefully is a better thing than to arrive was well exemplified by Key West. I was most struck by the handsome coffee-coloured Negroes (Cubans). I treated myself to some sort of lime concoction (they grow on the Keys), and to a picture postcard of the residence of Mr. Ernest Hemingway, and then promptly doubled back out.

I walked a good way across the next island and the shadows were beginning to lengthen before I was picked up by two superior young men in an expensive car. They were from New York and on holiday. The driver, who did most of the talking, said they'd intended to stay the night in Key West but, after looking round, decided against it. They were staying at Palm Beach; he was surprised that I found Miami tolerable. But when he spoke of books and films we were much in agreement. I was just starting to open out packed-away faculties of discrimination when we came to Hemingway. Yes, he was often to be seen in the bar at Sloppy Joe's and around the island, unshaven and barefoot: *'He's that kind of man!'* More than anything else the remark revealed the kind of man the driver was. Being the kind of person I was, the words were shocked into memory never to be forgotten. Attitude is indeed all; had he made a similarly disparaging comment on the President of his country or the Prime Minister of mine, it wouldn't have caused a ripple. As it was, tentatively forming lines of communication abruptly collapsed. He could hardly have become more alien had he suddenly developed fins and gills and slid down under the sea all round us. After that it seemed best to concentrate on the scenery. It was a spectacular night with the moon in and out of flying ragged cloud and sudden overcasting with downpours so torrential we were obliged to pull up. Long-legged land crabs pitched across the road. More than once the headlights revealed a pair of electric eyes of, it was thought, a racoon.

I left Miami in good time to reach St. Augustine, some three hundred miles, by evening. As usual the problem was getting out of the built-up area which here seemed to extend forever up the coast. My first lift came from a droll individual going to Fort Lauderdale - he said. Later, he was willing to make it Tampa, unless of course I preferred to sleep by myself.

Shortly after this I was picked up by a man whose face was so devoid of expression it could have come out of a mould. He said there was a truck going through to Wilmington, North Carolina, that always stopped at the gas station opposite his shop, and he personally knew the driver was a good fellow, sure to give me a lift. I could wait in the gas station - he would fix it with the attendant - he'd do this for me because he never liked to see a girl on the road. I should have been alerted by this last, since experience had shown that it invariably meant the opposite. Something of the sort did cross my mind, but he had it all worked out and was so sure of everything that in no time I found myself compliantly in tow.

I was installed in the gas station back room with a pile of magazines and a beer - which he at once changed for a coke, without comment and still without expression. Time passed, punctuated by assurances that the truck would be along any time now. In an interval between these, I cornered the attendant who said it should certainly arrive sometime that day, though you could never quite tell with trucks, anyhow, he reckoned that a ride that far was worth waiting for. After this I picked up my rucksack. The Mould came running across. This time he clarified the situation by pointing out that if by any chance the truck should fail to show up, at least I was sure of a place to eat and sleep.

I had not gone much more than a hundred yards when the attendant - who seemed to be cast as the cover man in this affair - drew up at the curb alongside to make what was no doubt considered to be a favourable financial offer. It wasn't at all a good day; in fact, it was one of the worst, and being largely my own fault, doubly aggravating. However, it seemed that the rest in Miami had effected a real regeneration, for instead of becoming despondent as in the south-central flatlands, this time the situation had a galvanising effect; and on the spot I made up my mind that no matter what, on this lap I was going to get to St. Augustine.

At length, as the built-up area at last began to thin, I was picked up by a pair of quiet, good-natured truck drivers. It was a large, heavily-loaded vehicle struggling along at thirty miles an hour, and by now it was pouring with rain. It was hot in the truck and the seat was hard; but at intervals when the rain let up, we got out to stretch and run round the truck a time or two.

In due course, and in the middle of a torrential downpour, we arrived in St. Augustine. It struck three as I got down. In seconds, I was soaked. As the truck rumbled away I found myself splendidly alone in the hissing rain: there was not a single lit window, and at once tiredness and cramp fell away. I felt extraordinarily strong and acutely happy. It had been a day of difficulties and setbacks; but I'd been determined to reach St. Augustine and I had, and I suppose it was this that made the deserted road of an unknown town on the night of the deluge seem such an ecstatic setting. I should be reluctant to reveal myself at any age - let alone late twenties - capering gleefully in puddles, safer simply to tell of being carried forward on a surge of high spirits, till at length I came to an all-night café and remembered how little I'd had to eat.

It was still pouring when I came out, and two youths who'd been in the café were waiting for me in their car. I said I didn't require a lift, but they drove alongside or took off round the block to meet me at the next corner. Coming up to a church with a commodious sheltering porch I quickly slipped inside out of sight.

The porch was clean and dry, it seemed as good a place as any I'd be likely to find at this time of the morning. I arranged my rucksack as a pillow and stretched out. I did get some sort of uneasy sleep for an hour or two. At one point I heard a car draw up, but it was only the fitful wind in the surrounding shrubs. Later, footsteps approached and ascended the steps to the porch - I squeezed myself deeper into the black shadow against the wall - but it was only blown water from the flooded guttering spattering the steps.

Dawn brought no let-up in the weather. As soon as it was light I was up and away. By the time I reached it, there were one or two people in the main Plaza, where sad pyramids of pitted cannonballs dripped steadily in the rain. St. Augustine had once been an important Spanish base and still had something of an Iberian atmosphere. I walked out along the edge of the water while rain off my head coursed down my back. Had I dived in and swum instead I couldn't have been more wet. But it was deliciously cool with my face a crystal waterfall and soft globes of water in the corner of each eye.

It was a truck or nothing now. I was too much of a liquid phenomenon to be received into a private car. In a little while, however, a private car did pick me up, and I was handed a clean car polisher to rub down with. This driver wanted to know all about me - he was probingly inquisitive - but for a change it was history rather than physique that interested him. I served what I fancied would satisfy. The journey to Jacksonville passed quickly as I related my curious life story - more curious to me than to him - and when we reached town it was difficult not to burst out laughing when I heard him earnestly wishing me and my husband the very best of luck.

By this time it had stopped raining. I went into a gas station cloakroom and squeezed out the worst of the wet. It seemed a good idea to make a point of walking through the town at a brisk pace to thoroughly dry myself. In the ordinary way such a prospect wouldn't have pleased but, in this instance, the opposite was the case. It was no longer Victory Night in St. Augustine but I was till buoyant. I recall floating joyously forward, wrapped in such a rosy view of my ability and character as to be full of pity for the rest of mankind so plainly not up to my standard.

Soon after this I was up in a truck of beans bound for New York: the men aimed to have them there by midnight the next day. I said I was going to Savannah, Georgia. The truck driver was a poetic-looking young man with a lock of dark hair that fell in his eyes. His thickset rugged mate couldn't have been more different. As we travelled, Rugged interrogated the Poet as to the time-limit, load, weight, and other relevant particulars; it appeared that there was not over much time - should the beans miss the Saturday market all would be lost. But the Poet had everything in hand, he knew it all, and at every juncture there was mention of Marilyn: the Poet - as every poet should be - was madly in love.

We were hearing more about Marilyn when the engine spluttered and we pulled in to the side of the road out of gas. Rugged looked grimly at the Poet who said he'd been assured that the tanks were full. Good fortune now came our way in the shape of Rugged's brother in another large truck. He was able to give us enough petrol to get to Pete's Place, the first re-fuelling point. But a few miles further on we were obliged to stop again. This time Rugged looked even more grim, since it was now evident that there was something wrong with the engine. Rugged rolled up his sleeves and got down into it, while the Poet waffled round, at one point knocking a pin in the carburettor. At last Rugged had everything right. But we were on our way only to stop again, for the second time out of gas. Rugged now hitched a lift to Pete's, while the Poet filled in time figuring the m.p.h. required to make the market, and wondering how late he was going to be getting back to Marilyn. It was dark by the time I got out.

Morning revealed Savannah resigned to the ramshackle, seemingly content to peel and crumble. It was the same at Charleston, South Carolina: aged, but comfortably relaxed the character and good looks still showing through.

Out of Charleston, I was lucky enough to be picked up by another long-distance truck. The driver was a perky, middle-aged Irishman. By the time we stopped for refuelling it was dark, and now a tousled lad emerged from the sleeper at the back. The Irishman informed me that he played ball for some team or other and was a fine fellow. The Fine Fellow took over, the Irishman got in the back, and at once the easy atmosphere was gone. I was asked if I'd had other long rides in trucks. Then in the same level tone, *'Well, if you don't get more friendly you won't with me.'* Without making a move he'd correctly assessed the situation. To be fair to the Fine Fellow, you could see his side of it. Hitch-hiking was common enough, but not a girl on her own. And his point about long rides was not without validity: most of us have an eye for the main chance that suits our needs. It was what I was doing myself.

I reached Virginia to find myself back in familiar country - deciduous trees and grass. I was given a lift by a salesman of sorts in a long car that swept forward, purring softly. The gentleman was large to match, and reeled off questions without the detachment of a social investigator taking a sample. It was the mixture as before with a variation in the last movement. On learning that I was going to New York to find employment, he asked what work I did.

'In an office.'

'Stenographer, huh?'

'No. Journalist.'

'Write, huh?'

'No. Art journalism.'

He thought for a minute. *'Pictures, huh?'*

'That's right.'

'Noods?'

I thought for a minute. *'No.'*

'No noods?'

'No.'

At this point there was a brief interval; then just as I was settling further into the luxurious cushions, thinking we'd come to the end of the symposium, he led off with, *What will I get if I take you to Washington?'* So cool! We were back with the Fine Fellow. North-eastern seaboard dominant seemed less a matter of appetite more of getting your money's worth. But like any other market it could turn out to be a gamble, and straight away I was picked up by a kindly couple who lived in the federal capital, and when we arrived, insisted on taking me round the sights before putting me down at the Y.

The Washington Y was welfare-conscious. Far from being suspicious, they had this pressing need to help. By this time, very likely, I looked in need of it; but it sounded more like the familiar preconceived response in reverse. In particular, they kept coming up with the Travellers' Aid next door. I was holding out to them the dollar for accommodation but they weren't interested. I tried explaining, but they were so sure I shouldn't be hitch-hiking they seemed not to hear. The Travellers' Aid was where I belonged, *'Such **nice** young ladies - just like yourself!'* (Perhaps they had nothing to do?) Then, *'But look at your clothes, they aren't warm enough.'* Still refusing to be moved on, I swore that my pack was full of sweaters.

But on my way out the next day I was caught. I made the mistake of inquiring at the desk which streetcar I should take to bring me out on the right highway. This time I was escorted next door where the nice young ladies just like myself would know all about that. *'It will only take a minute.'* Once more I repeated my question. The nice young lady just like myself looked startled. She excused herself and, after an interval, returned to conduct me to another room and kind helper to whom I said it again. It was taken, naturally, as an appeal for assistance, and as a result much time was spent at cross-purposes. At intervals I came up with my little question, but more and more faintly. I attempted to explain what I was doing, but either they couldn't assimilate it, or they didn't believe me. When I put it to them: wouldn't it be a ridiculous come-down to be assisted the last few miles? at least this had the effect of bringing the situation to a head. Most people didn't consider the Travellers' Aid a come-down, I was tartly informed. After this parting of the curtains, I summoned all my strength for one last presenting of my little question and learnt that they didn't know.

Outside I found a policeman; but by now I was perhaps feeling a trifle weak. Anyway I must have failed to make clear in which direction I wished to travel and consequently, sometime later, I found myself back on the highway going south. It was mid-day before I was through to the north which was still built-up. It was becoming increasingly clear that the east coast was not for hitch-hiking, and the nearer I got to New York the worse it was going to be.

As I passed a gas station, two neatly-dressed youths, standing by while their car was filled, called across, *'Going to Baltimore?' 'No, New York.' 'We'll take you to Baltimore.'* But I was looking for a lift going through, I was tired of getting stuck in cities, I said. A minute or two later they drew up at the kerb and the older boy, with great politeness, offered again, this time assuring me that they'd see I got through and out the other side. He was a good driver, the pace was just right, the atmosphere was relaxed and there were no questions. They took me well out of Baltimore and looked round for a good place to wait.

But instead of waiting, after the boys had driven away I wandered on down the road, calling to mind the difficulties I'd encountered getting into New York from the north. Quite a performance! From the south seemed all set to be just as demanding, but also - my native euphoria was quick to bubble up and point out - rewarding.

What presented itself this time was a monstrously long truck going to within ninety miles of New York. The driver was a well-developed man in early middle life, with hairy elbows out of a bright red jersey and flashing black eyes under a rakish checked cap, and once more appearances were nothing to go by. Here was my knight in shining armour! I was placed at once. He'd had an English boss. He said he knew a fair number of drivers and, with any luck, would be able to find one going the distance. We arrived at the Delaware River and while waiting for the ferry he went off on a tour of inspection, and came back to tell me he'd found a decent fellow who wasn't going far, but knew of another driver who'd take me on after that. By now the light was beginning to fade, the water looked leaden, the New Jersey shore was just visible in the misty distance. When the time came to say goodbye, the Rakish Cap gallantly shook hands.

I was taken right into Manhattan by a fleshy youth who was in no hurry; we were anyway slowed by fog, but he would keep stopping for gas, gum, coffee or food. He was also more than somewhat drippy, I was obliged to keep peeling him off, but he was at all times good humoured and ready to join in a laugh.

It was easy enough to be laughing at everything now: Married? Weight? Neck? Noods? While the Southerners' picturesque weakness for filled dates took an old-world charm alongside Yankee commercialism. It was now possible to see the long slow silent ride in Oklahoma for what it had really been - pure poetry from start to finish.

14

New York and London

The Greenwich Village Y put up a camp bed in the staffroom for what was left of the night. They were too full as well as too expensive for me now. I found a room for three dollars a week at the top of a tall house. On my first visit to New York it had been unbelievably hot. Now it was fiendishly cold. I had no gloves and was in no position to buy any. I could have done with ear muffs. Then came the blizzard. Having only a skylight and with the little room so cosily warm, I wasn't aware of it till I stepped into the street in the morning. There were these large white humps at the sides of the roads - there was one outside my lodgings - it wasn't until I was having breakfast that I remembered there'd been a car there the night before. It wasn't snowing now, and the ploughs were out, but in the main streets the traffic only hardened the snow even on Broadway and Fifth Avenue, and six feet piled up along the sides of the roads remained undiminished. This was real winter, compared with this our own were slushy imitations. I was lucky, it doesn't usually snow before Christmas in New York. As evening fell, the Greenwich Village shopkeepers lit fires of scrapwood along the sidewalks. Flickering on after dark it made a wonderfully thrilling, somehow splendidly Elizabethan, scene.

The white churches of New England. The Upper Mississippi 'Where the Falls of Minnehaha'. Grand Coulee - the bare-bones of wilderness. Flying high over the Grand Canyon. The flowering desert, the dramatic desert, the quiet desert. Northern New Mexico. And now New York in the snow.

There were other, more personal, collector's pieces. The Minnesota Schoolgirl: a celebration of us both. The Pencil Drawing: a meeting of minds. Casualty, upturn in the sunflowers and corn. Montana Dave, attitude and altitude. An Episcopalian angel somewhere in Nevada, Mrs. Minister. Greed and Shame; to ride the rods and the first refusal. American Plain, said collapse of the spirit in Oklahoma. The long slow silent ride, an Okie Idyll. Nocturnal Dance and floating out of St. Augustine. As for the escapade itself, so many people had admitted to similar urges, it almost looked as if it were a part of the human condition. Exposed in the human situation though, it was usually effectively smothered.

And now I was leaving the States. I was going home. I wasn't re-born. I hadn't changed. But although there could be no total immersion or overnight miracle, magic there was - had been all the time in the subtle osmotic pressures of people and places. And what had begun as a love affair with a country had ended enhanced, the promise proved.

I had kept in touch with the Pencil Drawing by mail. She and another girl had thumbed their way to New York where they now had jobs and new friends. I was introduced - once more got to know - two Swedish girls; this time one was an artist, the other wrote. These two strongly felt it was not right for me to be leaving their country without experiencing at least one decent home-cooked meal. Tourist Homes, YWCA, drug stores and automats were all very well, but could give no idea what American cooking was really like or the heights it could reach. Undaunted by my juvenile enthusiasm for chocolate ice-cream soda, pumpkin pie and cinnamon and raisin toast, I was invited to supper. It turned out to be a right royal dinner which has to be and still is the finest I ever tasted. I remember most vividly the magnificent chestnut soup that just about stood up on the plates.

In so many ways it was sad to be leaving. I'd come to America, brimming with enthusiasm and rashly prepared to disappear into it. To find myself content to be sailing home came as a surprise and disappointment. It put my 'tramp' in its place as little more than an adventure holiday. The quiet Pencil Drawing was the daring one now and she was living it, not playing a part, I thought, as once more we were waving goodbye.

After New York, London seemed particularly grey and sullen-looking. My aunt had moved again. She'd been there a week or more, though it was hard to believe: pictures were stacked, furniture, trunks and boxes still piled up and there were no curtains. She was seated in a small central clearing, entirely composed and relaxed, taking a picnic lunch. On a single-burner oil cooking stove a saucepan with an egg in it was coming to the boil. After the shock - not only did I have no parents to speak of, now I had no home either! - I looked again. In truth, a touching scene. But I was incapable then of anything approaching such a balanced response. In the forget-me-not blue eyes I only saw the same, inflexible innocence, now mixed with wonder, resignation and dilute affection.

I remembered the young Canadian bank clerk met six months before on the voyage out, we'd discussed books, played table tennis, even thought along similar lines. He had always wanted to do what I was going to do, but had settled for this, as he described it, 'tame trip' to visit the folks his parents had left behind. With a view to staying on if it felt right. But it hadn't. And here was I, also returned. I, too, had found I didn't want the Promised Land. Nor was I wanted here. Further, I had no money, no job, and no prospects. **I had failed** - all along the line. And instead of thanking my lucky stars, I burst into tears.

But as ever, I soon bounced back. It wasn't a question of success or failure - they were irrelevancies - you just had to soldier on, trying to make something out of whatever you had. I let it be known that I intended to write an account of my travels, I had kept a notebook going; and to the astonishment of us both my father offered a short-term bread and cheese allowance.

Nineteen thirty-nine lurched forward. Not that I was taking any particular notice; it was beneath my now splendidly-occupied undivided attention. But on the horizon, more and more plainly, fate was being spelt out. A time was coming - already hung over us - when no-one would be short of a job. The market was about to be deluged with a choice of mind-blowing opportunities and careers. A time was near when whole countries - much of Europe - would be in turmoil, physically and socially shaken out and scattered.

As for being re-born - I'd been running away from it. Here it all was with the labour, for me, for all of us, just about to begin.

III

THERE'S A WAR ON
1939-1945

15

A Question of Values

A Week in the W.A.A.F.s

The day after war was declared the facade of the Finchley Road swimming baths was reinforced with sand bags and guarded by a middle-aged character in a tin hat and boiler suit. A shelter, I presumed.

'No, Madam, this is a mortuary.'

For some time I'd been aware of the opinions of a number of more than usually percipient people. But the reasoning and forecasting had gone on too long: instead of bringing it nearer the war had appeared to recede. It had been in turn, shattering, thrilling, significant, boring, profoundly boring and finally not credited. In this day and age, among civilised people, it could never happen. So what **had** happened? Was everyone - were we all, mad? And when you came to look into it, there didn't seem much difference now between the sane and insane, except that the certified were safely locked up leaving the rest of us at the mercy of the manifestly much more dangerous people, allegedly in their right minds.

At twenty-nine, I was still, politically-speaking, unawakened. Yet at the same time, looking back, I seem to have been all my life a natural inhabitant of the territory between two opposing forces. Shifting territory, yes, but never right, always left of centre. Certainly, much younger and living in the country, I'd been dogmatic enough. When a canvassing personage visited us, she found me at the gate. I hung well over, blocking entry. *'She always votes Conservative, so you needn't bother.'* the woman was informed in tones of undisguised scorn. Politics was also Mr. Baldwin, who, on his own admission, would rather have been a pig farmer. How **feeble** of him then, to become Prime Minister!

I became strongly attached - you could almost say emotionally involved - with the Liberal *News Chronicle*. I feel sure this paper must have come into our lives along with the big ginger doctor, who used to come down to Plum Tree Cottage for away-from-it-all weekends. One Friday evening he turned up with a paper parcel full of sprats, which he tenderly and proudly laid out on our kitchen table. It was his idea that my aunt should cook us all a splendid supper. Unfortunately, most emphatically, it was not hers. What kind of a doctor he was I never discovered. He appeared to have some sort of fringe government appointment. I thought him the kindest, nicest and wisest man I had ever met. My aunt probably thought she'd had one doctor too many in her life already. Prising her loose from the *Mail* took a bit of doing. But the *Chronicle* was lively and popular too. Not popular enough, though, to withstand the giants. For me, when the paper finished, it came as a real bereavement.

Later, as a student in London, I held the view that I need not bother with politics because I knew nothing about it. I wouldn't expect a politician to tell me how to do my sort of work, it followed that I didn't expect to have to tell him how to do his. I knew myself to be left, I didn't see how any fair-minded person could possibly be anything else. It was as simple as that. True, there'd been the occasion when, at their suggestion, I'd gone with a group of fellow students to a left-wing gathering at the Albert Hall. No doubt I was considered promising material. But not only the time was wrong. While I was only too ready to give a joyous welcome to a social revolution, more than anything else I was an outsider - even in this. The instinct was to reject shepherding into whatever fold. I failed to identify and was repelled by the heated emotional climate.

Now, abruptly, these views were wiped out. I saw that politics was a matter over which a person might with justification become heated. I was up in arms for all the other simple people who woke up to find a waiting mortuary on their doorstep. I began to read more than the book reviews in the *New Statesman*, and to reflect on the strong left bias of many of the younger poets and writers. And not only the young, from the fighting front Hemingway had just reported the Spanish Civil War.

Out of a compelling sense of immediacy, this was a time of reportage - a time when events stood up and spoke out for themselves. Shocked into awareness, for me it was as if the environment had suddenly sprouted signposts all pointing in one direction. It was also something that supplied a need, a call to arms with justice as the banner. The unfairness of the system with its poor values was strongly felt. How could anyone not feel ashamed of a state of affairs in which those with the most got more instead of those with next to nothing and no means of helping themselves? It reached inside as religion had never done. Religion was fine and poetic, but on the down-to-earth level it pointed to a way of life that nobody bothered to lead. In any case the freeing of the people from an established hierarchy marking time on their backs was surely a Christian working aim?! It was also something that had to be done, could be done and seen to be done. And so it came about that a mixture of war and the left, shot through with more than a dash of Communism - or rather what I thought this was or ought to be - found a perfect fit in the vacant God-slot, neatly transforming catastrophe into crusade. In a state of some exaltation, once more I saw myself running with the tide, this time supported by purpose and surrounded by opportunity.

It was simply a matter of choice. For me, between the Land Army and the Air Force. The first had the most appeal: I saw a romantic picture of myself 'far from the madding crowd', and after all not much more than a year before I'd been planning to live in a tumble-down crofter's cottage out on the Hebrides. There was this urge, and now here was this opening. On the other hand the Air Force sounded dramatic and exciting, could only be picked up at such a time, and it seemed they needed women who could draw. So the Air Force won, as it was bound to do.

I was directed to an R.A.F. station north of London. Here, after a fashion, enrolment was proceeding for cooks, typists, and motor transport drivers, but nobody seemed to know what to do with artists, not even what to call us. First it was map-drawers, then plotters, closely followed by *'No, no, that's hush-hush, it's special-duty clerks.'* Did it really go on like this day after day? That's how I remember it. A young woman who acted as a sort of shepherd to intending recruits, came over to a group of us growing more and more embarrassingly familiar. *'You stand up and salute all officers and call them ma'am, and then we have parade and drill, and of course there's the uniform, and it really is* ***rather*** *fun!'*, she cried encouragingly.

At last the day dawned when even we were sorted out, accepted, and targeted for special training at an unknown destination. We were then told to hold ourselves in readiness for summons at any time and dismissed. Four weeks later our destination proved to be a grange somewhere in Middle England. Here a new set of officers took over. We were told that our job was not hush-hush - we could tell all our friends we were plotters, that we'd be staying not ten days (as we'd been told), but three weeks, and for this first one would be given the basics of a general training - 'made into good Waafs'.

Accommodation at *The Grange* wasn't fancy. We slept on three piece pallets called biscuits, and sausage-shaped pillows that creaked. There wasn't a looking-glass in the place. Clothes and belongings were stowed in airmen's wooden boxes, one at the end of each bed, painted grey, they were invisible in the gas-lit gloom that was all we were allowed after dark and guaranteed bloodied shins for all who failed to remember.

We were marched around the countryside like young Prussians, and when out of rhythm negotiating narrow stony lanes with untrimmed hedges, were loudly abused by the Senior Section Leader and commanded to sing *'Hang out the Washing on the Siegfried Line'* to keep in step. The clockwork performance of this same S.S. Leader was such that I was obliged to look quickly away, only just able to control with silent shakes, strong surges of hysterical laughter. On the other hand, my own performance wasn't funny - I felt totally idiotic. Looking covertly round, I could see no-one else in a similar predicament; at any rate on the surface all appeared deadly serious - to a woman, concentrating hard within to get it right while staring ahead with unseeing eyes. When it rained, we were issued tent-like capes. There was only one size. Mine swept to the ground, trailing lengths of tape that tripped me up. At least it lightened proceedings.

Even worse than marching was drill. Agile and good at games, in the gym, at school I flew over horses, hung happily upside down on bars, and whizzed up and down ropes; but when it came to floor exercises it was a different story. Being grounded was boring, but also I could never get it right. It was at once apparent that, unlike everyone else, unless I had time to think about it, I hadn't the faintest idea which side of me was which - I exhibited real talent for left right about turns. Games staff had learnt to live with it, but the armed forces weren't like that. Why wasn't there any running? If only someone had suddenly yelled *'At the double!'* I could have got into that someone's good books.

Discipline and unquestioning obedience were first principles in the forces. Orders issued from On High; our immediate superiors often seemed like transmitters, vehicles of The Voice or The Memo. It led to interesting situations. *'You can't be late in the forces - it doesn't exist!'* I was told on the occasion of an overdue appearance. Lectures were like this, too. You were allowed to wear a pin under your tie in the Army, but never in the Air Force, we were informed in a talk on etiquette. That same afternoon another officer, explaining rations, swore that white bread was superior to brown and fruit unnecessary, while we gazed, transfixed, at the pin under her tie.

The tossing together, shoulder to shoulder, of assortments of people from all walks of life who would never ordinarily have met, provides what has to be the most rewarding and warming of service-life experience in time of war. Even in our somewhat specialised catchment, it created a wider, more stimulating world. There were eight of us in the dormitory I was in - a Cambridge girl, a schoolteacher, an art student, two Harrods' shop assistants, an eighteen-year-old fresh from finishing school and a hearty collar-and-type who held a pilot's licence. The schoolteacher was our room leader. She'd been a Waaf longer than we had. Instead of passively waiting out the interval that followed after our acceptance, she'd rung up and pointed out that she'd given up her job. *'You mean your parents can't keep you?'*, had been the Company Assistant's gracious rejoinder. All the same something had been done. The schoolteacher had been working and drilling and collecting pay.

The flyer, one of the shop assistants and I discovered similar senses of humour, and found swapping anecdotes of the day in bed after lights out greatly releasing. We tried to keep our merriment quiet as we were not supposed to talk, and our room was next to that of the Company Assistant who ran the hostel. The schoolteacher had a cold and when we got badly out of control would start up a fit of coughing to cover up. So much force was she obliged to bring to this one night that it brought in the Company Assistant, wrapped in her dressing-gown, carrying a spoonful of liquid and some tablets. The liquid was **nauseating**, the schoolteacher informed us severely, and certainly something quickly put her to sleep, breathing like a bellows. It was back to jolly hockey sticks at the Girls' Grammar School - those not so far off jubilant days that ended in disaster.

On the last day of the week we were required to write a paper, answering ten questions. They were routine enough, but the first was 'What does service in the Waafs mean to you?' And when I saw this, I left a space, scribbling hastily through the others, and then got down to it. Here was the chance I'd been waiting for - to work off what was so urgently on my mind.

During those weeks of waiting, an event of importance had occurred. I'd listened to a radio talk, *'The Spirit and Aim of Britain'*, given by the Archbishop of York, William Temple, in which a churchman came down to earth, and instead of the usual inept pronouncements - here at last was Christianity intelligently applied to the real world. The talk was also printed in *The Listener*, so I was able to check it out and read it again and again.

> "...Our first step then, towards making a just settlement, must be a frank recognition of much wrong and failure on our side in the past...
>
> "Let us determine and declare that when the fighting stops, the terms of peace shall be drawn up in a true congress of nations, in which Germany, freed from the Nazi tyrants, shall take her place among the rest, but in which also the rights of the Czechs and Poles shall have first claim to consideration. If there are matters on which no agreement can be reached, let these be referred to a Court of Equity formed from neutral nations which are neither beneficiaries nor sufferers by the Peace of Versailles.
>
> "Nothing, surely, could so clearly establish the disinterestedness of our aims as such a declaration. Nothing, surely, could give the peoples of Czecho-Slovakia and Germany, so clear an assurance that they will receive justice so far as the tangle of facts bequeathed to us by history permits it and the wisdom of man can secure it. This frees us from the dreadful responsibility, and indeed the indefensible arrogance, of ourselves attempting to decide what is just and imposing it on others.
>
> "Before this congress of Europe should be brought all outstanding grievances and problems containing the seeds of future wars...and we must ourselves be ready for sacrifices provided the interests of minorities and subject peoples are safeguarded...
>
> "Many of us hope that the congress will pave the way for the Federal Union of Europe in which we see the only hope of a permanent settlement..."

The war all but dissolved as I saw from out of it spring a greater hope than ever before; something clean and fair and lasting. Here was a world turning-point where we could lead the way by becoming the instigators of a new world order: co-operation instead of competition; justice and equality instead of selfish national policies; away with dusty sovereignty, acquired property and complacent gold bars in the National Bank. We'd have to win the war first, I supposed. Would we win? Ridiculous question. You might just as well ask us to imagine ourselves dead as beaten. I was certain I was on the right track. I saw myself as formulating public opinion, and rejoiced. I tooth-combed newspapers and listened to other radio talks in an effort to find further identification, and because I worked so assiduously I found - or thought I found - firm, healthy shoots thrusting up in every direction.

And so it all flushed forth in answer to question one. I was aware - I continued on my way in triumph - that all this might not come about in my own lifetime. As I was really quite sure that it would, this was the one false note, prompted not so much by a scraping of caution, as floated forward in an attempt to reach less robust persons who might not yet feel strong enough to support so much so soon. It was something that I could supply even so tenuous a link with the existing state of affairs.

With an hour to go and ten questions to answer there was no time to read through what I'd written. But I was left with a feeling of intense well-being. That anyone could disagree with this blue-skied world of the future - this new, shining Europe - never for a fleeting moment crossed my mind.

The next day we were called into the officers' room, one by one. There was a sudden rush of nervousness and apprehension. Everyone was sure they'd failed or at least been responsible for some fearful, irremediable gaffe or other. Everyone except me. I was the last to go in. Inside was the Company Assistant in charge of us and a well-made Deputy Company Commander with red hair. They asked my aged and looked unbelieving, but I was used to this. They then asked about my previous occupation. Why had I left the B.B.C? And when I said to go abroad, they pounced. I see now that my answer must have been a great disappointment to them. There followed a sorting about to find my paper, which wasn't in the regular pile.

'I have to say that we found your answer to question one ***extraordinary***'. The Deputy Company Commander was speaking. It was the unmistakable character of the emphasis that created the air pocket that brought me plummeting to earth. And from the discussion that followed it became obvious that the two had never heard of Federal Union, but, going on my uninhibited elaboration of desired effects, took it to be a cover name for Communism.

'If you portioned out the world's wealth, each person would receive one and elevenpence', pointed out the Company Assistant. *'Which would keep a native for six weeks.'*, put in the Company Commander. *'Two to three months in many cases.'*, added the Company Assistant. I was at a loss. Hoary as the argument was, it was the first time I had heard it, and I could see no connection. I was then accused of planning to use the war as a convenient arena in which to plant highly seditious and inflammatory ideas. But when I said that if the principles of Federal Union could be

taken up and implemented at once, then peace might be possible straight away, one of them openly sneered. At this point I became excited and said I thought the Archbishop's broadcast infinitely more inspiring than Mr. Churchill's disgusting lip-smacking over sunk submarines. I went on to point out that the Archbishop himself had referred to Federal Union. To this, the Deputy Company Commander blandly stated that she knew the Archbishop personally.

I was called pro-German and a heretic, and then informed that the King cost less than the President of the United States. Money again. It had no place in my thinking - it seemed to me to block the view in theirs. *'You say we were too hard on the Germans after the last war,'*, went on the Deputy Company Commander, *'when the truth is we should never have stopped when we did. We should have gone right on to Berlin and completely smashed the country; then -* ***then*** *- nothing of this would have happened. That's what we* ***should*** *have done, but we didn't, we were too kind.'*

It was useless; every time I opened my mouth it made matters worse. As they saw it there was only one way out. Resignation. I considered this absurd, and said so. Difficult moments followed. Court marshal received passing mention. The dinner gong sounded. Orderlies pummelled at the door. The two consulted wrist-watches and exchanged tight-lipped looks.

Of course, it could rightly be said that not one of us really knew what we were talking about; but this is not a particularly unusual phenomenon, and we'd absorbed enough of the drift to know where we stood - under the banner of the establishment, they, and the less-fortunately placed, me. And however inept my answer, to them it was written testimony. They were only doing what they saw to be right. The situation was clearly of my own making. I felt a measure of serious unease. Out of school, and now out of the Waafs. You would have thought that by this time I'd have been able to rustle up a few grains of common sense, or at least find it in me to put a damper on the urge to come charging in, piping the good news in the worst possible place. I was thirty now. Would I **never** learn? In my teens I'd been something of a clown, it was a role I'd enjoyed playing. To wake up to myself as an innocent and a fool was not an encouraging progression. This laugh would be a long time coming. Meanwhile, I had no stomach for direct confrontation. Best bow out leaving as little unpleasant ness as possible.

The wording was theirs: *'I resign from the Women's Auxiliary Air Force after discussion with my superior officers because I find that my vision of the future is not in accordance with service in His Majesty's Forces.'*

16

High Hampstead

Dunkirk wasn't only amazing on the water. It was amazing on the streets, too. It created a feeling of oneness with others and the earth we stood on - when eye caught eye and pavement conversation with strangers. A never-to-be-forgotten time when being English and living on an island became suddenly sharp and real.

Once more shocked into action, I applied to the Ministry of Agriculture. But while I was genuinely drawn in this direction, my former mishap had been wounding and still hurt. One morning, shopping in the West End, I found myself in front of an R.A.F./W.A.A.F. Recruiting Office; the publicity in the window brought it all back and set me wondering. There was a different government now. *'In the **name** of God - go!'* You could hardly have it plainer than that. On impulse I went in. The officer inside was charming and understanding, even hopeful. A form was filled in. I hadn't expected to get as far as re-application. Outside, suddenly excited, I finished Regent Street at the double. Then a curious thing happened. As the picture of myself once more becoming a Waaf filled in and firmed up, so I was brought to see that it wasn't at all what I wanted. **What had I done?** The R.A.F. already had my particulars. Suppose they caught up with me before I heard from the Land Army? I took off again. This time in a bus, I couldn't get home quickly enough to see if that vital letter was waiting for me. In fact, I still had some weeks to go. But by the time I heard from the Air Ministry - inevitably turning me down - it had become a matter of no consequence. Balance had been restored.

My aunt was now over seventy, she was getting on, but she still relished a move and was looking about as eagerly as ever, and at this time for those prepared to remain in the capital, there were unprecedented opportunities. After the exodus at the outbreak of war, as time went on and nothing much occurred, many returned; but now, following Dunkirk - less frantic, more serious - it started all over again. And so it came about that she found a unique flat at a ridiculous rent up in the old part of Hampstead, almost on the heath. The flat, on the top floor, faced away from the heath but its view was sensational. Below us, Hampstead fell away to reveal the whole of London clear to the Surrey hills, every well-known building of any prominence could be picked out. At first such height and distance was unnerving in its total exposure - like being lashed to the mast. But this soon wore off and I grew to love it very much, even to drawing from it a kind of sustenance which was especially strong at night in the blackout when mysterious depths were revealed. Yet it was a sturdy, rather than a tall, house. Under a pillared portico a flight of steps ran up to the front door, while a modest, narrow flight descended to the basement which, at the back, was level with the garden. It was this falling away of the ground under us, carried on by the long sloping garden that gave the effect of dizzying height. Halfway to heaven, I called it. My aunt appeared not to notice. It was our position on the ground that delighted her.

This was a dreamed-about area, favoured by artists and writers past and present. For my aunt, property here was within a price-bracket entirely beyond her means. But not now. Keates Grove: did he write the *Ode to a Nightingale* under the mulberry tree in the front garden? Well he might have done. Church Row, with Constable in St. John's churchyard. He had painted on the heath and so would she. George Rowney had dallied in Hollybush Hill. She was in her element.

And the war didn't only throw up barrage balloons and the promise of bombs - it threw up very different phenomena as well. A culture boom. Free lunch-time piano recitals by Myra Hess in the West End, while along the Embankment art took to the pavement. And Hampstead promptly followed suit with weekend art exhibitions along the edge of the heath. Aunt was quick to join in. I doubt she picked up a commission, but she was a painter, showing her work, maintaining the importance of the artist, and sitting there on a folding stool beside a selection of her work, in the faded old straw sketching hat I'd known all my life. She looked as happy and fulfilled as I'd ever known her. Not only did she have the open country on her doorstep, she now had a gallery also.

Nor was this all. For inside, the house was as fascinating as its position and outlook. It belonged to an artist, who before the war had lived in the first-floor studio and garden maisonette. She was now permanently settled in the West Country, leaving the business of the house to her good friend, Miss Tytherington, an invalid of indeterminate age who occupied the floor above and carried out her duties most punctiliously from her bed. Besides being an invalid, Miss Tytherington was rather strange. When erect (rising time only) she presented a rivetting sight. She was very tall: her night garments swept the landing as she moved, slowly and carefully, from door to door. Almost bald, she wore a white veil, loosely swathed like a turban. The filmy whiteness accentuated deep-set shadowy eyes, and as at these times she was without teeth, the effect was of a refined skull in a cheesecloth halo. But these sightings were rare. We got up too late. By the time I came bouncing down to the bathroom (there were only two in the building), she was usually once more safely battened down in her bedroom, flanked as ever, provisions cabinet on one side, commode on the other.

She had no casual visitors. There was an elderly woman, at one time the family nanny, who came every day with the shopping and did what she could. From her we learned of two other sisters who had long since given this one up. According to them there was nothing wrong. And this was rather borne out by the old nanny's persistent cry from the heart, '*Oh, Miss Josephine, if only you would let me get you up!*' There was also a male factotum called Percy, who turned up once a week, or when required, to do anything heavy or odd jobs about the house. Apart from these her only visitor was a spiritual healer who also appeared at regular intervals and remained closeted for long, silent sessions.

She was said to be suffering from angina, and one would have thought that she must have been suffering from something. She had never been known to go out. Everything came to her. I can still hear her soft languid voice saying, '*Put it under the door.*' (usually a rent book.) I heard it so often that, looking back, she seems to have said little else. This under-the-dooring occurred when she was in but not 'at home'. At other times - though, of course there - she was neither 'in' nor 'at' home, and on those occasions the rent book and envelope containing money or it might be a message, was propped up against the bedroom door. This could be the situation at any time during the afternoon or evening, and meant she had retired for the night, when a wet bath sheet was hung over the fireplace (a precaution against gas), and cotton wool stuffed around the window frame, under the door and finally into her ears. She was a Whiteleys shareholder and received every week a large case of provisions, including, it was said, items frequently unobtainable in the shops at that time. She had once been discovered sitting on the stairs in a striking state of exhilaration. Assistance had ben waived away but not before a certain aroma had been detected. It was evident that she was drawn to more than one kind of spirit.

For all this, when you did attain an interview she was pleasing to meet. In the deep shadows the light grey eyes were kind, her opinions were generous and she was always helpful, '*Percy will do it.*' was another recurring refrain. And in business matters she was invariably competent and prompt. My aunt, herself sympathetic to unseen powers, got on with her well. Over their long acquaintance - through the war and way on after it - there was never the least trouble between them.

It was the first time my aunt had taken a top flat - inevitably the rooms were smaller than she was used to. But the light was good, and a door on the landing opened on to a narrow flight of stairs leading up to a large roof-room where trunks and clutter could be stored. A jittery typist occupied the rooms facing the front. But she was out all day, away most weekends, and often slept downstairs in a room in the empty basement prepared by Percy to the specification of the considerate Tyth. The girl was also already casting around for accommodation of out town.

It is incredible to me now that no-one every complained of my highly brio performance on the stairs. For as far as I was concerned, on a par with the view, the finest amenity of this Hampstead house lay in its splendid flights of stairs, wide, shallow, grcefully curing. Negotiating them was like dancing a cadenza - a beautiful, thrilling, sheer experience. I fancied I could make the descent in fifteen seconds, including bounding across the Tyth's landing and leaping from the turn of the lower flight to a thumped chord in the hall. There was then a syncopated effect for the door which crashed as I leaped the front steps to the final dominant on two feet at ground level. Sometimes as I dashed down Heath Street, dodging between the people, it occurred to me to wonder how old I would be before this delight in running abated. I was unable to believe that it ever would.

Meanwhile, where was the war? Then, just as we were beginning to settle into what looked like becoming another protracted interlude - it began to happen. Apart from being inaugural, this raid was nothing to speak of, but, being that, it had its effect. I woke to the throb of twin-engined aircraft and dull thuds. Two explosions rattled the windows. Gunfire followed. My bed was along by the window, I felt profoundly exposed - clear to the Surrey hills! I heard the nervous typist go downstairs. The sirens went and my aunt woke up. She got out of bed as I thought to prepare to go down to the basement. I was just about to follow gladly when she picked up the clock and took it to the window, *'Half-past three!'* She then got back in bed and snuggled down with a sigh of relief. Meanwhile, my particular pre-occupation was with my knocking knees - under the bedclothes it was true - but all the same clearly visible in the bright moonlight that flooded the room, curtains and blackout pulled back and window wide open. Unlimited fresh air was rule number one in my aunt's canon. Previous to this I'd thought knocking knees an invented music hall joke. I now found it only too real. Frantic silent commands had no effect, manual depression was contortionist, only marginally successful and anyway impossible to keep up. Fortunately, my aunt hadn't noticed and was by now snoring regularly, while I, shocked and embarrassed, had to wait still deplorably active, for the 'all clear'.

Almost at once I got my new marching orders. Five weeks at a School of Agriculture on the South Downs, within ten miles of the coast.

17

On the Land and in the Air

The college was on the edge of the South Downs, sharply rolling banks of fine green grass intersected by dusty white chalk roads. We were a mile out of the village but not isolated. Next door a large country house covered with creeper and surrounded by trees was full of Royal Engineers.

It was the end of August but still high summer, in fact it was Mediterranean, clear blue skies and a burning sun day after day turning us all shades of puce and brown. My arms were so sensitive that, turning over in bed, brushing them across the sheets was acutely painful. So much fresh air and exercise had other effects. We couldn't stop eating, we ate so much, it had us all laughing, we couldn't believe it.

Mealtimes, I sat next to a slim, engagingly fey nineteen-year-old city typist who came down to breakfast with the air of one alighting on a twig. We called her Tinkerbell. Opposite was Croydon, from the near aerodrome - not a healthy place to be at any time - she couldn't sit still and never stopped talking. No-one believed she was twenty-one. There's a husband in a searchlight unit, but we heard more about the dog. Any gap in the conversation was sure to be plugged with Croydon's dog. It could get a bit much. Till one morning when well-established and unstoppable as usual - it was five days now since she'd seen him - *'Do you suppose he's forgotten you yet?'* cut in young Tink brightly, finishing off the appalling whole with a merry peal of laughter. Then there's the girl I travelled down with and slept next door to. One of the few middle-class girls here. She looked a bit like a well-known film star and, true to type, menfriends, drinks and parties were all she talked about. The land seemed an odd choice. She was Lady Muck, the Marchioness, from day one.

The table behind us was noisy. The star turn, a sixteen-year-old toughie with two years' slog in a soap factory behind her, was making the most of being at large. She'd like to have been a boy and gone to sea. She and her pal made the best of a bad job, bumming rides to the coast and getting off with the navy: hanging around in the land for the chance engineer was not for them. The pal was a well-made seventeen years, one of those who breakfasted in curlers and only wore shoes to go out in. At first I'd thought the aspiring young tar a bit of a ruffian, but a morning digging in the cucumber house with the two of them quickly won me over, and now I, too, am a pal. They were staggered and awe-struck on learning my age, and now from the table behind it's the old girl says this, and the old girl says that, and they had better not disagree! Whatever had I been talking about? I seemed to have gained a disciple! The pal slept in the room on the other side of mine and now, when I take down the blackout and hang out my socks to sweeten, the chances are strong they'll be met with loud sniffs and suitably comic remarks addressed to the moonlit downs.

Some of the girls were 'regulars', trained at the college and then kept on as assistants. A good idea: we found them helpful, though they were strangely glum and set. I made friends with one of them - not less tired than the others, but at least awake enough to be aware that something was wrong. She was for ever making plans to escape. Carrying them out though - that was a different matter. *'But isn't it interesting'*, I asked, *'All these different people every five weeks?'* She replied, *'But they aren't different - they're all the same. We know it by heart. There'll be rough ones and refined ones - sometimes even county ones. Young ones and old ones. There'll be one duchess, one night-club queen and a nervous wreck. And the rest you only notice that they've gone.'*

Were they winded by our fits of excitement? Did our collective exuberance wear them down? Chock full of the joys of spring and midsummer combined we certainly were. It was five weeks of starry-eyed efflorescence for us, with, at the end, a prospect of further adventures. You had only to witness the bounce and sparkle of youngsters freed from imprisonment in some boring or senseless job; freed moreover, not into the madness of war, but into a real, life-giving, wholesome occupation. It had taken a state of hostility to close down firms dedicated to the production of wooden pips for other factories said to be making jam.

I began with General Farming. This was what I would have liked - how I had seen myself. I held a romantic view of the calling as aristocratic and spacious - a way of life. When I'd first applied for work on the land, at the interview I'd been curious about the Timber Corps. It was brushed aside. I was too small. I hadn't the **build**. I now experienced in General Farming something of what had been meant. I didn't think I'd be able to make a decent job of it. But even the lectures were off-putting. Discourses on the diseases of cattle made worse by lantern slides. We took down long tables of animal seasons, periods of gestation and so on which were only so many long words to us and calculated to inflict nightmares on the imaginative.

I took my turn on the tractor. Understandably not the farm's best machine, this one used for haulage called Pneumonia because it coughed so much. It also invariably expired in the middle of the narrowest country lanes, holding up Royal Engineers in all directions. But you had to admire its driver, a distinctly irregular Regular - a young woman whose over-the-top enthusiasm matched ours. She really loved that obstinate machine - to the point of extracting a sensual satisfaction from the sore throat brought on by its many sweats and exhalations (or so she thought), and she was inordinately proud of her oily dungarees, by far the filthiest in the college. But I wasn't made of such stern stuff. A couple of days with Pneumonia quite put me off. It doesn't matter if you can't drive, it's whether you have a mechanical sense or not, the Principal had said. I decided I had none whatever.

Next came milking and work in the dairy. But even before I was there I was sure I was in the wrong place. It could mean getting up before dawn...and then there was Tink who'd been down in the cowsheds while I was on the tractor. She had come in to breakfast after early-morning milking, in a fearful state, *'I hate cows, I loathe cows, I never want to see a cow again!'* We were given the beasts that were drying off to begin on. I carefully chose a nice-looking, large-eyed Jersey. I chose her because she was small, but also because we had to wash and comb them first and she was the cleanest. But when I attempted to get down to business she wasn't interested. After one or two surprise jets that misfired on to the floor or into my lap, the sulky beast recalled herself (or so I thought) and not a drop more would she yield. After a period of abject struggle, a regular took my place and did no better. I was then given a more productive brown beast with long white silky hair curling over its bag, which surprised me as I'd always thought that cows were bald in this area. But I still wasn't happy. For a small person it was a large animal and would lean on me. This being so, it was as well that I was held in position by the bulging contour of the beast in the stall behind. The two swayed and heaved, carrying me helplessly sandwiched between them, and I nearly panicked when one abruptly exploded, vibrating from stem to stern - it had coughed. I was even more nervous of the animal to the rear than I was of my own; it was being trifled with by a novice, too, but vented all its spite on me. At regular intervals I was sloshed by its wet, stroppy tail. There was only one interruption, when it (the tail) suddenly flew out horizontal, stiff as a rod...I didn't feel at my best, and prayed that the Principal wouldn't come round on a tour of inspection. She was a dairy expert, a near, bright, Scotswoman, said to be devoted to the herd. Anyone approaching the sheds with pointed fingernails was promptly returned to base, *'Don't you dare come near my cows with hands like that!'* The nice man in charge tried to be encouraging. One of their best milkers had begun by getting hysterics, *'She fell on the ground with spasms and screams. They wheeled her away on a fruit trolley.'* I failed to find this persuasive. The hours were daunting and there was Sunday work.

Tink said she wanted to do horticulture, and I was beginning to think that this would be best for me, too. Certainly the stodgy college diet was enough to drive anyone with a respect for what went inside straight through the gates of the market garden. Muck - sensible girl, horticulture from the start, would smuggle me out the odd apple or tomato whenever she could.

Once more I spoke to the Principal. It was a long, sad story. I hadn't been happy general farming, I hadn't been happy on the tractor, and I certainly wasn't happy in the cowsheds. *'How do you know you'll be happy in horticulture?'* she very justifiably inquired. Nevertheless, after ten days chopping and changing, the matter was finally settled.

It was a come-down, a terrible come-down, I was in no two minds about that. The grandeur of the land was not for me! For as against farming, market gardening was seen as niggling and old-maidish. And the men were like that, too. The gardeners were two neat little men with pointed noses and bicycle clips round the ends of their trousers. They were nice - I liked them - but while they were painstakingly explaining what we were doing, I would be wistfully recalling the rough, rubicund farm hands and bid, dark-brown bailiff. Orders from them were delivered in broad dialect unhelped by the steady chewing of perennial grasses, while throughout everything oblivious of the pallors of green young girls fresh from home, they would swear calmly, conversationally and in a stream. Whereas the gardeners would ask if a piled up wheelbarrow was too heavy, without a flicker the bailiff would order you to pick up half a sack of linseed cake, and watch you stagger with a look of tired resignation. Only once had I seen the old bailiff unbend. Pneumonia's driver had been sweating at the cranking handle again. After viewing the uneven struggle unmoved for some time, he suddenly spat aside and proclaimed, *'Let be girl - you'll rick your bloody guts out!'* One yank from him and the recalcitrant machine was trembling all over and raring to go.

It was lovely country and it seemed no effort at the end of the day to go out again. The downs were so steep that much of the time it was hands and knees; then over the top into the full force of the wind, sweeping strongly in from the sea. Here, hastily thrown-up defences reminded us of the danger that lay in wait.

Although we were beginning to get used to it, the invasion scare was still very much in place, and most of us had seen ourselves as arriving at the front, when in fact, as it turned out, we had left it, for on September 7th 'Black Saturday' the Battle of Britain began in earnest - with a **blitzkrieg** focussed on London. This literally stunning idea which had worked well in other countries - a series of lightning knock-outs with a view to easy, sweeping invasion - was to continue for fifty-seven consecutive nights before petering out into sporadic raids on other centres of population, thereby highlighting the invasion of Britain as the great non-event and arguably first real victory of the war. Night after night we lay in bed while relays of double-beating twin-engined bombers drummed overhead on their way to blast the capital. It was as if the sky was blotted out by a blanket of pulsing machines, systematic, rhythmic, uninterrupted. They knew there were no guns between the coast and Surrey, and flew low; sometimes it sounded as if they were just above the buildings.

Newspaper headlines screamed. Even the B.B.C. sounded disturbed. The telephone service was hopeless: when by a miracle you did get through it was only to the operator who, with the familiar phrase, *'There's a raid on.'*, forthwith disconnected you again. Letters were delayed - especially those coming from London. The morning's mail became our lifeline. Following the first frenzied rush, came a period of charged silence, then one after another extracts would be read out or re-told.

'My brother-in-law, fetching a tray of food from the house to the shelter, had it struck out of his hands by a piece of shrapnel a foot long.' It's from my sister. *'We swore there was a time-bomb in the garden, but the warden said no. Ten minutes later it went off. The house seemed to rise in the air and then, miraculously settle - I swear that dust billowed out from under the carpets. When we looked out across the back gardens the houses opposite were no longer there.'*

At these times I was almost ashamed of my aunt in comparatively healthy Hampstead.

There seemed to be a raid on most of the time, even during the day. *'There's a raid on.'* became a normal piece of occasional conversation. The nearest siren was five miles away, we heard it or didn't according to the wind. Nothing happened (to us). But then nothing really happened to us at night either. Extra to the inevitable drumming, we'd be shaken up, lit up, treated to crashes - on one occasion the distinct, raw splintering of wood. Yet, come the morning, everything was intact.

One more than usually troubled night I remember waking up, hearing girls running up and down the corridor calling for their friends, and matron's soothing tones. I then heard Muck moving about and two sharp taps on the wall meaning - I'm all right, how about you? To which I responded in kind. On my own I'd have been terrified I'm sure, but the company of others in the same fix seemed to support. Though basically all the time we were becoming acclimatised - able to take on more and more. The gruesome discord of damaged aeroplanes floundering out of control was the most alarming, and as it came nearer so did a number of unappealing possibilities. I thought of getting under the bed but managed to remain put. Then one morning we did have a result - scattered bits of Jerry plane in the yard. The men and early-morning milkers scotched the lot.

To us it was as it seemed: we were on a flight path, subject only to accidentals. That the raid on September 7th had brought into effect codeword 'Cromwell' - **invasion imminent**, we had not known. But then those supposedly in the know hadn't either - in their case of the despotic German Chancellor's last-minute change of mind: operation 'Sealion' was being postponed - we were **not** being invaded. Instead, the bombing of London went on. But all this is history, and like the war in the air remained well over our heads. Only momentarily disturbed, we carried on, still happy and excited, becoming more than ever sunburnt in the continuing extraordinary weather.

One evening three of us hitched a ride to the local town and went to the pictures. It was dark when we came out and there was no traffic - something we hadn't anticipated. It was only five miles but seemed endless. We saw what we thought was a flickering flare till someone, surprised that we didn't know, explained that it was a scattered bunch of incendiaries, this lot burning out harmlessly in a field. There were flashes and yellow stars and sudden, sickening glows on the horizon, but this was our scene now and it was a piece of cake compared with what we'd been expecting and what was going on elsewhere. Nonetheless, girls from Eastbourne and Kent had to leave to evacuate with their families. Then the Bayswater house where the Marchioness had a room was blitzed rendering poor Muck without a seat. *'Thank goodness I brought my trunk! I must get a job on from here now - **I have to**...'*

By this time most of us were beginning to think about jobs and discussing the lack of them. It appeared that unless you were a milker you hadn't much chance. The agricultural wage had gone up for one thing. It was also by now the end of September, extra help was unlikely to be needed before the spring. In addition, gardeners were said to be hardest to place, with jobs so few and far between as to be almost non-existent. This point had been made clear to me by the Principal when I was changing over. Not that I was expecting a job straight away. In London they'd stressed the point - *'You go down for training on the clear understanding that there's no guarantee of any job to follow.'* Unlike the services, the land was an open market.

But nobody really knew, and contrary to expectation jobs came flowing in with gardeners as well off as the rest. Moreover, to avoid returning them to the blitz area, it was a case of London girls first. To begin with I couldn't quite credit this, till a Brighton girl of my acquaintance had her job taken away when that of a Londoner's fell through. Soon most of us were fixed up. The Marchioness was going into Gloucestershire to garden for a retired doctor, 'a dear old lady', who turned out to b no end of a character, destined to lead poor Muck a fearful dance. I was going into Gloucestershire, too, but south of the channel, near Bristol. Tink was down for a market garden in Leicestershire. Croydon - against all advice, holding out for a job in Surrey - was one of the few not fixed up, but it was thought that she'd be kept on.

So. Stunned? Softened? Brought to our knees?! From where I stood it looked as if the blitz had provided just the shake-up we were in need of.

18

Land Army Gardener

I read and re-read the description of my job. 'Help with the digging', that was good. 'Must be able to work on her own', something of a contradiction, that was a bit disquieting. From the Paddington bookstall I bought *Vegetable Gardening for Amateurs*, one-and-sixpence, and hoped hard for the best. A few hours later, another confusingly large station. The train began to move, gathered speed and disappeared. The crowd thinned. I stood aside awaiting identification. It began to get dark. I dragged my suitcase back and sat on a seat.

'Are you for Chapel Farm?...' A young girl with a tense white face and black Eton crop stood over me. *'At last! How was I supposed to know? Where's your hat? Where's your green jersey? Since when have they issued blue shirts in the Land Army?' I think I should tell you'*, she said to me in the taxi, *'That you are the second. It's hoped you'll at least stay the week - the first only lasted three days.'* I asked her what had been wrong. *'Who knows; it changed every time she opened her mouth. It was thought someone older... You look sixteen, no wonder I couldn't find you.'* I could have sworn that she'd only just entered the station.

'Are you the farmer's wife?' I asked.

'***What!*** *Not likely - he's an old man!'* She rummaged in her pocket. *'Have a cigarette...I'm the cook.'* she added. I ventured to suggest that I looked more of a land girl than she a cook.

The taxi turned down a lane and drew up by a group of buildings fronted by a green. A small but superior-looking stone house had been built on to a cottage flanked by a wide farm entrance. A toy-sized, tumbledown church under a group of trees completed the picture. I was taken into the cottage and left in the sitting-room, where a folding table had been set up and a place laid. *'We'll take you down to your billet later, there isn't time now.'* In due course a nice-looking girl in a smart uniform with frilly headband and apron brought two boiled eggs and some toast. She gave me a lingering look-over, *'I'm Hazel.'* and departed.

Everything was going on in the room on the other side of the entrance hall; the connecting doors had been left ajar; there were thumps, crashes, and a splendid smell of roasting. After an egg and some toast, I was drawn to investigate. An enormous kitchen table was covered with dishes, pans, jars, shop-sized brass scales, boxes and bags. Primitive-looking implements with long handles and vicious knives were strewn about. With her back to me, the cook, in a white coat and tall chef's cap, was waving her arms like some frenzied magician over an array of pots and kettles on a long iron range. She was making sudden, staccato dashes and darts as she dumped tools and poured from pans. While I watched, she suddenly seized an iron rod and pierced it between the bars of the fire with a fearful clangour. At the same time, the pretty girl in uniform entered from the opposite door. Seeing me, she shook her head violently while waving me back. I retreated as directed, and ate the other egg. There wasn't anything else.

When the excitement had finally died down, the cook came in to inform me that no-one entered her kitchen - '**my** kitchen' - without permission. Even the old man knew better than that. *'He sends a message through Hazel.'* The inference was that I had no idea how to behave in a decently regulated household. As to that I was in agreement. For certain I'd never before found myself in anything remotely resembling this situation. It was like suddenly finding yourself on the stage in the middle of a play you'd never heard of. There's a war on, crossed my mind, but it didn't seem safe to laugh.

The next day was Sunday. On this day I met the Land Army Area Representative, something of a lady of the manor. She'd been at the previous night's dinner party. I was taken round outside, finishing up with the enclosed vegetable garden out in the corner of a field. Quickly ascertaining my ignorance (further humiliation), she assured me that I'd soon get into it - an intelligent girl... *'Barrow will be along twice a week to begin with, of course, and Mr. Sadleir will get any book or tool. You've met the staff. The cook can be difficult sometimes - cooks often are - but the parlour maid is amenable, a nice girl, I think you'll find. There are other land girls... You have a bicycle?'* I still hadn't met my employer. It began to seem possible that the previous girl had never done so.

'For goodness sake stop calling him the farmer!' said the cook, *'He isn't; Henry and Rod do that. He's in business. Off every morning. Parcels of butter and boxes of eggs go with him. Prime joints and salmon come back. Oranges and bananas - no problem. We're short of nothing here. With the Saturday dinner it's Christmas every weekend. Killing while it lasts, don't I know it! But you have the rest of the week to recover.' 'There's the old man - **him**'*, she jerked her head in the direction of the pantry, *'and four unattached sisters live round about. An ignorant bunch. We've worked for better people than this. Real class. But the war broke everything up - we had to get out of London, and this is nearer home. I'm worried about my mother.'*

I was intrigued by them both, especially the cook. She had character, was her own woman, I thought. She could be funny in a dry way, though on occasion, curiously morose. They were both twenty-one, though the cook looked older and Hazel younger. As she never put herself forward it wasn't easy to get to know the parlour maid. In all senses she was behind the cook, deftly adapting to her friend's shifting temperament. But the two of us did meet first thing when she came into the dairy while I was working the cream separator. She made butter. It appeared that the cook didn't come down till mid-morning, so Hazel did the breakfasts, orders for the cook came through her anyway, and she had to get up to take in the old man's tea. In the dairy she was natural and friendly enough.

Outside, 'Must be able to work on her own.' was right. I was by myself, away from the house and farm. To begin with I'd been adrift and depressed, but determined to stay six weeks. Orientation took time. It was autumn now. The mornings were often spectacular, heads of animals rose eerily out of rolling ground mist; across the sky ran reaches of white-feathered cloud with bars of pink and gilded under-edges. Later, I drew comfort from the shaggy donkey and elderly race horses out to grass in the meadow beside my garden, where hours of peaceful munching were interrupted by remembrance of things past - or so I imagined - as they suddenly came to life, rolled and snorted, kicked up their heels and charged round under the hedges.

Bert Barrow's 'Help with the digging' amounted to nothing, what with his chest, stomach trouble, the state of the heavy clay soil and the weather. The old man doesn't want him when it rains, *'What are the likes of I to do when 'tis wet -* ***starve****, I suppose!'* The first time he came it was planting broad beans. He found a piece of broken ground and showed me how to press them in with my thumb. Fresh from swotting it up in the gardening manual, I was a bit surprised and rashly murmured something about a trench with manure in it. He slowly straightened himself up, whistled in through his teeth, and gave out, with the air of one imparting a lifetime's wealth of accumulated wisdom, *'Well, 'tis like this - see me dear - 'tis only making extra work for yourself!'* And he pinches the seed - though there's a certain charm about it, it's done in broad daylight with a total absence of embarrassment, gardener's prerogative it's called. And when I'm obliged to come out with, *'What shall I do, Mr. Barrow, there aren't enough to finish the row, only some bits and ones with holes in them?'* I could see the edge of the packet in his pocket. All I got was *'They be all right, me girl, they be fine - thee plant 'un.'* So saying, he sat down on an upturned crate and extracted a Woodbine.

'Billet, modern cottage' turned out to be a neat brick cube, handy for the farm, being less than a hundred yards further down the lane. Modern compared with the ruin opposite - a genuine un-updated seventeenth-century peasant dwelling by the look of it. Modern, too, compared with the well-kept farm cottage; and the people, Ted and Dotty Trimmings, were a nice, youngish couple with a little one, and seemed sensible enough. But in the mornings I had to wash downstairs in the kitchen sink and they were surprised at my needing warm water. Bath? *'Yes, but we only light the copper once a week.'* Outside sanitation. But that was the least of it. It was their lifestyle that really defeated me. Evening conversation round the kitchen range, backed up by competition from the radio, all but drove me out of my mind. And the child screamed and charged about as healthy little ones will. I was rendered insensible - unable even to think. I couldn't retire to my room because the electric light was too expensive and anyway there was no blackout. The only peace, the one saving grace, came when they went to bed - fully-clothed - down in the Anderson shelter the good man had fixed up at the bottom of the garden. Dotty Trimming was highly strung and terrified of raids. Raids?! Where? As far as I could see the enemy hadn't yet discovered the West Country. But at last alone, really alone, I could stretch and breathe freely again - enough to become aware of who I was before falling asleep.

Mealtimes were awkward, too. My every move was keenly watched and they tried so hard to get it right: I had too many tools and platters. It was a situation that found both sides surprised - almost unbelieving - each of the other's lifestyle. Coming from a town they felt entitled to see themselves as a cut above the natives in this rural place. Certainly they were decent, nice people, but it just wasn't possible. We talked and agreed together that I'd better be looking round for somewhere else. And then it was the old, old story - that as I'd obviously had more than a state education, they were sure it was because I thought they weren't good enough.

So what were their thoughts, I wondered, as I slide effortlessly down to find space and succour with the Barrows? The Barrow bungalow was also modern, but included a respectable bathroom with warm water. I was given a nice room with a comfortable bed, blackout curtains and an electric fire for the evenings when I wanted to read.

Bella Barrow, older than old Bert who wasn't really all that old, was the worker. She never stopped. Their long garden had been turned into a smallholding, and the evenings were filled with feathers and fluff as hens were plucked and drawn, sinews snapped out of legs, claws cracked off like pistol shots and the table covered with trussed-up birds and bowls of innards. Poultry was difficult to come by at this time, so at the Barrows things were looking up. They had a small van and hawked around the area. Though this was usually Bella, Bert, like as not, would be sitting over the fire sipping hot peppermint for his indigestion. At all times of the day and in all weathers, out of the back door charged Mrs. B. to collect the eggs, feed the hens or finish off that big of digging old Bert couldn't seem to get round to. For this she invariably jammed on her head a knitted cap like a jumble-sale tea cosy, *'Dressed up scandalous!'* she'd announce brightly as she hurried out.

''Bye for now.' I'd call as I left in the morning, and *'Have a nice time'* usually caught me up halfway to the garden gate. The Barrow bungalow being right in the

village, I had to run the gauntlet of the main street. *'Land gir-rl!* ***Left****, right;* ***left****, right!'* yelled the delighted children, as I clanked up the road in my studded shoes. And should I so much as half turn round, *'Look at* ***she****, looking at* ***we!'***

There were no Barrow dogs, only cats - two lean, agile tortoiseshells. They climbed coats hanging on doors and walked the backs of wooden chairs. They'd shoot up Bert and take off on to the top of the tall store cupboard, their favourite nesting place. *'They do bide on 'ee'*. When they got too much in the way of Bella's feet at dishing-up time, she'd mutter something about dafty cats marching up and down and quiet them off with a dish of bread and water. They had to rely on hunting and old Bert for their protein. They wormed round his neck at meal times, rubbing his head and licking his ears purring like lions, and were fed titbits. They were called Big-Hearted Arthur and Stinker after the popular radio characters. Both were female.

I wasn't the only extra body in the Barrow bungalow. A young elementary school teacher stayed four nights a week. She sang romantic operetta around the place, and in the evening knitted endless lacy jumpers in tasteful colours. There was an opulent-looking pink silk eiderdown on the school teacher's bed, a present from the gent. in a silver frame on her dressing table - her boyfriend according to Bella. She kept her door and window shut because of the cats on the eiderdown. That Big wants to have his kittens on it is an **idée fixe** with her. But best of all she's the honourable originator of an illuminating description - in regular use by us all - of a Barrow bath. We 'Play polarbears'!

In other words, I was happily at home. We all were. For however bathed in gloom or ill (in fact he had cancer and died before the end of the war), at home and in the mood Bert could be very droll, he had a nice line in comic asides with inspired faces to match. What's more, he'd picked the right woman. She never complained, she never mollycoddled - just got on with it. In this household it never occurred to any of us to compare our backgrounds. There was no hierarchy, no standing on ceremony, Bella was far too busy. At meal times we simply got on with it according to our bent. As you'd expect Polar Bears was a shade 'refeened' - might even ask you to pass something. Bert and I were the primitives. I shot out an arm and fielded for what I wanted, he made enthusiastic slurping noises, drinking his tea which had to be scalding hot, and held his tools upright in his fists in between times using them. Last but certainly not least there was the old Gloucestershire dialect with its mixed pronouns and archaic words still currently in use. As a young under-gardener, Bert had a job where the lady of the house kept her husband's ashes in a casket on the drawing-room mantlepiece, and the maids refused to touch it; so every morning Bert had to be brought in to 'lift un and dust he.' Then, casting a knowing eye over their own mantleshelf, *'Well, me dear, no-one have dusted* ***that*** *this morning, and there be no casket on he!'* To me it was living poetry: I felt immense privilege, humbleness and awe.

Most Sundays, I went to lunch at the cottage and then stayed on. We played table tennis. The two had learned in a local club when in service in London, I in a college common room. I'd settled: dropped on my feet and found my place, I told myself delightedly, in the servants' hall!

When the old man came back with a sizeable box of young plants, scarlet wallflowers, he said, to go round the house, I wasn't pleased. I'd never heard of a bedding plant, and now that I had I was shocked, recognising it as urban display planting - in my opinion an insult to a natural country setting, at all times in poor taste, and in such as these an unwarrantable misuse of valuable energy. The two were a bit taken aback, and no wonder. I kept putting it off till the plants began to flag and the girls became concerned. *'We'll give you a hand.'* said the cook, and they did, kitted out in shiny wellingtons and rubber gloves, wound round with woolly scarves, and the cook had the kitchen clock in the pocket of her raincoat, the alarm set for when they had to go in. I was touched. It was their rest time.

Henry spotted us and came over to see what was going on. *'Got nothing to do inside, then?'* he said to the girls. *'You can talk! Hanging around, watching others work.'* retorted the cook. They'd given up on Henry, irritated by his unwavering concern, *'What do you do all day, then? Some old girl part-time could do it easy - 'tis never right with a war on...'* Or, should he be down with the milk when I came in with the vegetables for the house, *They can't never eat* ***all that****! What happens to all they left-overs then?'* And, for my benefit, *''Tis 'is pigs afore we, see - lower be we than they!'* As a result, the two had dropped being friendly to the natives, and locked my kitchen door.

Certainly there was a war on, and now it suddenly heaved over in our direction. The city ten miles away was badly blitzed. You could see the terrible red glow in the sky. And after that there were regular, less violent, raids on both the city and its dockland. Nightly disturbance became routine. To begin with every evening a stream of cars, crammed with the family clutching pets and valued belongings, fled the city and parked down country lanes bonnet to boot, getting what sleep they could. Bert's sister came to spend the nights with us, and then moved in when her house was hit.

Just as I was congratulating myself on how well I was getting on with the two in the cottage, there came a weekend when I didn't see them at all. They had to be avoiding me, I couldn't understand it. What had I done? The difference in our backgrounds meant I needed to be careful, though my natural, already-established strong left bias made for an almost foolproof situation. I didn't need to play a part - well, no more than a person usually does. They'd already been introduced to the gospel according to the *New Statesman*. They also knew I'd been thrown out of the Women's Auxiliary Air Force as a dangerous Red. They'd enjoyed that. The parlour maid had been particularly impressed. *'No-one would dare say they weren't Labour in Barnsley.'* she told me proudly, *'They'd get their teeth knocked out.'*

So what had gone wrong? I was worried. I had a standing invitation to visit any evening I wished, but had never taken advantage of it. Now, on a pretext, I did call. I could make no-one hear. The cottage seemed to be deserted. At last, looking wan, Hazel came into the dairy again. *'We've had a dreadful time!'* It appeared that one night two greying old girls from one of the cars had come to the door, begging hot water to make fresh coffee. The cook had taken them in and given them coffee with cream, and omelettes. They then all had a glass or two and exchanged life stories. Finally, hardly believing their good luck, as they left the visitors were presented with half-a-pound of butter along with a further invitation. Naturally, they came again. In the end the two could think of nothing better than to batten down the hatches and stay. Their evening were spent in a candle-lit back bedroom. *'It was horrible.'* *'You can be too kind.'* I suggested.

Christmas time arrived, festive and feudal. Presents were agreed on. Plough boy, Rod Bone, born into Sadleir service asked for a tweed jacket. (His father, an ex-territorial soldier had been snatched back on day one.) Henry, the hand - of only one year's standing - with suitable modesty asked for bicycle tyres which he could not get for himself. I chose gloves and the girls, compacts. Henry and Rod had turkeys. There was a present, too, for Ma Bone, mistress of The Ruin - their tied cottage further down the lane - and the cook was instructed to make her a pudding. I decorated with evergreen and Christmas Day found us with sisters everywhere, including two widowed ones staying in the house. The parlour maid flew back and forth and the cook was demented - though nobly backed up by Ma Bone lost in steam scrubbing pans in the scullery. Together they sailed through to calmer waters with flying colours.

I stood with Bert outside the bungalow, watching. Along the river an array of flares. Overhead the continuous steady drone of aircraft, this time sounding nearer than usual and broken by shattering outbursts from an anti-aircraft gun recently sited on the edge of the village. Crossing searchlights lit up odd strips of cloud sparkling with explosions. Beguiled by the pretty sight, it was easy to forget what it was all about. Then, suddenly, the lights veered in towards us, the drone changed to a roar and there was the sound of loose pebbles rattling in tin cans. Incendiaries, Bert said. The front door opened and we were grabbed inside, Bert's sister being sure it was machine-gun fire. The next minute all other sound ceased as the high explosive filled out and tore screaming down. I was in the passage. The bungalow seemed to heel over. I shot up an arm to ward off a wall or likely descent of the ceiling. In the kitchen I could hear them scrambling under the table and wondering where **I** was.

Bert re-appeared. He'd been out at the back, checking the sheds. He was convinced that the packet had gone down on the farm, though he had to admit there was no sign of fire, the only one to be seen was flickering in the direction of the docks - oil, by the look of it. But I was used to his tales of doom and noticed that explosions you were sure of as being in your own back yard usually turned out to have been a mile away. The family re-instated themselves upright in the kitchen and fetched out the teapot. I went to bed.

I was wakened by tapping on the window and voices. *'She peacefully sleeps while we're being bombed!'* It was almost light. They came in and sat on the edge of the bed to tell their story. The cook was still so agitated the whole framework shook.

Saturday night was dinner-party night. The lady of the manor (A.R.P. as well as W.L.A.) received a telephone message stating that enemy aircraft were coming up the estuary, showering incendiaries. Everyone trooped upstairs but could see nothing. A little later, the parlour maid, washing up in the pantry, heard claps on the roof and something fall on to paving, at the same time there appeared round the edge of the blackout a flashing white line. Ma Bone, in the scullery, saw it too and shouted through to the cook. The parlour maid grabbed a bucket of sand and was met in the hall by the old man. Incendiaries, she told him and quickened her pace. She privately thought it might only be one and was determined to get there first. The old man made for the farm buildings, there were barns full of straw and animals and poultry locked up. When he heard the screamer, he threw himself down. I was sure it was all over, he told them afterwards.

The house, being apparently untouched, everyone flocked outside. The fields around were peppered with incendiaries burning out in the grass. They were also in the farmyard. One had gone through the roof of a stable and started on some woodwork, and sacks lying around were smouldering. A nervous duck laid an egg on the cobblestones.

Back in the cottage, the cook refused to go to bed so they'd gone down the lane to check on the brick-cube couple. Dot and the tot were in the shelter. Ted and his mother, who was staying with them, were outside the front door engaged in a heated argument. She'd already been back twice, they gathered, then just as he was locking up for the third time she'd remembered her best hat and was refusing to budge with it. It's on top of the wardrobe she kept telling him. From the shelter a near-hysterical Dot was yelling at him to get a move on. Inside, the shelter was wet. He'd to mop out three inches of water, she told them, that's why we're so late. *'You never heard anything like the clatter of Dot's false teeth'*, appended the parlour maid.

Once more back in the cottage, the cook still wouldn't go to bed; they talked and made tea. However, by the time it was beginning to get light, she'd recovered sufficiently to show an interest in souvenirs. It was then that they found the crater - in the meadow next to the house, less than a hundred yards away. I was shown an evil-looking, brassy bit of bomb, the prize of their collection. On Sunday afternoon

I went to see for myself. Children were scavaging hungrily over the grounds. A soldier approached and demanded a spade to dig up a buried incendiary nose for his little boy. A steady procession of villagers in their best clothes passed to and from the crater. They were three or four deep round it, with babes and dogs playing on the outskirts. Huge rough chunks of sticky clay had been wrenched out and lay exposed in mindless disorder. Rod Bone disengaged himself to show off a shining silver unexploded incendiary. He'd just been round the farm with the old man, who'd kept muttering about and telling everyone what a terrible waste of money it had been. I was to get it, too, *'What a **waste** of money!'* Indisputably reprehensible business practice, you were given to understand. As for casualties, the whiskers of one of the farm cats had been singed to a black stubble.

The next day our feudal lord visited the vegetable garden, something he'd not done before. *'I'd like you to live in.'* he said. And when I didn't at once reply, *'Think about it.'* It was being done everywhere. Prompt action saved buildings. Later, I was visited by the A.R.P., W.L.A. lady of the manor. *'Mr. Sadleir is anxious, very anxious, and there's plenty of room in the cottage. The cook is also concerned - she would welcome some extra support, she has said so.'* Finally, Bella Barrow had admitted that under these new circumstances she could do with my room.

My chief concern was to remain on good terms with the two. I didn't see myself lasting long at Chapel Farm without that, and I didn't see our threesome having much of a future with me under the same roof. Visits to the cottage at weekends at their invitation worked well. And now it was all to change. Anything could happen.

At one o'clock I came in to lunch. As usual, there was no-one about. To begin with I'd found something laid out on a corner of my kitchen table. But by now all such high endeavour had been abandoned. It was true that I knew where everything was - what I could take. that was a different matter. I understood the difficulty. It was the cottage weekday timetable that caused the problem. Everything happened first thing and in the evening. The two had a late breakfast followed by their favourite meal, a grand fry-up in the middle of the afternoon.

I went upstairs to find a companionable book. It was windy outside and a draught blew the bedroom door shut. The next minute, the cook was in the room enlarging on the theme of her midday rest. As she held open the door, rolls of fluff blew out from under the bed and slid excitedly over the varnished linoleum. *'I don't suppose you know what to do with a broom'* said the cook tartly, *'There's a war on you know. I can't have Hazel coming in here, she has enough to do as it is. And while I'm about it something else, I don't like people eating meals off my kitchen table without a cloth on it, I'm not used to that sort of thing.'*

The old man's manor woman (Hazel claimed to have spied them in a clinch in the hall after one of the parties), pointed out that at any time now he'd be allowed only one full-time staff; fancy cooking was rapidly becoming a thing of the past, he would promote his parlour maid and get in more part-time help. I had only to hang on.

The end came sooner than most of us expected. All at once the contra-temps aped the war - it blew up and fell to earth, forming a new pattern. But this bomb didn't come from without. Carefully controlled, it came from within. It cost money but it got results. It became known that the old man had offered the parlour maid a goodly lump sum to stay on alone, plus the same again provided she was still with him at the end of hostilities. I had always thought of and seen the two as in tandem. Now, at a stroke, the proposition effectively clove them apart. It was a tense and terrible day with the cook accusing the parlour maid of mis-representing her to their employer. She got pretty drunk that night and had to be assisted upstairs. Hazel tried to undress her but was resisted. She was left tenderly laid out, still in her white coat, under a couple of quilts.

Before she left there was confrontation. I was blamed for everything. I didn't respond. Finally, *'You're **gutless**'* she spat it out, *'Haze needs someone to follow - to stand up for her. You can't even stand up for yourself!'* True, perhaps, to some extent; but to a far greater, wrong, for we were now at a stage where the parlour maid not only stood in for but also propped up her friend. Yet, to the cook, it must have seemed that everyone was against her. She had to set herself up for departure and this was something I wanted, too. I was fond of them both and upset that it had to end in this painful way. She was and, all these years on, remains, with all her faults if not because of them, one of my favourite characters.

19

Rising Together

The Parlour Maid and the Gardener

'Are you lacking anything - is there anything you'd like done?' the Old Man asked. I painted the front door blue and Hazel made new curtains. Bookshelves were fitted in our sitting room.

Ma Bone now came in every day. Hazel was still in service but with such a rise in status and pay she was not complaining. Above all, she wanted to better herself. Above all, I wanted to write. We were both determined to use our spare time to advantage. On Saturdays we bussed to Bristol and, instead of going to the pictures, went to the old *Theatre Royal*, the city's toy gem from the past, where the Bristol Old Vic put on a different classic play each week. One of these was a Restoration comedy called *The Constant Couple* and so regular was our attendance that this became our nickname at the box office.

The big department store in Queen's Road was Hazel's favourite venue for shopping. From the beginning, I chose all her clothes, and the materials for making them for us both. The clothes I liked, and Hazel, went well together, the one enhancing the other. She was a joy to dress. Her looks and trim, understated figure made it easy. And she really was skilful with a needle. This had led to promotion to lady's-maid duties in one of her earlier jobs. At Chapel Farm she'd already turned collars and cuffs on the old man's shirts to save coupons, and made new chintz covers for the three-piece suite in the drawing room.

After the department store, it was time for my treat. George's fine bookshop still stood at the top of bombed Park Street. *'I didn't know it was possible to spend an hour and a half in a bookshop.'* was all she said. And all I did was laugh.

We were both in a process of discovery - filling each other in as to our beginnings - goodness knows what she made of mine, compared with that of almost anyone at all it would have seemed extraordinary enough. I was in no such difficulty. Like a cat with a dish of cream, I lapped up all I could get of life in a Yorkshire mining village, where it appeared that her father was knocked up from the street in the small hours by someone systematically going round, banging doors and rattling windows.

Shortly afterwards, into a still dark and silent world, the men emerged and left on foot for the mine, carrying bread and jam in a tin box called a snap. For me it was transportation, no less. The wonders of Pabst's *Kameradschaft* coming to life.

He was a mild man, her father. His pay packet went to his wife in exchange for a small begrudged sum, the least she could get away with. In her view sheer wanton waste to be pissed up the wall at the back of the pub. She wore the pants and her creed was simple. Girls went into service to get out of home. They accepted a man to get out of service. They then found themselves, by law and circumstance, finally outmanœvred - inescapably tied down to the floor, the stove, the sink, the bed and the kids. This was what men did to you! She had nothing but contempt for the opposite sex, and a cutting tongue and a talent for scenes ensured that everyone else suffered, too. She was very likely well enough summed up by a sister-in-law calling to her young to make themselves scarce *'Here comes your Aunt, the Queen of England!'*.

A son and a daughter were born to these two. Ten years later, in error, another. Every trick in the book had been tried to see off the unwelcome present, including what sounded like shooting the rapids and belly-tobogganing down the stairs. But the mite hung on. This one was her mother's daughter. A rough passage! But in its less primitive way so had mine been. We had both missed out on one strongly fundamental, feeling climate. **We had never been wanted.** Upon our arrival no-one had thought to name us Joy.

Then came another period of emotional turmoil which Hazel remembered as 'living in a black cloud', when Your Aunt, the Queen of England's older daughter was discovered pregnant. Preliminary niceties, even as afterthoughts, there'd been none. Moreover, the boy had in mind emigration to New Zealand to become a lumberjack. New heights of hysteria were revealed, with the first cause repeatedly hammered home – **men**. The curtains were drawn. She refused to go out - or if unavoidable wore a black veil. Living turned into a protracted nightmare for them all.

The young couple married. Two nice people, they'd have done so anyway. The miracle was that the boy hadn't been scared off. But the parlour maid respected her mother and was upset at the lack of sympathy shown when she died early of cancer. Her father was experiencing a new lease of life, having promptly moved in with an accommodating widow. Home for Hazel when she needed it, was with her sister who had anyway virtually brought her up - latterly alongside her baby son.

Being actually exposed to Yorkshire family life didn't come until after the war, and by this time the parlour maid's sister was no longer living in a mining community. Nonetheless, it was an unforgettable experience. They all talked at once, yelling for dear life to get a hearing. I genuinely thought they were quarrelling, remembering Hazel's story of how her sister, more than fed-up with a teasing brother, had brought down the banjo (frying pan) so smartly on the top of his head as to draw blood and knock him out cold. Gradually, however, it sank into mine that what I was witnessing was no more than their regular manner of enthusiastic, familial, affectionate communion.

I hardly dared open my mouth that first weekend. Come Sunday, the lumberjack stuffed the two of us, wrapped round with rugs, into the sidecar of his motorbike combination, and we roared away to admire his new workplace, the city's fine park. And in the evening he performed like a virtuoso on the piano. After the birth, he had indeed gone out to New Zealand, stayed a number of years, and considered himself cosmopolitan. All of this was a long way from *Kameradschaft*, but at least it left that heroic scenario intact.

In view of how different the two of us were, we got on surprisingly well - that is to say she agreed with me over practically everything. I was the advantaged, educated one, the model. Comic, really, but compared with her I was, and I did everything I could to be an effective, beneficent raising agent. And she was as much of a joy to direct as she was to dress. Strongly motivated, persistent and seemingly infinitely adaptable. I never needed to push, only suggest - books, ideas, evening classes in French, a matriculation correspondence course. I need do no more than nod at a door and she was light-footedly through it.

She'd done well at school, but taking it further or staying on on her own as an unqualified assistant were options not favoured at home. The girl could read and write, add and subtract, what more did she need? A few years in London would open her eyes, top up useful skills - she'd live in and get paid. It made sense.

Teaching, as an objective, never actually came up, it was an assumption, and to this end the goal was acceptance into a college of domestic science. A foregone conclusion to us both.

Our differences in background and education put to good, mutual use, there remained character and temperament - here, too, were wide-apart differences that bit deep. She, over-emotional. I, too much in my head. But I was sure that it didn't matter. They were healthy, exciting differences that added spice to our lives. It seemed that nothing could spoil our accord. She was aiming for a more respectable and worthwhile occupation, I was set on learning to express myself in another, more native expertise. And the impetus was such that it swept a clear path and carried us forward handsomely.

Meanwhile, I was working hard, filling wastepaper baskets. Though I did have some small successes. Not that I thought of them like that, not at all, I thought I'd arrived! During the war it was easy. Competition was reduced, while those left behind were panting to know what was really going on - they were looking for the nitty-gritty behind guarded newspaper and radio reporting. They also wanted the human angle. Individual descriptions of what it was like to be suddenly caught up in situations totally opposed to all established, civilized normal practice. Understandably, the quality of the writing was judged very much secondary to the information conveyed. As far as copy was concerned, I could hardly have done better than get my silly self thrown out of the W.A.A.F.

A Land Army Training came out first - in a wartime, mushroom paperback, *The Convoy File*, edited by Robin Maugham. It was later re-printed in *World Digest.* Only the best was good enough = Cyril Connolly's *Horizon* and John Lehmann's *Penguin New Writing. A Week in the Waafs* and *Land Army Gardener* were submitted and both men wrote kind, appreciative rejection slips which were reverently kept till they crumbled away. Eventually, the two pieces were printed in hardback, *Leaves in the Storm*, a book of war diaries, edited by Stefan Schimanski and Henry Treece. The only review of the book that I saw was in the *New Statesman*, where they filled a good half page letting us know how disgustingly over-educated, sloppily self-sensitive and self-denigrating - in a word, thoroughly **sick-making** we were. I dare say they had a point. Myself, I was over the top to be in such company, almost all names and including Spender, Gertrude Stein, V.S. Pritchett and Henry Miller. And of them all, I, and I alone, had two pieces printed!

Oh what a wonderful war! And on the creature-comfort level it was the same.

IV

POST-WAR
1945-1975?

20

A Shortage of Teachers

Further Adventures in Education

Hazel was pushing steadily ahead. She'd got a job as house-mother in a progressive boarding school in the south-west. While we were still at Chapel Farm, Elizabeth Jenkins's book *Young Enthusiasts* came out, a novel based on her experiences in two such schools. We were both fascinated and decided that she should try to find a slot in just such a school. We tried Bedales first (I dictated the letters), but they were fully staffed. As it turned out she couldn't have done better. Once more small was beautiful. The staff were understanding and interested, helped with the correspondence course and recommended a good City of London crammer.

My friend was on a clearly-defined path, heading towards the one thing she wanted to do - had always wanted to do. My own situation was nothing like so satisfactory or straightforward. I was already qualified, yes, but that was part of the trouble. By force of circumstance I was being impelled towards the one thing I did **not** want to do - had never wanted to do. An acute shortage of teachers, my training, the holidays, the prospect of a salary again instead of a minimum wage - all conspired and contributed. I had no choice. In the matter of jobs it was different. A plethora. I enjoyed going over the vacancy notices from scholastic agencies - letterbox lottery! Picking plums, I called it. But whatever I called it, the bottom line was always the same.

It was to last ten years. **Ten years of teaching in seventeen different schools!** It would be impossible not to be ashamed of such a record. True, most were filling-in, but too many were not and in only one of these was the agreement honoured for a respectable length of time.

I began cautiously in a Midlands girls' high school and gave in my notice at half term. After that, with the end in view - only six more weeks and I'd have served out my sentence - it wasn't really so awful.

Toe in - toe out. It didn't help that I had no teacher-training. Instead of the usual Art Teacher's Diploma - a broadly-based qualification designed for schools of general education - mine was a specialist's degree in painting for teachers in schools of art. But for this, I had to be a practising artist and I hadn't continued to paint.

Obviously, the next school was going to be crucial. It **had** to be right. 'For one term only'. **That was it** - just what I wanted, and so it proved. Today, I see it as the most fortunate of all my appointments. If this one had turned out badly, too - I really don't know - anything could have happened... It was a large, prestigious public boarding school. I went up for the interview and stayed the night, and to my surprise I wasn't appointed, but they were let down and I was still free.

In the course of my teaching career I never ceased to be struck by how much the headmistress made the school, its strength and weaknesses, its heart, the very spirit of the place derive from her. At the high school the headmistress had been curiously disengaged - it was as if she was going through the motions - and instead of supporting her staff she leant on them. Whatever she had been cut out to be, clearly it wasn't a leader.

The situation in my new school could not have been more different. This headmistress had no such defect. She knew where she was going and saw that she got there - and on time. Morning prayers were whistle-stop, readings at the double, hymns first and last verses, then with a crash of chords the great hall promptly cleared. This headmistress could have come out of a family of field marshals, she was a large, firm lady with a high chest and indelible presence. Only temporary I might be, but I was not overlooked. The strong music department was directed by a handsome woman of continental appearance, consort - it was said - to the Generalissima. Other more than probably committed couples emerged. There was even a recently deserted maiden for me. I was given to understand that I was exactly the sort of person she needed, and beyond question she was being similarly encouraged.

Again - and most remarkable of all - although I was only temporary, my future in teaching was being considered. Although by now nearing forty, this was only my second appointment - but with smaller classes, and from the top a strong basic discipline that held - indeed the whole boarding school set-up was supportive - I found I could manage well enough. She gave me a first-rate testimonial. It hadn't occurred to me to ask - I hadn't known that I could. When I went in to thank her and say goodbye, she said to me kindly, '***Always** wear a hat for an interview, dear; and if you have occasion to stay the night, on **no account** carry a knapsack.*

Several schools on, with a term or two off when there wasn't anything - or nothing that tickled my fancy, or what looked exciting on paper turned out to be not at any price - once more I began to despond. I wanted to settle. **I needed to belong**. All this flitting and flirting, it wasn't decent. I noticed that the better the school the more successful I seemed to be. In any case, by this time, I'd attended an excellent 'Art for Schools' summer holiday course and felt equal to anything. The second prestigious public boarding school with an opening in my speciality was even more so than the first (some would have described it as the most prestigious of them all). And this time the appointment was permanent. With no disrespect to the kind Generalissima, I went down for the interview without a hat, and was offered the job on the spot.

It was January, the weather sharpish, the staff were wrapped up in layers of sweaters, thick hairy tweed skirts and ribbed stockings. What was wrong with the central heating, I wondered? But we were in a deeply rural stately home. The luxury hotel of a once fashionable watering place had posed no such problems. Then I noticed the dogs. Dogs everywhere. All the older staff and establishment figures - the Sister, the Housekeeper - seemed to have one (indulgently referred to on the Old Girls' Network as the 'outlets'). Lunchtime, I had hardly put down my knife and fork when a tin dish shot diagonally across the long refectory table, successfully targeting my plate. A vegetarian-more or less, I'd left some meat - contributions for the most important member of the staff: Dodo's dog. Do-do's dog went with her to classes, he was elderly and slept most of the time.

That the headmistress made the school in this case was unquestionable. She was co-founder. It embodied her ideas. The school was not progressive, but more than a glance had been taken in that direction. The timetable was regular enough, high academic standards were required, but outside the classroom the girls enjoyed more personal freedom than was usual. This headmistress passionately wanted her school to be a happy place. To her it was more than a school, it was home, one which she wished to share with us all. It was this element that made the school special.

It followed that staff meetings were strongly familial. They were held in the sitting room of her private quarters, older staff in stuffed chairs, younger ones on cushions on the floor. Those not concerned with the matter in hand knitted or mended their stockings, others corrected or scribbled in notebooks. Dogs would their way in and out. It was informal to a degree - under the circumstances - out of this world, with no-one more at ease than our totally unschoolmistressy head - every inch the loving matriarch.

My immediate predecessor had been an artist, a painter of delicate watercolours. I ordered sugar-paper, long-handled hog brushes, enamel plates, bun liners and unlimited powder colour. I floated a few imaginative ideas, and we were off. Literally. It was if I'd released a tidal wave. The work went round the art room four deep, down the stairs, along the school corridor into the dining room. *'I take it that you are as amazed as we are?'* murmured the Matriarch. And I was. It was awesome.

The staff boarding house was still filled with evacuees. There were staff in caravans in the grounds, the rest of us were scattered about the village. Along with two younger mistresses, I was in a period cottage with a separated parent and a whole flotilla of low-bellied, yappy little dogs. My two colleagues went home for the weekend. The two schoolgirls returned for the weekend. I remained for the weekend, and understandably wasn't popular.

The school timetable created difficulties. Games in the afternoon meant evening teaching of as far as possible non-academic subjects. It also meant being stranded in the school for the afternoon - it wasn't worth cycling back to the period cottage. Effective relaxation amounted to an hour or so before going to bed. But I was lucky in my two young companions, both Old Girls of the school. One had a marvellous sense of humour, the other was creative - a tall, darkly-beautiful girl. I loved them both with a sweetly simple uncomplicated acceptance never felt before and only glancingly experienced since.

I stayed two terms. At that point, a record. *But we're such **nice** people, dear'* put forward the Matriarch, sadly, touching me lightly on the arm. And it was true. She was. They were - **they were**. But I knew it wasn't for me.

I had never been to Wales. A direct-grant day and boarding school in southern Snowdonia was chosen for the locality, and it didn't let me down. The school was another matter. The trouble with so many middle-grade boarding schools was that they couldn't or wouldn't employ the right number of house staff. You come in on some first-class specialist degree and find yourself hemmed in by duties - meals, taking the lights, church, the Saturday afternoon crocodile. At least, as a non-academic, I'd never had a form - that is until I entered the Principality.

In the Principality I was a booking clerk in charge of lists, notebooks, a register, a drawer full of cash, and an assortment of purses, as far as I could see all of them marked 'Jones'. On my half day - I repeat, **my half day** - I scooped up what looked like enough wherewithal into some commodious draw-string hide pouch (circa the Middle Ages) and did my little ones shopping - soap, toothpaste, hair grips, stamps, knitting needles, birthday cards 'One with roses on it for my granny!'.

And every week the domestic science mistress pressed the boarders' Sunday frocks with the kind of flatiron only found in museums over the border. **Slavery**. And yet...

I was lodged in a house in the grounds with two other new staff. Along with a land girl, graphically described as Jones the Spade, who was courting, and Games (known as Lewis the Legs). The Legs was an old-timer and friend of the head. Every evening she disappeared into the main building, leaving us with the place to ourselves. We came together at the end of the school day to compare notes and die, laughing.

The Midlander, a tall girl with glasses, taught juniors and was keen on the theatre. Younger than us - it was her first job - the Dish was dashing to look at with shining black wavy hair and light blue eyes. We learned that at Oxford she'd been an all-round failure with only a second, and, worse, thwarted as to her main objective. She explained how she'd steadily cultivated three prospective partners, only to be three times neatly ditched at the end of the year, *'I don't understand. I thought of everything. Tell me what I did wrong?'*

'You had not effectively cast yourself', laid down the Midlander-cum-Drama Director..., *They'd have seen you waving your net a mile away.'* she concluded. *'Which one did you like best?'* I asked, gormlessly fascinated. *'Oh, I don't know, any one of them would have done, they were all intelligent.'* The Midlander pounced - *'Another mistake! They're the slippery eels. If you'd focussed on some decent fellow reading for the Church you wouldn't be here.'* *'No - I'd be in a far worse fix'* capped the Dish as we fell about laughing.

When the Dish developed a heavy cold and decided to stay in bed, she had her temperature taken. The senior mistress visited and wrote down what her classes were doing. She'd hardly had time to snuggle down for a second time when a procession of staff began, bearing piles of books for correction. But, when we'd recovered our breath, she had to admit, *'I felt terrible. Jones Geography lost her one free period.'* The Dish thought the Welsh old-fashioned and slow, but her stratagems ended in comedy. Theirs worked.

In the noisy, bi-lingual staffroom, all talked at the same time. One way and another the Welsh can certainly talk - it doesn't matter what about, they'll always manage. I was a bit stunned to begin with, but, like the ever-present sound of rushing water when you live at the foot of a mountain, I soon learnt to let it flow round me. Rhiannon Richard took the harp and, of course, they **all** sang. It was a foreign place, novel and attractive, its people comfortable and warm. You could lose your heart here.

In the school the trouble was too many English girls sent to be safe from the raids and kept on. They tended to take over and sit on the easier-going natives. The head was an Englander. The Dish wasn't bothered, but such casting upset the Drama Director and it upset me, we didn't think it right. In the little town, they were so proud of their school. When they discovered who we were they couldn't do enough for us.

Straightaway I fell in love with the little town and its mountain. Out of my bedroom window I looked up to Cader Idris - the Seat of Idris the Giant, legendary astronomer, poet and philosopher - and every day it was different. The Midlander, who knew Snowdonia well - it was her holiday playground - took me by the hand to show off its wonders, and I woke up a devotee.

On being first introduced to bog and bright green juicy mounds of starry sphagnum moss, I was unable to resist stripping off to bounce and splash about on the springy cushions. The water was so piercingly icy it could have come from the Pole. The startled Midlander looked nonplussed, unsure if there was something wrong with me or lacking in her. There was a touch of the Red Queen and Alice in Wonderland in some of the sequences thrown up in the early days of our relationship. I was fond of the Midlander and grateful to her for introducing me to this exciting new world. I was only a humble scrambler, but that was enough. I could plunge down scree - I'd been promised a chimney. At this point in my life heaven was a mountain.

Distinctly a highlight of that packed term in southern Snowdonia was a visit to Llyn Cwm Bwchan. Most mountain water is bubbly and excited, but this little lake was unmoving. On the opposite side, a mountain came down to the water's edge to meet its reflection, making a single unit. There was something sweetly perfect about this scene, it was as if the mountain were on its knees before the beautiful image, innocently unaware that the source was itself.

And as we stood at the edge of the lake, knee-high in water, I looked down and saw that just under the surface each leg was the hub of a ring of tiny fishes, fanned out round it. They were busily nuzzling our legs and flicking their tailfins with obvious delight. I could feel nothing but cold. Was it the warmth? The taste of the sweat, or perhaps the fine hairs freely on end in the clear water - did they think it some new sort of seaweed? At the slightest move they were gone in a flash - but back in a matter of moments, they savouring us, we entranced by them.

On our way back, we discussed the feeling we had, that it was possible to communicate with the spirit of a place. The Midlander felt sure that this was because we were always alone. We had to ourselves something the summer crowds had the effect of dissipating. The only person we sometimes saw was the Man of the Mountain. Man and dog crossed over the seat of the gifted and scholarly giant every day. We were always saluted. But one day, he stopped. It was unusual, he told us, to find others on the mountain in December. Then a smile and a nod and we were off in our different directions.

In no more than a week or two I'd be off for good, I reflected. I'd given notice to leave at the end of the term. The other two, as good girls should, were staying till the end of the school year. Neither went back to teaching.

No men! - it's unnatural. No free time - that's illegal.' stated the Dish. *'Put that in your letter, I dare you'*, suggested Jones Geography. *'I shall work out my year and move on.'* declared the Drama Director, standing tall for one of her centre-stage-hogging speeches, *'But when my mother dies I shall buy a cottage up here.'*

Unabashed, straightway I fell for another permanent post in a tempting locality, a small private independent boarding school in Westmoreland. 'Preference will be given to a candidate fond of country living.'

To the north!

As soon as I got there it fell into place. I was interviewed by the retiring headmistress. It was a modest stately home on the edge of the dales. A river, plopping with salmon, bordered the ground, fishing rights went with the house. To begin with, in the holidays, she had fished there herself I was told. A catamaran was tied up. Along by the river the grounds turned into a wild garden, landscaping not often seen. The Persians had a word for it: Paradise. White ling and cherry trees. It was claimed that assistant mistresses bathed naked in the moonlight on hot summer nights. It fitted! In such a setting, how could they not?

Nearest railway station twenty-five miles, small market town one-and-a-half miles. No village. No public transport. In this school even the headmistress rode a bike.

You would have thought the Lady of the Leaping Salmon, a colourful woman, rich in character, would have been a hard act to follow. The new headmistress had no such qualities. She seemed uncertain, she lacked presence. Her morning greeting to the school sounded as if she didn't properly understand how she came to find herself in such an unlikely situation. But in this rested her appeal. The school felt it, too, for as if by magic from the floor rose up unanimous reassurance and support.

In fact she was warm and easily likeable. (Had the colourful character been a bit much for them, I wondered.) She loved Paradise and was often encountered strolling by the river, usually accompanied by the senior mistress, a sharp-nosed brunette of some elegance. From the head a smile and a wave. None such from the senior - she worriedly scanning the waterside undergrowth as if anticipating the imminent emergence of a serpent.

On the first Sunday after my arrival, I had gone for a bicycle ride taking in three counties, adding Lancs. And Yorks. To Westmoreland. A plaque on the wall of a cottage informed me that it had been a school known to Charlotte Bronte and thought to have been the model for 'Lowood' in *Jane Eyre*. We were not only at a confluence of counties, but types of country, too. Around our school it was pastoral enough, the view from the church in the small market town had been painted by Turner and lauded by Ruskin, but a mile or two over the river rose the western fells of the Yorkshire Dales. Calm, open and spacious. Curlews floated on the upper air. The globe flower grew. Straggling lines of skinny black-faced sheep roamed unconfined, their thick coats hung down and swung like kilts as they foraged in the tough coarse grass. Economy and grace.

The school staff were mostly Lancastrian or Lake Dwellers. If only I had found a committed Yorkie of the order of the Drama Director. But I didn't, and it didn't matter - she had done her work well. I went hostelling in the Lake District and, wonder of wonders, for two whole years I was happy and contented.

Not long after Paradise, I was being interviewed on the other side of the dales. The headmistress was pleasant enough but seemed at a loss as to what to say, which was disconcerting because I couldn't think of anything either. Suddenly she said, *'I was expecting you tomorrow - didn't we say the 8th?'* *'Oh, how awful - I don't **think** so'* I answered. *'But you may have done.'* I added, since she seemed in need of reassurance; but I knew that they hadn't. The senior mistress came in and the matter was referred to her. *'Miss Painter has arrived!'* *'So I see. How nice!'* She beamed, we shook hands. *'Yes, but I thought it was tomorrow.'* pursued the headmistress doggedly. *'Oh no, was it? I shouldn't think so.'* She bustled out.

When sent for, the school secretary looked at me thoughtfully but declined to comment. At this point, in self defence, I produced the letter. The head put on her glasses and slowly, very carefully, read every word. *'Yes, well in this case I think we can take it that it* **is** *today...'* She hesitated, then in a confidential aside, *'I have it on paper upstairs in my chest of drawers.'* Before removing her glasses, she examined me intently. *'You don't look at all well, dear. You have good health, I hope?'* *'I always look like this.'* I answered shortly, beginning to feel fed up. The next set of revelations concerned the art mistress. She hadn't been told, it was her half day, she'd gone out, the art room was locked, the key couldn't be found. In the end I was taken outside to look in through the window.

The weather was dull, the wind cold, but after tea, momentarily, a shaft of lemony light broke through a rift in the cloud. The headmistress stood up, *'Such a nice day! Shall we go in the garden?'* By the time we got outside, the sun had given up and gone in for good. It wasn't the day for a stroll, but she seemed not to notice. What happened next was nothing short of transformation, as a weak, ineffectual figure filled out into someone warm and alive, confident and exceedingly well-informed. It was as if she now found herself supported on all side by loving friends and close relations.

The grounds were undeniably impressive, in fact quite an arboretum, with many tall mature trees, including an enormous ancient Cedar of Lebanon propped up in the middle of the main lawn at the back of the house, its flat black branches spread out in ominous stages called to mind *'My Father's house has many mansions'* and the *'House of the Dead'* paintings of Paul Nash. And this in turn reminded me that the school had been founded by the Quakers. At the time, like the town, the school had 'lapsed', its head 'sympathetic', its status 'affiliated' to the Society of Friends.

We walked down by the lake, large enough for an island, with nesting swans and wild duck. *'I hope you are not too advanced'* she put forward. It appeared that a previous art mistress had taken the children outside to **feel** the spring - **fill** themselves with it. She was not against, she was quick to assure me, but they'd done little else.

Although they were not really at all similar, it was difficult not to be comparing this school with Paradise on the other side of the dales. This one was larger, much larger. A boarding school, it also took a very considerable number of day girls from the surrounding busy, urban area. The grounds were as good, if not better, and as in the other, bounded on one side by a river. No salmon, no, but with an unobstructed view across into the city park, you could have been in the heart of the country, when in fact a first-class shopping centre was only five minutes away.

The two headmistresses had characteristics in common. Oddly, for heads, they were both backward in coming forward - they appeared to find public relations difficult. At assembly, their performances were comparably low key. In the smaller school it was not so marked, you needed a good ear. In this, so much more crowded, setting it really did sound as if the speaker was fearful that one morning no-one was going to respond, or some unidentifiable bright spark from the floor would sing out a mocking challenge to the modestly-presented greeting.

Nonetheless, here as everywhere it was the headmistress's school. Everyone, but **everyone**, had a garden and gardened. **Everyone** belonged to the flourishing Field Club. Although an out-of-school activity, its importance over-rode all others. Wild flowers lined the corridors. Bird song was breathlessly listened for, chiff-chaff and tree creeper sightings piously recorded. And this strong pastoral predilection spilled over on to the games field with juniors playing tennis in their spare time on an outside court ankle-deep in buttercups and daisies, a fallen branch propping up the sagging net.

It was a respectable summer. The head was rarely inside. You might catch glimpses of her - it might be anywhere in the grounds - her tall figure bending over a shrub, suddenly straightening up out of a border, or on her knees before a formal bed. For certain she knew intimately every plant in the place.

'You know, she's an extraordinary woman, she isn't interested in people at all.' complained someone in the staffroom on a tetchy note. So what **is** she interested in?' I asked as if I didn't know. *'Well - **flowers**...'* We then learned that on high days and holidays, she hires a car out to some frontier of wilderness, and walks and walks... returning exhausted but ecstatic, holding a single gentian. You had to admire it. And the school worked.

On the while I didn't care for high schools, the classes were too big. But there had been exceptions. My favourite was up in the fens of East Anglia, in a small town with a towering cathedral, wheeling birds in endless sky, and an old-fashioned school full of fireplaces. There was one each end of the art room. A man was kept going full time, filling scuttles. And the food! Superb home cooking, worthy of grace, I couldn't believe it; but the kitchen, it was explained to me, was full of loving mums.

My second trip east was different. A much larger centre of population, too near London. I'd been in the place no more than a fortnight when I learned that the art mistress had been pronounced unfit to return to teaching, she was being pensioned off, and the headmistress was looking to me to carry on till the end of the school years - **two** terms. The news quite put me off my evening meal as it was taking every bit of all I had to steel myself into staying out the current one. The place was more insurrection than institution. The descendants of Boadicea and Old King Cole were very tough cookies indeed. Past troubles with discipline had been hiccups by comparison. But at least it would end in April. Or so I'd been fervently telling myself.

So what was going on? To put it in picturesque terms, I was having the stuffing knocked out of me. As bodily experience, it was a battery - a terrible jarring. After some of my classes I'd come away feeling stunned - figuratively - yet at the same time most palpably I was being clammed between the eyes. Walking back to my digs, along darkening streets I'd find myself pressing my fingers over my forehead.

Was this some sort of retribution? Was I being paid back in kind for the mayhem I myself had created at their age? I do hope not. Suck a lack of subtlety could undermine a person's confidence in higher powers. The correspondence I drew then, and still uphold, goes back further - to that hugely-accommodating black leather armchair in my father's consulting room. It was the same sort of extraordinary, out-of-this-world experience. Only the location of the trauma was different.

In class, I helped those who were interested and wanted to learn. The wild element was ignored. I never opposed or responded - I went out of my way to make no connection (wind to their sails), but I suffered. I suffered all right. I was shamed. I knew only too well who was in charge and it wasn't me.

The headmistress appeared to have no more appetite for the battlefront in her school than the rest of us, but she was better placed. Hedged in by secretaries, she sank herself in admin. And protective theories, leaving all else to a strong senior mistress who held up the place like a pillar. Even so, it was a staff regularly depleted by sickness and collapse. Previous to this I'd never heard of girls screaming at mistresses, or mistresses walking out of classes. Even those who lived in the town were thinking of pulling up stumps.

For myself, distinctly a ray of light at this time had been the application for a summer term on the Continent. A finishing school, I imagined. Happy outdoor classes of polished young ladies were pictured, with me convalescing to the tinkle of cow bells in the Swiss Alps.

With the end of the term a week away. I was sent for. They couldn't get anyone. If by the end of the term...could I be persuaded? **The examinations**.. And I even agreed. But the gods were merciful. *'She's coming from Camden Town'* revealed the head, her eyes bright with hope.

Was she **escaping** from Camden Town! I couldn't help wondering.

21

Refuge – Relics and Remains

Interlude

At least exposure to the young revolutionaries of the east alerted me to a very real situation. I became a woman strongly motivated for change. What was I **doing**? I'd never wanted...all these years...I'd done my bit. It was more than time to be moving on. But where and into what? I still had to earn a living.

Even more urgent was the need for some sort of base. My mother was coming up to ninety, she was always pleased to see me for a day or two - more than that upset her routine. The flat was so small, and anyway there were two of us now. Worse, Tythrington was in a serious state of decline, only just holding on in her flat - propped up by Percy, and a heavily-bribed home help who, every morning, washed the sheets the laundry refused to accept. And when the Tyth died, the house would be sold with the one vacant flat and three sitting tenants - cheaply, and, almost certainly, to some unscrupulous purchaser who would systematically set about making their lives more and more uncomfortable until they left.

By now Hazel was at college in Bath. A friend she had made down there had a relative who owned a house let out in unbelievably cheap flats. Peanuts - literally. The 'girl' - she was probably my age, I judged - had a house job in my friend's hostel. Sheas said to have private means, and worked when she felt like it between serious bouts of bird-watching - it could be anywhere. *'I live there myself'*, she said of the house, *'I get fed up at home. It gives mea perch in the town and privacy, too. I rent a large room with a neat kitchenette - only seven-and-six. But I'm not there a lot, and while I'm away you could have it for that. It's decently furnished'*, she added, *'And when something falls vacant I'd see that you got it.'* The 'girl' had a fringe and glinty eyes behind glasses. Plainly I was of no particular interest - my younger, better-looking friend, that was a different matter. *'It's right by the Remains and the Abbey'*, she continued, *'And in front there's a green with a huge spreading tree. What more could you want?'*

I wondered.

'Just a pile of old junk!' said my friend, *'Forget it.'* But she knew that we had to

find somewhere. *'It's not flats, it's a slum.'* said another, *'Don't go near it.'* But I did and at once fell in love with it.

The house was covered with creeper and featured an antique shop with a double-bowed window. The shop was run by a pocket-sized vibrant brunette, ever beavering away in the background. She lived there herself and collected the rents. On the face of it the Vibrant Brunette was something of a jolly-hockey-sticking figure but she also had strong teeth and a deep bite, fortunately usually reserved for short-sighted local authority with a mind to clear away heritage and build high-rise.

'Oh yes, you'd think she owned the place, and house nothing, she imagines she runs the city as well', said the glinty-eyed 'Watcher, who, apart from my friend, didn't seem to care much for people.

From Arthur Mee's Bath, *St Hugh's Press*

Elton House! The superb shop-front took up almost half the lower facade, and over the basement instead of the usual flat grating the novel and rare crinoline irons rose up in a graceful curve to the wall (so that when the fine ladies moved forward to peer in the window their wide skirts were discreetly depressed, denying any rude fellow below a view of their knickers.)

Inside, the stairs were old and worn, but beautifully proportioned - wide and shallow, delightful to skim down - the short flights turned back on each other, divided by half-moon landings roomy enough to turn a sedan chair - in my time they featured the only plumbing, communal taps over sinks. While for anything further it was down the flights and across a leafy yard strewn with bits of architectural ornament, broken statuary and other wonders, to a flimsily-partitioned double - and here's hoping you'd remembered to bring your own blotting. But what of that! In those days we were still young enough to find it good healthy exercise and no end of a joke.

From my sub-let window, I looked down on the leafy yard and over the roof tops to the downs, fringed with trees nice enough. But from aside in the bijou powder-closet kitchenette, I could see the heads of the emperors posed round the Great

Roman Bath, and felt mightily privileged.

The Abbey, though blocked from view, was very much with us. The bells rang time passing every fifteen minutes and three times a day played hymns and country airs, a different one for every day of the week. Other on-site attractions and amenities included being within spitting distance of Woolly's and Marks and Spencer. But best of all, on the other side of the green was Evans the Fish. 'The cleanest shop in Bath.' (And still frying today!) You could set the table, flash down the flights, bound across the green, and be back with your precious package to slap on the plate still piping hot, for an unsurpassable supper.

The 'Watcher was as good as her word and in due course we became fully-fledged tenants renting two small rooms at the top of the house for five shillings a week, and, as she pointed out, you couldn't store your stuff for that.

The following summer I returned to Bath to find Hazel in a state. It was the end of her third year, an exciting time with everyone sending for application forms and getting fixed up. But not one of hers had any effect. No grammar schooling meant no interest. She burst into tears. I was astonished. Surely she wasn't still thinking of herself as under-privileged? *'All we have to do is write an accompanying letter'* I said, and, seeing her achievement for what it was - a tour-de-force - I composed a suitable enclosure. And after that it was simply a question of which one to choose.

And so began a period with the two of us teaching, but as we never taught in the same school, town or even county, we still only met in the holidays. My friend moved on from her first job, to better things as head of department in a new comprehensive in Cornwall. She was now living in a fascinating one-up-one-down converted garage, a popular choice down there in those days.

By this time the 'Watcher had a place of her own, a small stone cottage with genuine sloping floors, a brass carriage lamp by the door, and fine open views across country. Only I was left still disgracefully living from pillar to post

'What does your friend teach?' asked the Vibrant Brunette one day as we stopped on the stairs for a word. And, on being informed, *'My dear - **how** clever of you!'*

Earlier, someone had said to me, of the two of us, that if I went on to do nothing more with my life, at least I'd made hers. I never repeated this. I thought nothing of it. Being what we both wanted and had been working towards, what had been achieved simply seemed natural. But this later, sophisticated observation was in a class of its own and much too deliciously funny not to be shared. It was an **inspired** remark - wildly, outrageously untrue - never for one moment... Yet at the very same time it was a perfect fit, hitting the target with the effortless precision of an arrow from the bow of a Zen master. But also, and importantly, it was between the Vibrant Brunette and myself, and should have remained that way. Exposed in the workaday world it was always going to be open to misinterpretation.

But I saw nothing of this then, and at the telling was far too carried away to notice the sort of response I was getting. To me the remark was live - **quick** - a sparkling paradox that encapsulated so much. In any case, at no time had I thought myself 'clever'. Lucky, yes. After all I'd never expected to find a partner, I lacked that sort of confidence - had seen myself missing out. But I hadn't. Lucky, yes - exceptionally.

When the owner of Elton House died, the Vibrant Brunette acquired the property. And at once everything changed, as it was bound to do. The place being entirely out of sync. With the present. To begin with, most of the tenants had been originals - to us they were ancients. They were also poor to a degree that must have been almost Dickensian. One or two were still in place. This was their home. It was also the home of the Vibrant Brunette - figurehead no longer - and one of the first things she did was put pressure on us. I complied at once. I was seldom there, my friend just a name on a bell. I went down to the garage in Cornwall for most of my holidays. It wasn't a proper use of the amenity. Unfortunately, the garage was furnished. This was awkward, but I reckoned that by a process of stacking, piling and infilling, we should be able to hang on in there until we found something affordable of our own. It would mean losing the dining area of our living room, that was all.

I remember the day our belongings were moved. Meeting us on the stairs, the Vibrant Brunette made some passing, jolly remark and my friend let fly with a slashing rejoinder. Like many effective teachers, my friend enjoyed conveying to others what she strongly felt. All the same, I was astounded. I missed a tread and had to claw hold of the bannister. She'd hardly been in the place! It was with some trepidation that I went in to say goodbye. But, *'I really don't know what to make of your friend'*,was all she said, as over the top of her glasses she gave me a thoughtful look.

22

The Last School

Body and mind

Two years on from the killing fields of the east, I was still teaching. Once more it was summer. I was in a south-western boarding school with a gentle, appreciative headmistress. I'd filled in there before, for a term, this time it was two - in effect I'd been with them a year - a relaxed situation. We were sitting about in the staffroom with cups of coffee, I bemoaning my fate, when the lead I was so desperately waiting for slipped neatly in place. Someone's kid sister had just finished training for a new profession called occupational therapy, no **not** physio - **occupational**. Medical, yes, but it was arty too, she explained.

It was about rehabilitation and healing. How recovery could be enhanced and speeded up by activities, creative and practical, selectively applied. It was also about lifting people out of morbid states of mind. Its emblem was the phœnix, flaming, renewing - out of the ashes another beginning. I was impressed and excited. I soon discovered that occupational therapy as a profession had originated in the States, and been pioneered in this country by a Miss Mcdonald, who had gone on to found - in Oxford - the first school.

Out of the ashes another beginning

And so it came about that as once I had piloted the parlour maid, I now faced putting myself through the same hoops. Following familiar guide lines - only the best is good enough, and always begin at the top - I promptly got in touch with Miss Mcdonald and went up to Oxford for an interview.

From where I was on the Somerset coast, reaching Oxford took the best part of a day. However, I needn't have been anxious about the return journey as in twenty minutes flat the interview was over and I was on my way again. She was, indeed, a remarkable woman, always to the point and not one unnecessary word. She asked questions and listened intently. She regretted that in her school at the time there was no niche - as she put it - where I could usefully be fitted in. In the Midlands, however, it might well be different. That was the place to try. *'Tell them you've seen me'*, she ended.

All the way back, in my mind I went over and over that short, packed interview. Particular interest had been shown in the description of my defeat on the battlefront to the east. *'Are you a **perfectionist**?'* I'd been asked. Fortunately, I knew just enough to know that it wasn't a good thing to be. I hoped not, I'd answered. The train swayed from side to side as I went on mulling over that uncomfortable question, till in the end I was forced to conclude that the answer had to be, yes - rather more than somewhat - I was.

Disregarding the great lady, I tried for the school in the West Country first, but they had no **niche** either. The school in the Midlands, however, replied at once with an invitation. It turned out to be attached to a large, handsome, exceedingly expensive psychiatric hospital. I was received in the school as an emissary from On High. *'How **is** dear Miss Mcdonald?'* I managed to suppress a strong desire to tell them I hadn't had time to ask. (A pity, they'd have enjoyed it. The American best-seller, *Cheaper by the Dozen* was recommended holiday reading.) It was soon arranged for me to have two classes of patients in the hospital. I'd take my fellow students for design and keep an eye on them in the hostel, where I could have a study-bedroom on the ground floor. Nothing could have been more easy. The place was full of **niches** calling out to be filled. Understandably, I suppose. Myself, I was unaffected: if anything it was a fascinating additional challenge.

The Principal was sure I'd have no trouble with the practical part of the course, but unfortunately the most difficult part came first - the basics of a medical training with emphasis on orthopœdics. Psychiatry followed psychology. The standard was high, too high she inclined to think - occupational therapy didn't attract the academically-minded, nor did they usually turn into better O.Ts. *'We began by making the course too easy'* she explained, *'but now I think we've gone too far in the other direction - so **many** failures.'* Finally, would I stay the course? *You seem to like moving around!'* Two years on, I was to sit two three-hour papers in psychiatry, and get distinction.

I thought of it as my miracle situation, and so it was. As to 'duties', even the refractory class in the main building (the real nutters) was a piece of cake to me. There was no antagonism. They were each sealed in their own particular prison. They drank the paint water. One man always christened himself with it and then stood on his head; he was always polite, even apologetic, but equally insistent - the minute I turned away he was at it again. There was nothing you could do, so I settled for making the class as happy an event as I was able, and if they didn't notice at least I benefited.

As for my fellow students, they were such **happy** maidens - **filled** with the joys of spring all the year round. I loved them all - well, **nearly** all. Unfortunately, though, such qualities didn't make for committed students. Myself, with half my life behind me, I was nothing if not single-minded, I genuinely relished the training I was getting. Splendid for life as well as a career was how I saw it.

Being with the students always refreshed and invigorated, but I missed companionship. Thirty years divided us. Most of their parents were younger than I was. But some companionship did come my way. A small weekly class for anyone talented or interested was held in a summer house in the grounds. As far as I could see these patients were just like anyone else. One in particular I felt sure was more sensible and better balanced than I was. Yet on paper she was deeply into schizophrenia. Another was an artist, considered by many to be one of the most severely disturbed. She was my age, and we at once discovered a mutual friend - a fellow student of hers who had gone on to the Royal College. She was never in any way difficult or even strange. It was a free situation in which, I like to think, we all benefited.

Another artist, a sculptor, was said to be the most dangerous patient in the hospital. Enormous blocks of stone were delivered but came to nothing. In woodwork, he carved cute shelf-sized lucky pigs with leather ears and a lick of paint. They were given away or sold for pocket money to spend in the canteen.

These two artists could be seen as the stars of the establishment. They were arguably the most interesting, but in no sense typical. Beyond question the profession most strongly represented was medicine itself - especially psychiatry. These were the great days of the drug largactil (chlorpromazine). Electro-convulsive therapy and insulin treatment were also frequently used. It meant fewer locked doors, with the freedom of the building and grounds open to many patients for the first time.

It wasn't until I went on outside clinical practice in the local mental hospital that I met my favourite character. He wasn't in my class, but kept trying to gate-crash, only to find himself blocked by the charge nurse, a huge, white-coated fellow with the figure of a base-line rugby football player. The patient was small and lightly built, it didn't seem fair. True, he thought of himself as Napoleon Bonaparte, but that was not his appearance. He looked like an addled Eliot. As soon as I saw him I noticed the resemblance to the poet. In fact, he was a native of the Channel Islands, who'd worked for some years in France. But none of this tied in with his hair - plastered forward and licked back with a pinch at the front, twiddled up to an uncertain point on top of his head.

'But I want to do some knitting, sir, the lady said I could.' He wasn't well enough behaved, I was told. But he persisted, and, in the end, he got his way.

'What's he making, is it a vest?' asked the big man. It was undeniably a curious shape with gaping holes. He was always delighted to be put right and then forged vigorously ahead with his own variations as before. When I told him it was 'individual', he was tickled. *'Is it? Looks fine to me. Just the thing for the car! When I finish this I'll be doing one for the wife.'* He was always enchanting to listen to.

When the going was strong, he owned the hospital, Selfridge's and the Marble Arch. *'I've been given a Rolls. An exceedingly large lump sum has been settled on me. With millions coming in each day it was nothing to him. I've written to the Bank of England.'* I was assured as he tore off a piece of newsprint, carefully folded it down to size and slotted it into the hospital mail box. Straight out of the text-book into real life - 'delusions of grandeur' in person!

Somehow I managed to get him off the terrible knitting, onto a rug in herringbone stitch. He got on better with this - could even see when he went wrong and was pleased by the green areas in the pattern. *'My Intelligence Corps colours!'* Fact or fancy? And when I spoke of the design as 'symmetrical', he at once picked up the word and dandled it. All the same I couldn't help feeling mean, he really loved that unbelievable knitting. The dilemma was resolved when he was given permission to do a short session every evening before going to bed.

Unlike the rest of the class, there was hope for the addled Eliot. He'd been put on a stringent new heat treatment, and if his body could tolerate this long enough, it should have been only a question of time. Splendidly, classically deranged as he was he'd been able to take this on board, he knew he'd been seriously ill, but should now get better. And this mixed situation was reflected in his behaviour - sensible enough, at other times clearly enclosed in a flamboyant world of his own.

He was already looking less addled. *'I talk too much'*, he said of himself, *'I must get on with my work!'* We reached the stage where he saw that the others put their things away tidily at the end of the morning, he then ran round putting the room to rights. *'They **are** funny, aren't they?'* he said of the class. But I didn't find them funny. I couldn't get through to them. I put their work right and that was it.

Then came the morning that changed everything. I arrived to find him waiting for me at the hospital entrance. *'Miss! - at two o'clock this morning my mind came back! Yes, I'm all right now.'* And he was - he remembered his past, he knew who he was, and all that stuff about elephants, yachts and cars was only because he'd been ill. The trouble had been general paralysis of the insane, G.P.I. a late manifestation of syphilis that usually appears eight to twenty years after infection, causing fearful havoc in both body and mind.

But syphilis, I soon discovered, was more than just one disease, it was an Empire - a marshalling of sophisticated bacterial organisms - agile, thread-like presences with a taste for whizzing round in the most vital parts of their host. They also had a talent for acting under cover, imitating other infectious diseases, T.B. and leprosy for preference. But this time they'd been outmanœvred - this particular late-flowering performance had led to extinction.

So it happened like this, did it? The scales simply fell away! Even the big man was stunned - he had never seen anything like it. All but wiped out by penicillin, even then (the late Fifties), the last stages of what had once been called the Great (or

French) Pox were very rarely encountered.

Touching on the delusions, I asked if at any time he'd felt the least doubt. No - none, it couldn't have been more real, I was told. What's more he'd never seen a bar of gold, and there they were, stack upon stack, by the vault-full. That he retained any of these memories into normal consciousness surprised me. Though some areas did appear to be missing. What struck him as most curious was the business of naughty French songs at breakfast. They had certainly proved popular. He was being approached by patients and personnel from all over the hospital, registering their appreciation. But he couldn't sing and didn't know any. Given his history, this seemed unlikely. But we all know that even normal memory plays tricks, and any man suddenly stripped of all he possessed (no matter how come by) was more than likely to be in some degree of shock. Again, with self-consciousness re-established, shame and guilt would be lurking in the shadows. He would want to be seen as sober and respectable. Unbelievably, he became boring. But change was going on continuously, this flat grey patch would soon disperse. All the same I caught myself looking back with nostalgia to the good old days, affectionately remembering the one time he'd 'misbehaved' - with the remark that in his opinion a bite out of my arse should prove especially tasty. I received this in the spirit I hoped it was given - while prudently maintaining a stiff frost to discourage any further observations of that nature.

By the time my clinical practice in the hospital finished, he was going home every weekend. He was picking up but still looked under strain. He'd been admitted sick - a triumphant Napoleon. He was going out cured - as it appeared - sad and defeated. The hospital had saved his life. He had now to prove himself. The small business his father had started had folded with the war. He had been the firm's traveller on both sides of the Channel. The café he had opened in the Midland town after the war had now been sold. To hold on to the roof over their heads, his wife was giving private lessons in French. There were two young boys. That he would find a third way forward and prosper once more no-one with a working knowledge of the man doubted. His native initiative and will to work had been on the way back well before two o'clock that historic morning.

Out of the ashes another beginning

Outside clinical practice, in the town's General Hospital, was also in its different way a revelation. I remember moving forward under an imposing stone arch with above it the carved inscription *DEPARTMENT OF PHYSICAL MEDICINE*, and on into a busy, noisy, untidy O.T. room. And then it hit me. It was so unexpected it came as a shock. People were **communicating** with each other. They were making jokes, laughing, pulling legs - it was friendly and natural. I felt a strong surge of happiness, followed by a state of lightness and lift, almost levitation. It was only a work-a-day scene, I recognised that, but it was also a way of life left behind and forgotten. At the end of the day I walked slowly back to St. A's, pondering. I was fascinated by the training I was getting at the school. I was happy there, too - **though**... I came to the conclusion that the first half of our training amounted to a virtual immersion in the mental side of our work. An exaggeration, but placed as we were some degree of this was inevitable. That I'd been so totally unaware was what alarmed me.

Later, amazement and relief took over. I felt as a prisoner might on being suddenly freed by an overturned sentence. **Prison?!** Well, granted, a special kind of prison. For despite new drugs and procedures, there were still locked wards. The scissors in my uniform pocket were on a cord attached to my belt. In every workshop, tools were counted out - and in again at the end of the session, should anything be missing no-one left the room till it was found. At all times in the hospital the maintenance of restraint, the need for caution hung heavy in the air - sustained concentration on the worst that could possibly happen was all about us. Not that any of this had worried me at the time. Not at all. Released by that quaint first day in physical, however, it had all come flooding forth **demanding** to be looked at in a different light.

As far as I could see, hardly any of my fellow students had it in mind to stray from the fold. It was as if they had no alternative. Presumably the selection of this particular school in itself was a form of acceptance. In addition, the unnecessarily high physical medicine examination standard didn't help, the Principal hadn't exaggerated, it was daunting. First and worst was Grade I Anatomy. Even I could extract no pleasure from this, and until it was passed you were in no position to take Grade II. There were students who got no further and finished their training unqualified. Application and sheer slog ensured that I passed in anatomy at the first attempt.

It occurred to me that I was probably the most committed of us all to the psychiatric. There was no doubt in my mind as to which of our alternatives was the most exciting and important. And already it had given me so much. I was leaning about in my **niche** surveying the scene. I was sure I'd discovered my groove. I'd even gone on to picture myself in the role of art therapist.

Two major periods of outside clinical practice were still to come, both physical. For these we would be distributed about the country into what were considered to be the best-run departments. As far as our training went, this should re-dress the balance, and perhaps it would not be too late to change one or two minds. Though the happy maidens at the height of their powers, bursting with muscle tone, all vigour and bounce, were hardly at risk. In any case, after no more than a year or two of professional experience, most - if not all - would be married.

Before me lay fifteen years to retirement. But I needn't have been so bothered about my future. When the time came it sorted itself out with **inspired** precision.

The Last School

Occupational therapy had barely reached Cornwall, but there, waiting for me, was one open slot, of a kind that had never - would never - have entered my head. Domiciliary - visiting homebound disabled. **And it suited me perfectly.**

The psyche the soma a *medic* diploma!
3 restorative years among
maidens of 20
me all engines firing
about to be 50
from the top of the Burnham
to the base of the Whitley
(even more niggardly)
rich - in all other
job domiciliary
wheels a necessity
Cornwall the scenery, could be on holiday
no
happier
helper.
Free-ranging, smooth-riding
right through to half-sixty.

These memories end in the summer of 1959 when Phyllis was 'about to be 50'.

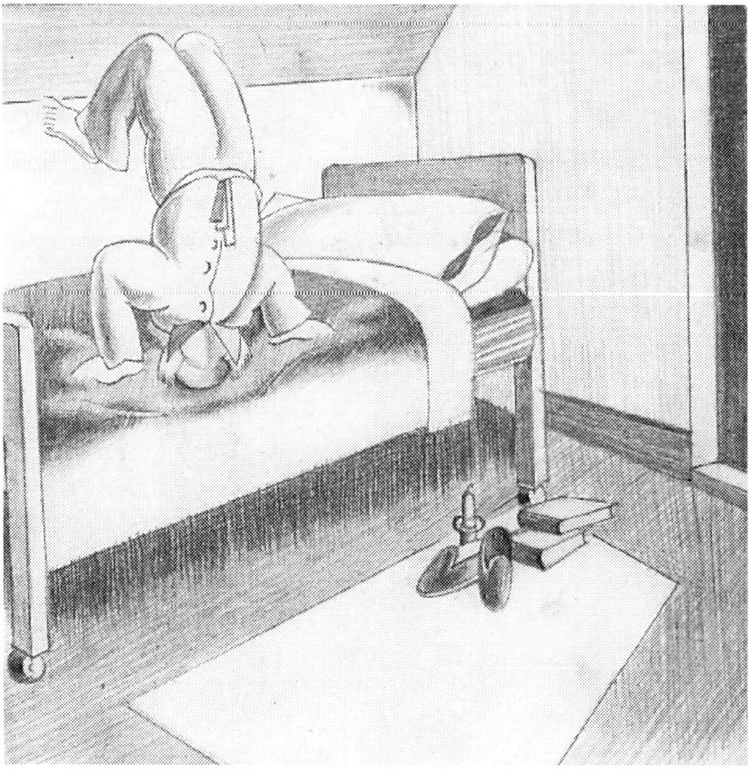